W9-CFZ-352

Some reviews of Peter Lemesurier's *The Great Pyramid Decoded*:

A very, very remarkable book; at the end of reading it I felt that either I should throw it out of the window, or that I should throw every other book out of my window and just keep *it*.

Anthony Smith, BBC Kaleidoscope

A most remarkable book which should be read by all.

New Humanity

Mr Lemesurier is a pyramidologist beside whom most pyramidologists look mere triangles.

Sunday Telegraph

Some reviews of his *Gospel of the Stars*:

Coming back to read ordinary religious literature after this book is a 'drop' into the shadows of ignorance.

Science of Thought Review

A work which exhibits a deep sense of order and purpose.

RILKO Newsletter

And some reviews of his *The Armageddon Script*:

Of compelling interest . . . 'hooked' to the last page.

New Humanity

This is a fascinating book. It is a product of painstaking research and inspired interpretation. I do recommend you to read it.

Radionic Quarterly

ABOUT THE AUTHOR

Born in 1936, Peter Lemesurier read languages at Cambridge and holds the Associate diploma of the Royal College of Organists. He has been a musician, jet-pilot, trimariner and teacher. Now writing and lecturing on new age subjects, he is the author of *The Endless Tale*, *The Great Pyramid Decoded*, *Gospel of the Stars* and *The Armageddon Script*, and the translator into English of Peter Michael Hamel's *Through Music to the Self* and Horst Hammitzsch's *Zen in the Art of the Tea Ceremony*.

the Cosmic Eye

A Traveller's Guide to Inner Space

Peter Lemesurier

The Findhorn Press
1982

ISBN 0 905249 55 0
First published 1982
Copyright © Peter Lemesurier 1982

All rights reserved. No part of this
book may be reproduced, except for quotation or review,
without the written permission
of the publishers.

Set in 11/12 point Garamond by The Findhorn Press
Printed and bound by Unwin Brothers at the
Gresham Press, Woking
Published by The Findhorn Press, Moray, Scotland

Cover design by Elke Kempa

TABLE OF CONTENTS

PART I — DESTINATION SELF

1.	The Prisoner in the Iron Mask	9
2.	The Karmic You	13
3.	You and Your Soul	18
4.	The Prince and the Pearl	28
5.	The Dilemma of Duality	34
6.	You, the Dreamer	43
7.	We Who are the Dead	54

PART II — SYMBOLS OF DESTINY

8.	Ordeal and Initiation	69
9.	Thou Art That	79
10.	The Turn of the Tide	97
11.	The Symbols at Your Door	118
12.	The Cave of the Archetypes	131
13.	Rhythms of Being	145
14.	The Magic Circle	159

PART III — THE NEW INITIATION

15.	Return to Source	175
16.	The Cult of Earth and Fire	189
17.	The Great Awakening	197
18.	Over to You . . .	204

Classified suggestions for further reading	213

Part I
Destination Self

Challenge: Halt! Who goes there?

Fear is the natural and traditional reaction to the unknown.

Especially when that unknown is your own deeper self.

The same basic gut uncertainty is reflected in the supplementary challenge, 'Friend or foe?' You know perfectly well what your response will be if there is no answer, if the unknown insists on remaining unknown.

You will shoot first and ask questions afterwards.

And the corpse will tell the tale.

But remember that it is not necessarily a corpse because it was a foe, nor a foe because it is now a corpse. It is an assumed enemy, a real casualty, only because you have not succeeded in identifying it.

*   *   *   *   *

And so, as it turns out, is the deeper you.

1. THE PRISONER IN THE IRON MASK

Man, know thyself.
Inscription at the Delphic Oracle

Who do you think you are?

If often asked, the question is rarely answered. Understandably, perhaps.

Pressed on the matter, you might well answer it with a name. Failing that, you might equate yourself with a job, a position, an address, a relationship to property or to others. You are Joe Soap, or a student, or an office-worker, or number three in the hierarchy, or the person who lives at number twenty-seven, or the owner of the blue Suzuki, or Jane's cousin. Or merely the sum of your past achievements.

This, at any rate, is how most of us habitually identify ourselves.

And yet if you really are your name, who were you before you were given it? Who were you before you acquired your job or your property, before you realised that you were related to anybody else, before you achieved anything worth mentioning?

Who, by the same token, are 'you' now?

The question is one that this book is designed to help answer. But one thing is certain.

The designations that I have just listed are mere roles. Even your name is only a pseudonym. They are identities that you have adopted, attitudes that you have struck, masks to conceal the real you.

Like children, we never tire of dressing up.

And so we lose ourselves in a world of fantasy, a kind of Greek drama on a planetary scale. Forgetting our real identities, we take on the roles that fate has assigned to us and imagine that they are our real selves. We don an actor's mask—a fixed, unchanging death-mask—and animate it with our own life. We become walking, talking images of the dead, true victims of mortality.

Yet we are undeterred. But for our mask we should feel soft and vulnerable. The mask gives us a sense of security. Its very hardness and stiffness keeps the outside world at bay, preserves the distinction between 'I' and 'not I'. We call it our personality.

Appropriately so.

For, in ancient Rome, *persona* was the actor's mask.

* * * * *

But if your personality isn't your real self, what is? Is the real you the actor who is underneath the mask? Or is the actor in turn yet another mask, a deeper layer of pretence?

There are some who propose that every character in the play, and even the play itself, is but a dream in the mind of a single author. The idea has its attraction. So how would it be if it turned out that the author who wrote the play is also playing all the parts?

In which case you are not only acting and playing every word. You *are* that word.

The word made flesh.

* * * * *

Perhaps the thought is too overwhelming. Certainly it is highly speculative. It is unlikely to appeal to those who are unfamiliar with religion or metaphysics.

So supposing we leave the broader canvas and zoom in on a particular corner of it—the question of who assigned us our roles in the first place.

Who, in other words, is the casting-director?

To the ancient Greeks, as I have already suggested, it was Fate itself that was the villain of the piece. Or rather the Fates—those three malevolent females who spun for each new-born child a complex web of destiny from which it could never escape. The scheme was born of sheer malice, and since there was no escaping from it, people could express their humanity, achieve their latent nobility, only in terms of the fortitude with which they bore that fate and the valour with which they fought it to the end.

Life was a cosmic tragedy. And so, on stage, it was literally through their great tragedies that the Greeks depicted that ancient struggle. The guilts and fears of childhood, the subconscious impulses towards incest, murder and hatred of one's kin, the conflict between duty and free will, the eternal war between society's demands and the inclinations of the individual—such were the themes to which the drama returned again and again, the same themes which the later Freud was likewise to identify as basic to our inner experience.

To the Greeks it was fate that inflicted these traumatic circumstances, deciding both one's *persona* and one's subsequent destiny. To the psychologists of over two thousand years later it was an equally traumatic mixture of heredity and environment that decided the issue, and so moulded both personality and resulting behaviour. No doubt that was why the Freudians, no less than the Greeks, saw the re-experiencing of those events as a powerful tool for inner healing.

For the wheel had come full circle.

Once again the ultimate cause of the process, the real villain of the piece, was blind chance.

Perhaps this was inevitable in view of the Judaeo-Christian background of the later thinkers. For a God who wilfully allots one-time bit-parts to men and women—whether as beggar or king, genius or idiot, athlete or cripple—is not easy to distinguish from mere chance, or even from the malevolent Fates of Greek tradition. Even under the Christian dispensation there is no hope of self-redemption, no escape from the allotted role. Our ultimate destiny depends in large measure on how we react to the circumstances in which we have been arbitrarily placed. Our redemption, when it comes, is an almost gratuitous reward from 'out there'.

Deus ex machina.

True, the God of Christian tradition is credited with having a purpose for it all. It is assumed—somewhat generously—that He knows what He is doing. But it is all a great mystery. The workings of His mind are unfathomable. It is not for us to ask the reason why.

All of which is a far cry from another and equally venerable set of assumptions, typified by Hinduism and Buddhism. For here both blind chance and celestial tyrants are alike discounted. For every effect there is a cause, and every cause is in turn the effect of earlier causes. The universe is logical: it proceeds from the *logos*.

In the beginning was the word.

And you, equally, are a function of that *logos*, that word, that universal expression of natural law, that game of cosmic consequences. Between you and it, in fact, there is no real distinction. And so ultimately it is you who have chosen your present role, you who have chosen other roles in the past, you who will choose further roles in the future. It is a process of self-discovery. You are a piece in a cosmic jigsaw-puzzle, a piece which needs to try itself out in many different situations until eventually it discovers its true shape, slots into its rightful place in the scheme of things.

And so the cosmic picture is gradually built up, the universe rediscovers its true identity—the picture on the box. Until eventually it realises that it, too, is but a piece in an even greater jigsaw-puzzle.

The future of the universe, in these terms, is at least partly in your own hands. By discovering your own true self you help to promote its evolution, to fulfil its destiny.

In any terms, however, the process of self-discovery needs to begin and end with self-understanding, with realising that much that you though of as 'you' is actually imposed from outside, and that most of the rest is imposed by yourself. To start with you may be afraid to remove the mask, to discard the outer clothing. Perhaps our taboos on nakedness are symbolic of something much more vital. Obsessively we prefer pretence to truth, fantasy to reality. The tendency is a typical form of psychosis—literally a disease of the soul.

Nevertheless, little by little, the outer, dead layers of the onion can be removed. Sometimes the process may bring tears to your eyes. But the pain is not fatal, the anguish is only temporary. And despite your fears the onion turns out not to be hollow. There is, after all, something vital inside. Something which gives life. Something whose discovery at last brings true self-confidence, true self-assurance.

The real you.

So supposing we start by looking into your *curriculum vitae*, the history of your soul?

2. THE KARMIC YOU

Of these two thousand I's and we's,
I wonder, which one am I?
Jalal'ud-Din Rumi: *Shamsi Tabriz*

Before Abraham was, I am.
Jesus of Nazareth (Jn. 8:58)

It's all your fault. It was you who chose your parents, your relations, your sex, your school, your teachers, your friends and enemies. It was you who chose your body, your illnesses, your accidents, the times of your own birth and death. And you chose them not for fun, but because you needed the experience.

These are among the possible consequences if one of the most widespread and time-honoured theories of 'you'-ness is correct—the doctrine of reincarnation.

What does the doctrine propose?

Basically that you have existed for ever, and always will do. But then this immediately re-poses the problem raised in the previous chapter—who or what *are* 'you'? Perhaps we should start by establishing what 'you' are not.

Clearly for a start 'you' are not your body. The vast majority of its living cells have died and been replaced within the last seven years or so. The rest have had their entire molecular structure renewed not once, but several hundred times. Yet you still claim to be the same 'you' as seven years ago—though the rest of us have only your word for it.

Or is a car still the same car even after you have replaced all its parts?

13

Then again, were I to lose both legs I should still feel just as totally 'me' as I did before. Further amputation would leave the situation unchanged, until only my head and my torso were left. Yet if you then undertook the further amputation of one from the other to determine which really corresponds to the 'I', you would be likely to stop getting any answers at all.

Logic might suggest that the 'I' corresponds to the brain, whose cells at least are with us for life. But quite large sections of the brain can be removed without any diminution in the feeling of 'I'-ness—right up to the point where further surgery results in there being no more feelings anyway.

It seems to be all or nothing, and to a remarkable extent 'I'-ness seems to correspond to aliveness. You are essentially the life that is in you, whether you describe it in terms of your individuality, your sense of 'I', or the bundle of unconscious psychic energy that the ancients, for want of a better word, dubbed the 'soul'.

And there never was a time when this 'you' was not.

The germ of it was already there before the solar system cooled and the molten planets became spinning worlds of rock. Asleep in the mineral kingdom, it stirred in the plant, awoke in the animal, became conscious in the human.

And so it entered the realm of cause-and-effect whose law is the law of 'karma', the same universal law that Newton expressed so succinctly in his third law of motion: 'Every action has an equal and opposite reaction.' Everything you do returns to act upon you. Pigeons come home to roost. The ripples from the stone you threw into the universal pond eventually return to the point of impact.

Kick the cat, and karma, without any assistance from the cat, will sooner or later exact its revenge. Not necessarily in kind, but still in a way that is both appropriate and educative. Help a friend—or better still an enemy—and karma will eventually bring an ample reward, perhaps in this lifetime, perhaps in the next. The profit-and-loss account is carried on to the next sheet.

It is not a question of life after death, for there is no death. The real 'you' cannot die even if it wants to. Rather is it a matter of life after life.

The flame passes from candle to candle. Compelled by the state of its karmic account, the all-knowing 'soul' chooses body after body, human incarnation after human incarnation, each exactly adapted to its current psychic needs. Whole groups of 'souls' repeatedly incarnate together to settle their karmic debts; as mother and daughter, as brother and sister, as employer and employee; first one way, then reversed, then from a different angle entirely. Any given experience may be pleasant or unpleasant, but the 'soul' knows it to be necessary, and cannot resist the compulsion. In short, it 'judges' itself.

So, at least, says the theory. In the light of this, what seem to be gratuitous acts by others are seen to be no more than your own judgements on yourself. Far be it from you, then, to presume to judge *them*.

All of which ultimately means that you are what you have made yourself—the self-made man or woman. And you are both cause and effect. Not only is the present 'you' the result of your own past thoughts and actions; your present thoughts and actions are even now building the 'you' of the future. A lower or a higher you, a more brutish or a more enlightened being, or even just an ordinary mortal. Hence those inconvenient inequalities of birth which we all try so hard to forget, frantically covering them up with legal and linguistic taboos. Hence the Mozart or the Einstein, the idiot or the cripple. All are potential 'you's. Do not be too hasty to stick on labels, then, for who is to say that the challenges taken on by the idiot are not even more advanced than their Einsteinian counterparts?

Up the ladders, down the snakes. On and on goes the cosmic board-game, until you realise that things can't go on like this. Living is really only another name for dying. Every visible cell of your body is already dead; most of the dust in your room is dead bits of you. You are subject to the ultimate in mortgages—for by the very fact of your living you are pledged to die. And whether you call it living or dying, the process inevitably brings with it much pain and suffering—if not for you, then for countless millions of others. For pain is a large part of experience, and pleasure is merely the other side of the coin. They are the two tools of all learning.

Yet one thing is clear. The chief cause of death and suffering is neither cancer, nor heart disease, nor starvation, nor even old age.

It is birth itself.

Nothing, surely, could be more obvious.

But how do you avoid birth, stop the wheel, cut the everlasting circle?

The method, basically, is to destroy the sense of 'I', for 'I' is an illusion. It is simply another way of saying 'not you'. And yet if 'I' am the life that is in me, and 'you' are the life that is in you, then we are both the same life, the 'aliveness' that is the life of the universe itself.

I am the universe playing at being me. You are the universe playing at being you. We are but two leaves on the same branch. Fully know and act upon this fact, and there is no more you and me, yours and mine, us and them. Other people are merely different names for yourself. The door between us is opened by the key of love—the love that loves your neighbour as yourself.

There are no more debts, because there are no more debtors. Therefore no more karma, no more rebirths.

It is in this moment of realisation that you achieve a further step towards your destiny. For you have become one with the universe, one with the great World-Tree. All that is, is you. Even all that is not, is you. Only You Are. Only I AM. Through you the universe achieves consciousness.

*   *   *   *   *

An attractive idea, you may say, but where's the proof? Well, the main proof of the pudding is naturally in the eating. And you are eating it right now.

But presumably what you are really asking for is objective evidence of the reality of reincarnation.

Much research has been done on the subject. Some of it (notably that of Stevenson*) has been rigorous and scientific enough to confirm beyond all reasonable question the reality of a number of people's experience of previous lives. Psychologists' experiments in age-regression under hypnosis** have produced similarly impressive results. Patients concerned have been successfully taken back in time to re-experience events in the embryonic state before birth, then back further still, when there have been numerous cases of a sudden 'jump' to another time, another place and another physical identity.

All these researches, however, have depended upon one assumption. Memory has had to be taken as a guarantee of identity. It has been pointed out that some sort of 'trans-time' telepathy could provide an equally good alternative explanation. But by the same token it could also provide the explanation for your own insistence (based, no doubt, on supposed memories) that it was you who were occupying your own body more than seven years ago.

*Ian Stevenson, M.D.: *The Evidence for Survival from Claimed Memories of Former Incarnations* (published in U.K. by M.C. Peto, 4 Oakdene, Burgh Heath, Tadworth, Surrey) and *Twenty Cases Suggestive of Reincarnation* (American Society for Psychical Research, 1966).

**See, for example, Bernstein's *The Search for Bridey Murphy*, and *Many Lifetimes*, by Joan Grant and Denys Kelsey (Corgi, 1976).

16

As usual you simply have to believe what you are ready to believe. If, like generations of men and women stretching far back into the mists of prehistory, you feel reincarnation to be too obvious a fact even to need discussing, then you need do little more than ask yourself what it implies, and act upon the answer. If on the other hand you take the supposedly scientific view that nothing exists outside what is perceptible to your five senses, it would be a waste of time to point out to you that you are treating the assumptions of science as if they were its findings. Still less would it be worth arguing with a Christian who insists—rightly or wrongly—that the Bible doesn't sanction a belief in reincarnation.

People believe what they want to believe. The wanting comes first, the believing second, and the reasoning a very poor third. It is a matter of predisposition, whether inborn or acquired. And in terms of reincarnation theory we have chosen that predisposition precisely because it happens to be the experience we currently need.

Thus most European and American children turn out, as luck would have it, to be nominally Christian, most Indians to be nominal Hindus. The latter, unlike the former, generally believe in reincarnation. Or should we for 'luck' read 'karma'?

But then you don't have to believe in reincarnation. Fishes don't believe in the sea.

3. YOU AND YOUR SOUL

Everything, the whole of existence,
can be seen to have its origins in a
single source—universal life energy.
Lyall Watson: *Gifts of Unknown Things.*

I'd like us to take another look at the idea of 'soul'. I said earlier that what the ancients used to call the 'soul' seems to correspond very largely to the life that is in you. Then I went on to suggest that, to the extent that we all share the same 'aliveness', our sense of separateness is an illusion. It is the same universe that lives through each of us. There are not many, but only one. And you are it.

Implicit in this idea is the notion that the universe itself is somehow 'alive'. And it is this notion that I should like to try and clarify a little.

Especially in recent years the tendency has been for the scientist to look at the universe as if it consisted of a series of disconnected bits. The physicist, the chemist, the biologist, the astronomer, the geologist, the mathematician—all have tended to confine their studies to their own chosen sphere, or even to a further subdivision *within* that sphere, except in those inconvenient grey areas where two or more spheres overlap at the edges.

The days of the da Vinci or the Goethe are gone. The scientific all-rounder is no more.

Let me say at once that I am not blaming anybody for that attitude. The scale of the universe is so unimaginably vast that any *complete* knowledge of its workings must be equally vast. Unimaginable—and therefore unknowable. And the universe is growing all the time—or rather our knowledge of it is, which amounts to much the same thing. There is not the slightest sign to suggest that, as our knowledge increases, the remaining area of ignorance is decreasing.

Quite the reverse.

In science, then, as in other areas of experience, the Jack-of-all-trades is nowadays likely to be the master of none. So scientific knowledge remains fragmented. In consequence the universe itself seems to lack cohesion and perspective. The vision of wholeness is gone.

But it was not always so. Towards the end of the nineteenth century in particular there was a distinct feeling in the scientific air that the complete description of the working of the universe was only just around the corner. You sense it above all, perhaps, in the writings of H.G. Wells. The nature of matter and energy had been satisfactorily defined, the eternal laws which governed their interactions were regarded as virtually cut-and-dried. Darwin had shown convincingly that the earth's living species were subject to the same overall scheme of things.

If you had asked one of the scientists of that era to describe the universe, he would probably have likened it to a mighty machine, all of whose parts functioned blindly and mechanically according to known and predetermined laws, which were in turn the inevitable consequences of the nature of matter and energy themselves.

This is still the picture in the mind of most people today, and even the pervasive view in today's schoolroom. In science, as in religion, there is always a time-lag of a century or so between an idea's birth or death and the general acceptance of that event, even among the educated.

But by no means every scientific researcher would now be prepared to support so simple a view. The notion, admittedly, dies hard. Fortunately so, perhaps, for the desire to corroborate it still seems to be the mainspring of most 'pure' research. And yet the more advanced the nature of the work, the more non-committal the 'pure' researcher is nowadays likely to be. As a result of work in the spheres of radio-astronomy, quantum theory and high-energy physics in particular, the old certainties are turning into worrying doubts.

The closer we try to approach the ultimate basis of matter, the further it seems to recede; the more we try to comprehend the real nature of energy, the more insistently it eludes our grasp; and the deeper we delve into the natural laws which seem to govern their interrelationships, the more inadequate we find them to be.

At the basis of matter there seems to be no substance, at the basis of energy neither true waves nor true particles, at the basis of the natural laws no independent reality at all. Reality seems to retreat almost as the square of the researchers' advance—the more we look, the more it isn't there. Matter-as-such, energy-as-such, and the natural laws themselves look as if they are going to turn out to be mere mirages, ghosts, figments of our imagination, words about words, convenient ways of describing our experience.

Which is more or less what the Buddha always said they were.*

The old verities—and in particular the mechanical picture of the universe as a kind of cosmic machine, built up from known parts according to unalterable rules—are already more than half dead. In their place a new image is arising.

For the worrying phenomenon I have just described—the tendency for what you are looking for to run away from you even faster than you pursue it—is almost the exact equivalent of that involved in my earlier description of the search for the real 'you'. The basic reality which continues to elude the researcher cannot be identified with any one of the universe's known constituent parts—neither matter, nor energy, nor any particular set of natural laws. It appears to be simply some kind of underlying dynamic which is to the universe much as your own 'I'-ness is to you—and which, we deduced, was life itself.

Can we then regard the universe itself as being 'alive'?

Certainly the universe as a whole doesn't satisfy the traditional criteria of eating, breathing and reproducing—not, at any rate, so far as we know. But we should beware of confusing words and definitions with reality—a characteristic tendency of post-Renaissance European thought. The three traditional criteria may be applicable to terrestrial life, but it is entirely conjectural whether they will prove to be valid in extra-terrestrial contexts, unless we stand the notion on its head and deny that the proverbial Little Green Men are alive because they don't satisfy the three traditional criteria.

In other respects, however, the idea of a 'living universe' is starting to gain a measure of acceptance—though this may only be another way of saying that it is becoming fashionable. It is beginning to be generally realised that every part and aspect of the universe is in some way related to and affected by every other, just as the ancient philosophers in their supposed ignorance always maintained. The whole thing is one gigantic organism. Its members are the galaxies, its sinews the whole gamut of natural forces, its flesh the great star-systems, its cells the suns and planets, its molecules the chemical compounds, its atoms the

*Compare Fritjof Capra: *The Tao of Physics* (Wildwood House, London, 1975).

elements. It is moving, growing, evolving, and—strange to relate—it seems to know where it is going. Always in the direction of greater complexity. Always in the direction of expanding consciousness. Here on the cell that is Earth we are on the very frontier of that evolution, witnessing and participating in the inexorable process as it unfolds—from inorganic to organic compounds; from single-celled creatures to multicelled organisms; from the lowliest life-forms, through plants and animals, to conscious humankind.

And thence where? Only the cosmic being itself knows. Or perhaps it doesn't know.

And so in us, and in the plant and animal life of our Earth, it is the universe itself that is at work. It is the universe that in everything around us is eating, breathing and reproducing.

It is the universe that is truly alive.

Similar considerations apply to Earth itself. Gaia, says the increasingly well-known hypothesis*, is a living being that has produced us to further her own evolution—and will destroy us if we obstruct it. Almost too late the ecologists have come to realise the truth of the idea. If we pollute her atmosphere or her oceans, if we over-exploit her resources, if we upset the balance of nature that is her body-chemistry, Gaia will sicken. And if she sickens, we die.

A living universe, then, and a living earth. The idea has its attraction, yet you may feel that it is too incredibly far-fetched. Give the scientists time, you may say, and they'll come up with the answer. Of course they will. It is the job of science to come up with answers. There is, after all, an infinite number of possible answers to come up with. The history of science is a never-ending series of new answers to old questions.

But is there such a thing as the right one?

* * * * *

Or perhaps you would prefer to look at it from a different angle. Life—aliveness—exists. It exists on earth; it probably exists elsewhere. And somehow it has arisen out of what was there before. It was already there in the molten rock of the spinning planet, already there in the subsequent mineral elements; then, as we have seen, it stirred in the plant, awoke in the animal, became conscious in us. Even if we reject the idea that it is itself alive, the universe has within itself the potential

---

*Compare Lovelock, J.E.: *Gaia—A New Look at Life on Earth* (O.U.P., 1979)

of life.

It is this idea which seems to have struck the ancients with particular force. Here, they felt, was something undefined and intangible which lay at the very basis of reality itself, and the characteristic of that something was that it gives life.

What should it be called? 'Glonk' would have done very nicely. So would 'splidge'—any word that would allow the notion to be slotted into the thought-patterns of language, shuffled around, discussed, peered at, looked into. But the ancients weren't given to inventing new words just like that, out of the blue. They preferred to adapt old words, words that would tell you what category of thought you were meant to fit an idea into, props that would help you make sense of it.

And so they came back to the human model, to humanity as the measure of the universe. It's always a good recipe. We understand best what we can relate to ourselves.

"What is it that gives life?" they asked. "What is it whose presence in us means life and whose absence is a sure index of death?"

Breath.

So 'breath' they called it. They were under no illusion, of course, that it *meant* breath. 'Breath' was simply the name they gave to the cosmic life-giving principle for want of a better word. And they were careful to be perfectly scientific about it, for they knew nothing about where it had come from or where it was going. All they knew was that it was here now. They did not theorise as to its nature, nor did they turn it into a god. As Newton was to do with earth's own force of attraction, they merely named it and observed its effects.

Breath. In Latin, *spiritus.*

Spirit—the universal principle which, whatever else it does, gives life. And since its absence would necessarily mean a dead universe they assumed it to be fundamental to all existence.

Spiritus said the Romans, *pneuma* the Greeks, *ruach* the Hebrews, *ka* the Egyptians, *atman* the Hindus, *chi* the Chinese, *ik* the Maya. But that was only the beginning of it; soon it had become Brahman, Amun, the Hidden One, the Unfathomable, the Formless, the One, El, Allah, and not least, God.

For God, say the Christian scriptures, is spirit.

But there were dangers in all this. Name a thing and you start to picture it, define it, imagine that you have power over it. The indefinable life-giving principle gradually becomes a cosmic entity, the solar disc, the earthly fire, a descending dove, an old man in the sky. We create God in our own image.

And so the Buddha refused to discuss the idea, the Hebrews were forbidden even to name it aloud. Perhaps it had been a mistake to treat the idea as a noun in the first place. Perhaps, as Moses realised, it should always have been a verb.

Ehyeh. I AM.

At all events, there it was, the concept of spirit, the 'livingness' of the universe, the 'livingness' of the human race. The I AM that admits of no YOU ARE.

And so where does soul come into it?

Basically it comes in where humanity's roots come out.

*　　*　　*　　*　　*

A piece of rock does not think of itself—if it thinks at all—as separate from its environment. Neither, presumably, does a plant. No less than the rock, it is totally enmeshed with the world around it, totally at the mercy of the elements, the seasons, the succession of night and day. But with the evolution of the animals, life started to uproot itself, became mobile. What was 'out there' started to be seen as separate from what was 'in here', until in ourselves the notion became obsessive. I am me, you are you, and never the twain shall meet. Independence is all.

No wonder we need love.

Thus we enter the illusory world of duality, of this and that, of here and there, of now and then. So vital does it become to us to demonstrate this independence that it soon becomes axiomatic that that is better than this, there is better than here, then is better than now. We become restless animals, cosmic nomads, always on the move, always fleeing from our ancient roots. Fugitives from time and place, fugitives from ourselves.

We set out across the face of the planet to explore its seas and deserts. We take to the air, plumb the depths of the ocean, blast off for the stars.

And always 'because it is there'; never 'because it is here'.

At the same time we feel impelled to get there—wherever 'there' is—faster and faster. Speed is of the essence. Lurking at the very back of our minds seems to be the thought that if we can only travel fast enough there need be no this, no here, no now at all. It will be instant that, instant there, instant then; independence to the ultimate degree.

Yet it is all an illusion. As soon as we get 'there', it becomes 'here', 'that' becomes 'this', 'then' turns into 'now'. Our much-vaunted independence is only relative. We carry within our veins and arteries only a limited amount of the primeval soup from which we sprang, and we must constantly replenish it with food, with water, with oxygen. The range of temperatures and pressures within which we can operate is infinitesimally small by the standards of the universe. Our bodies are little more than highly vulnerable semi-rigid bladders which have achieved a measure of mobility by growing a bony projection at each corner—our arms and legs.

And unfortunately we have let ourselves be carried away by them. Carried away to the extent of imagining that the life-force within us is quite independent of the life-force out there. And it is this 'individualised spirit' to which we traditionally give the name 'soul'.

This too, then, must be an illusion, but even illusions have their purpose. It is to our obsession with achieving physical independence of our environment that we must attribute the extraordinarily rapid evolution of human consciousness during the last century or so. And it is to a similar preoccupation with the welfare of our 'soul' that we can perhaps attribute the parallel evolution of our deeper awareness through the ages. Our concept of 'spirit' may have become individualised, but it is still 'spirit' for all that.

And so religions and philosophical systems sprang up to serve the concept. Many of them still flourish today. They will continue to flourish until the concept ceases to have any usefulness, and probably long after that.

On the one hand, spirit; on the other hand, soul. In the red corner, God; in the blue corner, me.

But eventually the truth will have to be faced. There are not many, but only One. The spirit that moves in the universe out there is the same as the soul that inhabits your own inner universe. Brahman is Atman. *Thou art that.* Hence the commandment to 'love the Lord thy God, and thy neighbour as thyself'. For to love is to become one.

And the sooner we realise it, the better.

Various analogies have been put forward to illustrate the idea. Like all analogies, they are imperfect. Like all analogies, too, they are merely words about words, symbols for symbols. But here, for what it is worth, are two of them.

Imagine a chain of islands stretching out to sea. They are called A, B, C, and D:

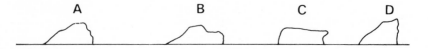

Island A stands for your soul, B for mine, and so on. They seem quite detached, quite independent. Yet we are letting ourselves be deluded by the sea of our own consciousness. If we now bring in our underwater cameras, the picture changes:

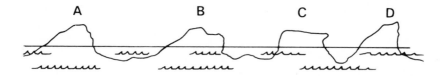

We suddenly become aware that all four islands are merely the peaks of a single, semi-submerged mountain-chain. That chain we could call the 'soul' of humanity itself, the particular 'aliveness' that manifests itself in us all. And what of the bedrock of which that mountain-chain is merely an extension? It is of course the underlying 'aliveness', the life-giving spirit, of the universe itself, deep, concealed, almost un-detectable except to a deep-sea diver or a mariner with an echo-sounder, but there nevertheless, firmly and indubitably there, the ground of our very being.

But perhaps our first analogy was too static. For a more dynamic pic-ture we could take the waves of the sea:

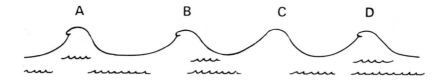

Here your soul is represented by wave A, mine by wave B, and so on. Once again we all think of ourselves as different, independent entities. Yet here, even more clearly than before, it is obvious that we are all merely functions of the sea itself. Driven by the wind of cosmic evo-lution, we puff ourselves up into great billows of egotistical foam and imagine that we are somehow independent of the universe, acting upon it from outside. Yet we are doing no such thing. We ourselves are functions of the universe. The water—the universal spirit—does not even travel with us: it merely oscillates in vertical eddies and returns to its point of origin. The universe continues on its inexorable way, intent upon a destiny of which we know nothing.

Nor are we the unique, unchanging selves that we often imagine ourselves to be. The shape of any given wave does not stay constant for more than two seconds together. The soul, if there is one, is in a constant state of flux. It needs only a windshift or a collision with some rocky shore to reduce a wave forever to the nothingness from which it came. And eventually, with the calm of the evening, the truth is revealed for what it is. The waves are re-absorbed, the sea once more becomes a single, shining Oneness. There is only the breathing of the ancient deep.

The breath that is spirit itself.

Yet even islands have their *raison d'être*, even waves have a logical place in the scheme of things. They are there because it has suited the purposes of cosmic evolution to put them there. And so it is, perhaps, with the concept of soul. Perhaps it is in the nature of spirit, the life of the universe, the cosmic thesis, to provide, through the evolution of consciousness, for its own analysis—the arising of the concept of separateness, of individuality, of 'soul'. Perhaps it is inevitable that it then proceeds, through the further expansion of human consciousness, to beget its own antithesis—the denial of both soul and spirit that is characteristic of our own age.

Thesis; antithesis.

But the argument does not stop there. Classically it goes on, via whatever catalytic process, to a final, greater synthesis, the synthesis which not only concludes the argument, but goes on to act as the thesis of the next cycle.

Thesis; antithesis; synthesis.

Perhaps it is towards that synthesis that we are now heading. Plumbing the consciousness with which the evolutionary process has provided us, we are now—if unwittingly—deepening our awareness of the 'aliveness', the cosmic spirit which we share with the universe itself, so that in the end we shall be able to live not merely from our individualities or 'souls' as disconnected entities, but directly from the spirit that is common to all of us—just as Jesus of Nazareth seems to have been able to do from the moment of its 'descent' upon him at his baptism. Thus we shall become the arms and legs of that spirit; the 'body of Christ' in the words of St Paul; the *Adam Kadmon* of Hebrew tradition; the *Purusha* of the Hindus. And in that moment a new, immortal, Cosmic Being will be born, a being of which each individual is but a single cell, a new colonial animal in the universe's eternal drive towards ever greater complexity. And no doubt that event will be accompanied by an even greater leap forward in universal consciousness.

* * * * *

Where, then, do we begin? First, inevitably, with the deepening of our awareness. Here we could take the 'cake of consciousness' as another crude analogy:

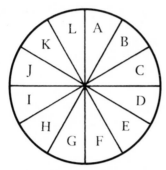

This time the cake represents the total consciousness of the whole of humanity. Slice A is your slice of it, slice B mine, and so on. At the surface level, the edge of the cake, there is a great deal of shallow awareness and a large quantity of sense-data to process—the circumference is maximum in length—but we are quite definitely separate. As we deepen our awareness and work our way down towards the centre our outer consciousness decreases with the width of the slice. At the same time there is less of 'you' to oppose less of 'me'. We seem to be heading in the right direction. Just before we reach the centre of the cake we are at a level where our consciousness of sense-impressions is almost nil, the depth of our awareness is maximum, and 'I' and 'you' have almost disappeared as separate entities.

Suddenly we hit centre. 'I' and 'you' have disappeared completely; yet in that moment we have become one, not only with each other, but with the whole cake. In becoming nothing we have become All. The still centre of me turns out to be the still centre of the universe itself.

The way to the universe lies not outward, but inward. The journey to the centre of the soul.

And so perhaps it is time for us to strike camp and hit the road again. Where there's a will, says the proverb, there's a way, and setting out on the first part of that way means sitting right here and learning to turn within. The technique of meditation.

A journey of a thousand miles starts under your own feet.

4. THE PRINCE AND THE PEARL

The road onward lies inward.
Anton von Webern

Once—but not necessarily upon a time—there was a young eastern prince whose beloved had given him a precious pearl in token of their betrothal. Ecstatically he bore it in his hands as he rode homeward through the forest, dreaming of the day of their marriage.

The day was hot, the road wound on and on. But at evening the prince came to a clearing where there lay a deep and silent pool. Dismounting, he made his way to its edge in order to slake his thirst. Still his eyes were only for the precious pearl. Perhaps that was why he did not see the boulder in his path. Imagine his desperation as, suddenly tripping headlong, he saw the pearl jump out of his hands and disappear in a flash into the depths of the waters.

What should he do?

What *could* he do but wade in after it, search the bottom frantically, grope hither and thither after that lost promise of future bliss?

It was all in vain. His movements merely stirred up the mud from the bottom of the pool and destroyed all chance of spotting the pearl. Already the light was beginning to fail. Soon night would devour the forest.

And so the poor prince, cursing the boulder, had no choice but to make the best of it and camp where he was for the night, in the hope of resuming his search once more by the light of dawn.

Needless to say, the prince slept not a wink that night. Dawn found him still squatting damply at the edge of the pool, peering miserably into the depths. Still no pearl was to be seen. Only the dim reflections of the late stars quivered in the gnats' ripples, ringed by the dark, upside-down images of the trees.

Then, as the sun arose out of the morning mist, he spotted a soft, cool glint at the very bottom of the pool. Immediately he flung himself headlong into the water. With strong strokes of arms and legs he clawed his way downwards into the depths. But the pool was too deep. His breath ran out long before he could reach the pearl. And when, returning to the surface for air, he was ready to dive once more, he saw that his movements had once more clouded the water. Once again he had to wait for it to clear.

One hour. Two. Three. Only when a fourth hour had passed did the prince once again catch a glimpse of that beckoning glint in the depths. At once he flung himself once more into the water. And once again the result was as before. Repeatedly throughout the day the prince made desperate efforts to reach the pearl, until evening fell upon a prince even more dejected than before.

After the exertions of the long day the prince at last found sleep. As the third day broke, he awoke with a new energy and alertness, and made his way straightway to the edge of the pool. There in the morning coolness he stood and waited, contemplating once more the reflections of the late stars quivering in the gnats' ripples, ringed by the dark, upside-down images of the trees.

And as he waited for the sun to come up for the second time, the prince suddenly had an idea. A little to his right, an old tree-branch hung far out over the water, almost touching its surface. If he could somehow lower himself from it gently into the water, he might avoid stirring up the mud. But in that case, how to solve the problem of breathing? And how could he possibly reach those elusive depths where the pearl lay?

It was then, as the sun was emerging from the mist, that he had his second idea. He had lost the pearl because he had tripped, and the cause of his tripping had been a boulder. Now it was that same boulder that must recover the pearl for him.

And if you had been there beside the pool as the soft glint of the pearl once more responded in the dim depths to the call of the morning sunlight, you would have found the prince clutching the heavy boulder tightly to his body as he lowered himself gently from the overhanging branch into the pool. Quietly the water closed its fingers over his head. The weight of the boulder carried him swiftly and effortlessly towards the bottom. Down and down he sank, willing the boulder to take him ever deeper. Breathing scarcely mattered, for his body was still. It was the boulder that must work for him now. Opening his eyes, he peered downwards into the watery gloom.

And there, suddenly, was his pearl coming up to meet him. In the same moment as the boulder came to rest on the bottom he had already stretched out an eager hand and grasped the precious jewel for all he was worth. Releasing his grip on the boulder with the other hand, he let the buoyancy of his body bear him effortlesly upwards again. With a rush he broke surface and, gulping down the good air, swam vigorously to the bank.

Thus, where much toil and struggling had failed, an effortless and simple technique had regained for the prince his precious jewel. Instead of fighting the forces of nature he had used them and worked with them. Non-action had triumphed over action. No wonder the prince sang out in joy as he clambered from the water, holding the pearl aloft in the morning sunlight. His destiny was assured, his marriage as good as celebrated. He and his beloved would live happily ever after.

And the entire forest re-echoed to his song.

*   *   *   *   *

Only a fairy-story, you may say. And you would be right. But fairy-stories, like many ancient myths and traditions, often have more to them than we think. Like the pool in the story they have hidden depths. What you see in them at first sight—like the reflections in the pool—is often their least important aspect. And deep within them, if only you will let them flow over you, may lie some hidden jewel of great worth.

For the prince in the story is the seeker—you or I—and the pearl is the 'soul' that we have lost and seek to find again. As for his beloved, she is the universal self, the I AM, the eternal source from which arose that 'soul' and to which it is destined eventually to return.

The seeker, bearing inwardly the promise of that final reunion, stumbles. That stumbling is the biblical 'fall'; the boulder is the prison of physical relativity. The question is how to find the 'soul' again, that key to the ultimate bliss of cosmic reunion.

Frantic action is in vain. The direct assault results only in failure. The elusive goal merely disappears from view. It is hidden in darkness—the 'dark night of the soul'. Only memory still testifies to the fact that the 'soul' is there at all.

The seeker may believe that only actions justify existence, but the actions thought to be the most vital are for the most part totally ir-relevant, even actively harmful. They merely cloud the issue. Even more darkness results.

And it is only when things are seen in a completely new light that the seeker realises the mistake. Nothing is achieved by fighting circumstance. The secret lies in working with the flow of the universe. If it is the seeker's destiny to go through hell, then it must be gone through—in order to come out again on the other side.

And so it is by using the very cause of the 'fall' that the seeker finds salvation. Aquiescing in physicality, quietly accepting the 'darker side', almost by magic the goal is achieved. And the technique is no more than a stillness, a surrender. The surrender that is the very meaning of the words 'Islam', 'Subud', 'Om'.

The stillness of meditation.

* * * * *

What *is* meditation?

Does it involve adopting weird postures, holding the breath, chanting magic spells, going into trances, dabbling in Black Magic?

Emphatically not. It does not even involve sitting cross-legged—unless you prefer sitting that way. And it certainly is not only for inscrutable orientals. Meditation is as old as the hills, and has figured prominently in every major religion. In some it is described as 'prayer', in others as 'contemplation', but as generally understood the term refers simply to a wordless activity aimed at achieving non-thought—or at very least the realisation that your thoughts themselves are not the real you.

Meditation is simply a technique for relaxing the body, stilling the mind, allowing the deepest 'you' to speak. In psychologists' jargon it is 'the relaxation response'. To those who practise it regularly it provides spiritual refreshment, mental calm and physical regeneration.

You need to be physically still, breathing regularly, and relaxed. A typical sequence might be as follows:

1. Sit comfortably but erect. The spine is straight, the head upright, the eyes closed.

2. Breathe deeply.

3. While continuing to take long, deep breaths, consciously relax each part of the body in turn, starting with the toes and finishing with the throat, the jaw and the area of the eyes.

4. Now bring the consciousness to the tip of the nose. Concentrate on the feeling of the breath as it passes in and out of the nostrils. If the thoughts wander, bring them gently back.

5. Next feed in some positive thought—'peace', perhaps, or 'love'.

'Light', 'wisdom' or 'strength' will do equally well. Visualise yourself breathing in that thought; then, as you breathe out, feel it flowing down from your head and flooding through your whole body.

6. Now forget the breathing. Simply let youself go. Listen to the silence. Go deeper still. If thoughts arise do not stifle them. Merely bring them back to the tip of the nose, then let go once again.

7. When you have had enough, deepen your breathing once again, and send out with each outbreath the same thought with which you began—visualise it spreading in a ring to all those around you, to your friends, to your companions, even to your enemies if there are any, and finally to the whole of humanity. Everybody should benefit from your meditation and the peace it brings.

8. Finally 'come back', stretch, and feel the new vigour and freshness within you. Carry it into your everyday life.

That is one technique. Others involve concentrating on a particular word or phrase (a 'mantra'), a colour or series of colours (generally starting at the red end of the spectrum and finishing with the violet), a flower, or a circular or spiral design (a 'mandala'). You can meditate on most things—Lewis Carroll would no doubt have meditated on the smile of a Cheshire cat. You can meditate while falling asleep, meditate while walking. And, rather like sleeping on a problem, meditation can be a fruitful source of ideas, of solutions, of new initiatives.

Yet it is not easy to learn a skill from printed words on a page. To learn to ride you need to come into contact with a horse, to learn to sail you must have a boat, and to learn to meditate you should first find someone who practises it, and then ask to be taken through a session. One of the inevitable consequences of allowing yourself to 'flow with it' seems to be that whatever helpers you need will appear of their own accord just at the moment when you need them.

If one technique doesn't suit you, try another. When you have found 'your' method, try meditating regularly. If possible aim to spend perhaps fifteen minutes in meditation morning and evening. After a few weeks stand back and assess the results.

If they are negative you should abandon the practice forthwith. Meditation is not for you—or there is something in your psychological make-up or conditioning which prevents you from benefiting from it.

If you find that you are more at peace with yourself, more at one with the world and everybody in it, more aware of your own inner thought-processes and motivations, then meditation is clearly for you—just as it already is for thousands of others across the planet. And it may be that a world of meditators would be a better world—for meditators are unlikely to be fighters. Perhaps that is why a special room is set aside for meditation in the United Nations building in New York. Certainly it was the view of the organisation's second Secretary General, U Thant, that it was the meditators who ultimately would save the world.

Meditate, then, and be at peace. And one day, apropros of nothing, you might even try meditating on the story of the Prince and the Pearl . . .

5. THE DILEMMA OF DUALITY

Earth lives . . . and now, through the agency
of sentient collections of cells on its skin,
it begins to feel self-conscious.
Lyall Watson: *Gifts of Unknown Things*

Perhaps the ultimate goal to which meditation gradually leads is the realisation that we and the universe are one and indivisible, whether physically, mentally or spiritually. And yet, whether we like it or not, we are born into a relative, dualistic world. Our senses, our thoughts, our culture and above all our language speak to us constantly of a world of opposites.

But it takes time.

To the new-born child there is no this and that, no I and you. Everything is 'I', everything is 'this', everything is 'now'. There is no space or time. The brain has not yet learnt to interpret the incoming messages into pictures of a separate reality 'out there'. To the infant those messages themselves *are* reality.

Then comes the urge to suck. The need, for the very first time, is supplied by something 'out there'.

It is literally at its mother's breast that the new-born child, struggling dimly over the edge of the beginning, receives its first lesson in duality.

But the lesson needs time to sink in. There is no rush. The child will learn in time. For a while yet it can be allowed to luxuriate in its utopian kingdom, to imagine that the universe is but an extension of itself, that its every will is reality's command. The child is small, harmless, defenceless. It threatens no-one. No need, then, to fear the child's will. Humour it.

It is some time before fear sets in—the parents' fear of the power of the child. Now the growing infant must be reduced to its true size, individualised, separated from the rest of the cosmos, weaned of its sublime illusion.

Divide and rule.

It is at this point that the child starts to learn in earnest the difference between 'I' and 'you'. The lesson is rubbed in. The measure of the increasing gulf between 'I will' and 'you will' is a cry of anguish. The wider the gulf, the louder the cry. And who is to say that the child is not right?

It is this cry that signifies the cutting of the true umbilical cord—the cord of consciousness.

Now the lessons come crowding in thick and fast. The floodgates of duality are opened. To I-ness and you-ness is added it-ness. First of all, only it-when-it-is-there-ness; later on, it-even-when-it-*isn't*-there-ness. Not to mention they-ness. And all of them coloured by various degrees of niceness and nastiness.

Categorisation has set in.

Meanwhile, right from the first, they start working on your mind. They drum their own code into you, brainwash you with a ready-made scheme for organising all these new ideas. Constantly, morning, noon and night, they croon it over you, whisper it at you, bombard you with it from all angles. They even set it to music.

They give you *language.*

And as soon as you accept it, as soon as you take the bait, you're done for. The *real* you, I mean.

Language is the apple in your Garden of Eden.

Henceforward you will have knowledge, but knowledge only of the world as *they* see it. Knowledge of duality and the world of opposites.

Knowledge of good and evil.

Here, there is the beginning of what you now call consciousness. In the beginning was the word.

Through it you were taught, little by little, that reality consists of a finite number of 'things' and 'actions', all of them capable of interaction, and subject to subtle qualification by means of a range of ready-made 'attributes'. To the eternal and divine trinity of noun, verb and modifier you were taught to defer without question, even before you were ever taught explicitly of the doctrines surrounding their existence. Their kingdom, you were taught, is reality itself, and beyond it lies no other kingdom. The declensions of the entire universe are encompassed in their ineffable and incomparable paradigm.

Of course you never questioned the idea then. You may not even question it now. You may be unaware that these assumptions are basic to the language you use. Yet by your use of it at this very moment you are still, even now, deferring to their authority.

The basic function of language is to communicate—to communicate between the now-separate 'I' and 'you'. And yet, curiously, it sets about the task via a process of separating and distinguishing.

In the pseudo-world of actions we distinguish between coming and going, bringing and fetching, eating and drinking, living and dying. In the pseudo-world of attributes we divide big from small, good from bad, old from young. Via the here/there dichotomy we create space, via the now/then distinction time, via the mine/yours duality alienation. And in the pseudo-world of things we divide the general from the particular, and the particular from everything else.

A word is a means not of naming but of negating. We name only to the extent that we wish to distinguish.

'Look at those cows,' says the little girl in the train on the way to the seaside. They may be young bulls, but to the child it is literally a matter of indifference. She merely wishes to draw attention to those large brown four-legged things with horns on, which are not telegraph-poles, not tractors, and in particular not sheep, horses or goats. The word 'cows' therefore fills the bill. To her at this moment, bovine sex-distinctions are not of the essence. Were she a farmer it might be a different matter.

To us Westerners, snow is snow, camels are camels. We do not need to make the myriad fine distinctions that are essential to the Eskimo and the Bedouin. Lacking the need to make such distinctions we lack the words to make them with.

On the other hand, 'I want three pieces of furniture please' might meet with a mixed reaction in the furniture store. The shop-assistant, after all, has a right to assume that you won't ask for lettuces or S U carburetters. What is needed is a further degree of distinction, some information from you to the effect that what you want is not-tables, not-beds, not-sideboards, not-kitchen-stools—and the assistant is not paid to play guessing games. In short, the word 'chairs' will quickly elicit the correct response, and a few more distinctions—large/small, dining-room/easy, hard/soft—will soon produce several examples of the desired article. You then need only to make your final choice—narrowing down the various possibilities until you find the one which most nearly accords with the image (*not* the chair) which you had all along in your mind.

Again, the child who is taught to say 'blue bus' every time it passes the door has perhaps never seen any other sort of bus. The word 'blue' has no function here; it has nothing to distinguish. 'Blue bus' is simply a means of distinguishing it from the telephone-box, the house opposite, the gnome in the garden, a van, a car or the postman. Strictly speaking, then, we ought to write it 'bluebus'.

Because when the child is taken to see Aunt Edna in London it will doubtless see the bus's red counterpart, which will undubitably be a '*red* bluebus'. Consider the parallel cases of green blackboards, red greenhouses, grey whitewash. Only now does the child need to express the distinction which language is designed to supply.

*   *   *   *   *

Meanwhile the greatest distinction of all soon looms up and establishes itself in the child's psyche—the eternal divide between 'mine' and 'yours'. We devote untiring efforts to turning the child into a property-owning autocracy. We even teach language with the aid of the concept: 'Is this *my* train set?', 'No, it's *my* train set'. Then we are suprised when the child starts to affirm its independence.

Yet the process of distinction goes inexorably on. We teach the child values, inculcate attitudes. Good is not bad, bad is not good. Nice is not nasty, polite is not rude. Even people are turned into animated labels, walking categories. Nothing is allowed just to *be*. In short, we spare no effort to turn our children into microcosms of our own culture-structure, to re-create them in our own collective image. And we measure our eventual success in terms of their surrender to the dead system that we have imposed on ourselves no less than on them. Their originality is our failure. To preserve 'us', to maintain our own illusion, we kill 'them'.

Nothing is more precious to us than the stained glass with which we surround ourselves. For anyone, even a child, to break it and let in the pure, undiluted light of day is a crime against nature. For the child who asks dangerous, fundamental questions such as 'Why does it keep on getting later all the time?' there is quite simply no answer.

But the most crucial moment of the whole process comes when we finally teach the child to read. Now at last the whole world can beam its ready-made opinions into the child's malleable brain, scream its blind slogans, declaim its dogmas into receptive eyes and ears.

The child doesn't stand a chance.

How strangely appropriate that the process traditionally starts with

'A for apple', the apple that is the symbol of our fall from grace, our entry into the underworld, our death.

*   *   *   *   *

Not that it is wrong to recognise that there is a duality pervading existence as we know it. That duality, for us and our senses, is indubitably there. The danger lies in two characteristic assumptions of the approach that I have just outlined—the approach based on linguistic categorisation.

The first assumption is that the categories of our language correspond to reality, and that reality can therefore be totally understood through the spoken or written word. This assumption is widespread among Protestant Christian sects, as well as among Muslims, Cabbalists and the more amateur dabblers in relativity, quantum mechanics and high-energy physics. You can detect it, too, in those who react emotionally against abstract art because it doesn't allow them to make those categorisations—'What *is* it?'—which alone for them correspond to meaning and reality. Only in music is there any wide acceptance of the idea that a work of art can just be allowed to *be* for what it is without categorisation, and even here it is often assumed that a piece of music can be fully appreciated only when it has been analysed.

Nevertheless the snow and camel analogies I made earlier should help to dispel this particular linguistic illusion. Our ancestors fashioned our language—largely subconsciously—as a tool, not as a metaphysical system, and so its categories simply reflect the model of the universe which most conveniently serves our traditional way of life. Metaphysics of a kind this may be, but its main criterion was always usefulness, not truth.

Speakers of other languages are heirs to slightly different symbolic systems, and therefore carry in their heads differing models of the universe about them. Speakers of Swahili do not categorise the phenomena of the world in exactly the same way as speakers of English, still less the speakers of the Australian aboriginal languages. The spectrum may be differently divided, shapes differently categorised, sizes differently grouped, animals, birds and degrees of human maturity differently classified; nouns may acquire tenses, adjectives imply differences of gender, verbs affect nuances of tense, number and probability unknown to speakers of other tongues. Even between such closely-related systems as English and French the differences are considerable—more than sufficient to engender marked contrasts in the

38

understanding and assessment of the world 'out there', and particularly of human behaviour. Small wonder, then, if the children of bilingual marriages, and especially those who are brought up to speak with each parent in that parent's native tongue, sometimes display difficulties of psychological adjustment.

Among speakers of Germanic languages—including English—there is a marked tendency to assume that once an idea has been given a name it represents a reality. Students of German philosophy particularly will recognise the tendency, which no doubt also had its part to play at the time of the Reformation, with all its emphasis on written sources. Crossing the Atlantic in the ships of the North American colonists, the notion was subsequently to flourish as happily in the New World as in the Old, particularly in politics ('democracy', 'freedom', 'participation', 'rights', 'standard of living') and in advertising ('new', 'bigger', 'better', 'Brand X' and a whole range of 'special additives' unknown to science).

Words, then, do not necessarily correspond to reality. And, in particular, *reality itself is not subject to the dualism of the language we use to describe it.* This common, if pardonable, delusion is the second great assumption against which we need to be on our guard. Perhaps it is in our proneness to draw this particular conclusion that our real fall ultimately consists.

Of course there is an observed duality throughout experience as we know it. There is light and darkness, heat and cold, summer and winter, seedtime and harvest, life and death. In our own bodies we observe the duality of male and female, bear the very stigmata of duality. The whole universe revolves around the vast cosmic forces of attraction and repulsion, in the apparent motions of sub-atomic particles no less than in the apparent wheeling of the galaxies and of the planets in their orbits.

But note the two words 'apparent' and 'revolves'.

For those orbits are neither right-handed nor left-handed (scientifically the difference cannot be defined) but *either,* depending on which way we look at them. Could it be, then, that *all* polarities—and thus the whole of existence as we know it—are functions of how we look at them? Are they *all* apparent, *all* relative—dependent upon the observer, the relater?

Do they perhaps look different 'from outside'?

From our position within it, certainly, the whole universe seems to resolve itself into a vast cosmic tournament between the polarities and sub-polarities of the atom. Solidity is a myth, substance an illusion.

And yet what is it that is so polarised? What is it that produces the bewildering phenomena observed by high-energy physics? We do not know. We can never know. Our senses, and our instruments which are their extensions, are designed to detect only phenomena, not 'things' themselves—what happens, not what is. We are aware of reactions, not of that which reacts; polarities, not that which is polarised. Even at the level of everyday existence, we observe only observations.

And so when we come down to the barely-detectable level of the atom's internal structure we are at the very frontier of the knowable. We may speak of matter and energy, mass and velocity, particles and sub-particles—not to mention wavicles and quarks. But these are words rather than things—words whose purpose is to create for us a mental model of the atom, a convenient coat-rack on which to hang our observations of phenomena. They are words about thoughts, and thoughts about we know not what. What is ultimately producing the phenomena, what it is that is actually polarised, must always remain for us unknowable, a closed book. A no-thing.

Indeed it may be just that—nothing.* The same, blissful nothing that seems to lie at the very centre of our own being.

Of course, at this point I am attempting to do the very thing that I have just suggested cannot be done—using words to describe the indescribable, just as generations have tried to do before me. It is rather like using blinkers in an attempt to see more clearly, or chains to break out of prison. It is the old bootstrap-problem all over again. Perhaps silence would be more appropriate than words which teeter on the edge of nonsense—for non-sense the ultimate reality inevitably is.

Yet certain things can be said. At least language can identify the identifiable. That is what it was designed for. And so we can identify for a start those notions that are *not* valid. This was the Buddha's way of tackling the same problem. It is useless, for example, to side with one polarity or the other, to try to destroy the 'opposing forces'. Opposition can bring only reaction, the ceaseless swing of the pendulum of opposites, continued subjection to the shackles of karmic action-reaction. And think what would happen if you succeeded. Take away the black squares from the chess board of existence and there would be no white squares either. Take away the black players and there would

---

*Not my own speculation, but a respected scientific theory, first put forward by cosmologist Edward P. Tryon, of the City University of New York, in 'Is the Universe a Vacuum Fluctuation?', *Nature,* No. 246, 1973.

be no game at all.

If there is no darkness in the observed world, then there can be no light. If there is no evil, there can be no good. Without death, there can be no life. Without opposites, in short, there is no existence, only pure being. Yet whether we like it or not we *exist*. And it is as existent beings that we have to act.

But to what purpose?

The dynamic of duality, it seems, is the method whereby the basic cosmic unity evolves to produce a new unity, a higher essence. And humanity, itself the fruit of the polarity of male and female, is intimately involved in the process. Not only as its observer, its relater, its catalytic agent, but as the summit of the earthly evolution through which that process expresses itself. It falls to us, then, to build the new world-house, using duality as our bricks and mortar.

At every level of our world of phenomena we exist at the intersection of two cosmic arcs, at the interface between two worlds. And only we are aware of the fact. It is only in and through our consciousness that the chaos of disconnected perceptions can become a unified field of awareness whereby the dualities of space and time, of mind and matter, of physical and spiritual may eventually be transcended. And so it is from the spark of human consciousness, flashing between the two poles of duality, that the next step in the cosmic process must eventually arise. From thesis and antithesis a new synthesis will spring, a new foundation for a further upward leap. Through us the universe achieves self-awareness. And the universe itself, some say, must be transformed.

*   *   *   *   *

The immediate task, then, is to penetrate beyond the veil of mere duality, beyond that largely artificial world which our senses observe and our language remodels and categorises. And in that world beyond the senses, in that kingdom beyond words that is also the silence of meditation, we may re-discover the ancient oneness that lies beyond all categories and distinctions, beyond sex and race, class and dogma, religions and moralities, opinions and judgements—indeed, beyond belief.

The distinctions become blurred, the dualities resolved. Things simply *are*. The returned innocence of the new-born child, the childlikeness which alone grants entry to the Kingdom of Heaven. No longer is there any distinction between self and other, between heaven and earth, between God and man. The frontiers are down. From the union of opposites a new humanity is born. The world begins anew.

And in anticipation of that sacred moment the Buddha sits down to meditate under his Bo-tree, Moses and Jesus on their mountain-tops, Muhammad in his cave. All are transfigured. In England the later Isaac Newton reclines under his tree until the legendary apple brings sudden awareness. But this time it is the apple, not man, that falls.

The apple of enlightenment.

The penny drops.

I AM.

6. YOU THE DREAMER

Mind is the builder.
Edgar Cayce

Admittedly we have just been speaking of a vision, not reality. There is nothing substantial about a vision. But then, as we have seen, there is nothing substantial about reality as we know it either. And if visions themselves are not that reality, then they have a truly extraordinary way of becoming it.

It is as though vision were the essential first step in reality's becoming.

Once upon a time nobody on earth, as far as we know, had ever run a mile in as little as four minutes. It was not that they lacked the muscle-power or the practice. It was not that the laws of gravity or aerodynamics were different. It was not that the food was inferior.

It was simply that the vision was lacking.

Nobody had ever achieved the four-minute mile for the simple reason that nobody had ever imagined that it was possible—whether in those terms or any others. It was inconceivable. And so, not having been conceived, it was never born.

Then, one day in 1954, a British doctor named Bannister achieved what had hitherto been impossible. A mile in 3 minutes 59.4 seconds. The world stood amazed. There he was—a man, not a god. There he was, still alive, still breathing. There were many who had witnessed the event, and many more who would do so on television.

And then what happened?

Suddenly everybody started to do it. Within a short time no distance-runner was anybody who hadn't run a four-minute mile.

Soon it got to the point where only four-minute milers stood any chance even of reaching the finals of international events, let alone of winning them. In more senses than one a milestone in human evolution had been reached.

Why this sudden outburst? Why had the impossible suddenly become possible?

Simply because a man had had a vision—a vision of himself achieving a distant goal. Having created that vision, he went on to develop techniques to ground it—to bring heaven down to earth. And its translation into physical terms then made it possible for others to share the same vision, to make it their own. Seeing was believing. And having achieved that faith, they could go on to move mountains.

The road of human evolution is marked by a myriad such milestones.

It was in 1522 that Magellan's ship, the *Vittoria*, at last came home after completing the first known circumnavigation of the globe. That event, too, represented the fulfilment of a vision—a communal vision which had been incubating, growing and unfolding in the mind of Renaissance humanity since at least the time of Columbus. Once again it was not lack of people or materials that had prevented its earlier realisation, but one of imagination. The vision was all. Thus grounded, the new vision could now give birth to other visions.

First the solo circumnavigation. Perhaps it was inevitable. that the first to achieve this should have been a former ship's captain—one who, having already sailed the seven seas, had the materials fresh in his mind for building his house of dreams. And so Joshua Slocum, setting out in 1895 in his little *Spray*, embarked on his epic three-year voyage.

And thereby gave birth to other dreams.

For if the world could be encircled by a single man in three years, why not in two, or even one? Why not emulate the clipper-ships, stoping only once, in Australia?

And so Slocum's grounded vision—which had already produced a number of successors—combined with that of the clipper-captains to produce a new dream. Meticulously its dreamer explored the accounts of earlier mariners, pored over the charts which recorded their observations, re-created in his own mind the whole of the voyage he was about to undertake, until for him it became a living reality—a reality subsequently focussed and intensified through the writing of his book *Along the Clipper Way**. And it was in 1966 that the 64-year-old

*Francis Chichester: *Along the Clipper Way* (Pan, 1967).

Francis Chichester, already a sick man doing battle with the ravages of cancer, set out to bring his own particular vision into triumphant manifestation.

The next step was inevitable. The difference between the dream of a one-stop circumnavigation and a non-stop one was merely a matter of two years and a change of dreamer. And following Knox-Johnson's 313-day voyage it was only a matter of time before Colas (despite one stop) reduced its duration to 167 days in his trimaran *Manureva* and Blyth, defying the elements, encircled the globe 'the wrong way'—against the prevailing winds and currents.

It seems that we can achieve anything we set our minds to. But it is the setting of our minds to it that is the crucial event. What is then set in operation is nothing less than a universal law—the Law of Creation or Manifestation.

Basically this law states that *whatever the mind can fully conceive will eventually come to birth.* And there is of course a corollary: *whatever comes to birth does so because it has first been conceived in the mind.*

The implications of this law are considerable. Implicit in it is the idea that thoughts are real things—as real as anything else. What is thought today is done tomorrow. As a man thinks in his heart, so he is.

We are such stuff as dreams are made on.

*   *   *   *   *

The process can perhaps be seen most clearly in the growth and development of a human child. Even before it is born the baby's limbs start practising the movements which will allow it to crawl and, later, to walk. Already the neural passageways are being opened. Something in the child already foresees the crawling, walking being that it will become, and fashions it accordingly. And if at this stage the mental and neural impulses are absent, the child will never walk of its own accord.

But the child has yet more growing to do before it becomes an adult. And in order to achieve that transformation yet further processes of anticipation must take place—processes both of body and of imagination. The child begins to play. In its imagination it creates its own adult world, takes on a multitude of grown-up roles. Continually it tests, experiments, learns. Already it starts to visualise its future life, its future role. And if the adults around it can discover that vision, help the child to hold it and feed it, the vision will grow and unfold until it is eventually fulfilled.

Traditionally our educational systems have imposed their own vision on the teachers, who have in turn imposed it impartially on their pupils. In general it has been a vision of prescribed academic achievements—a vision focussed by intermediate lenses along the way, in the form of periodic examinations. And all the while the system remained faithful to its own principles, that vision too tended to produce its own inevitable manifestation, its own degree of success.

But it need hardly be said that the imposed vision did not necessarily correspond to the natural vision of every pupil—or even to that of the majority of them. There lay the injustice of the system. For many pupils, experience was always incompatible with the vision, and so the vision, unnourished, quickly withered and died. Left to themselves, there is no doubt that they would have chosen other paths. As it was, they simply became academic failures, and often, by extension, social failures as well.

For some, however, the vision was always close to their particular dreams, while for others the leap of imagination was not so great as to be impossible. For them the imposed vision became a guiding light, producing its own measure of achievement.

More recently there has been an increasing trend towards attempting to allow each child to discover and manifest its *own* vision. The trend is truly humanitarian. Unfortunately it tends to be defeated by sheer weight of numbers, pressure of administration and rapidly-changing educational fads and fashions. Above all it tends to be defeated by a conflict of visions. At the end of the process society often still demands fulfilment of an academic vision which, in the initial (and crucial) stages of the process, is almost entirely lacking. Neither vision is adequately fed and cared for, neither picture is properly focussed, and failure too easily results. It is little short of a miracle that, despite everything, the 'humanitarian' vision still manages to win through to manifestation as often as it does.

But then that is what the Law of Manifestation is all about. If the vision can be created and held, the impossible becomes possible.

It's the thought that counts.

*   *   *   *   *

What transformed the western world at the time of the Renaissance was not some new breed of people, not some mutation of the brain. It was a new—or rather a very old—vision of humanity's place in the cosmos. *Genus homo* started to see itself as the true measure of the universe, a semi-divine being in harmony with its processes, able to understand and eventually control its forces. It was that vision that led directly to

46

the development of our present-day science and technology, that vision whose manifestation is our modern world.

Mentally, spiritually, and of course physically it was the vision of our Renaissance forebears that ultimately created *us*.

Later thinkers went on to create further visions. The industrial revolution arose out of the dreams of such men as Watt and Stevenson. The age of flight—one of humanity's most ancient dreams—had the visions of Montgolfier and of the Wright brothers to thank for its eventual realisation. The physics of the atomic age was in due course to take root in the vision of Einstein.

Now enter the great science-fictionists. As well as the submarine, Verne had already foreseen the blast-off from the tip of Florida, the landing on the moon, the return and splash-down in the sea. The vision was eventually manifested in precisely those terms. Soon Wells was to envisage aerial and tank warfare, and later Clarke the communications-satellite. Those dreams, too, were duly fulfilled. And remember that these last three were writers rather than scientists. Having conceived their visions, they held them clearly enough to write about them and describe them in meticulous detail. In the end their dreams became as real in the ether of their minds as if they had been made of steel. Then the dreams were shared, reinforced by thousands of avid readers. Those dreams became communal thought-forms. And finally the thought-forms were charged, given life by the emotional spark of the narrative or by the sudden, excited awareness of new possibilities. The feelings subsequently experienced by their readers helped catalyse the process of manifestation. And so the visions duly entered the realm of the physical, as properly-fashioned visions always do.

Even the death-ray and the great leap through hyperspace are only a matter of time.

* * * * *

How does the process work? How can you operate the Law of Creation to further your own evolution? How can we all use it to help achieve our destiny?

The obvious place to seek the answer is the biblical creation-account, where the technique is set out in detail for all those who have ears to hear or eyes to read. The technique is here attributed to God. Presumably, then, what is good enough for God is good enough for you.

As the author of the *Tao Te Ching* puts it, 'Knowing the ancient beginning is the essence of Tao.'

The first command in the Genesis-story is 'Let there be light' (Day One). The vision must first be created—the vision that is the very stuff out of which all that follows must be fashioned. But there is an important condition written into the text. 'God saw that the light was good', it says, 'and he separated light from darkness.'

It is of paramount importance to see that 'the light is good', to see that the vision is one which you *really* want to create. Have you really foreseen all the consequences of your visionary act, both for yourself and for those around you? And not just the pleasant consequences, but the unpleasant ones too? Might the supposed blessing turn out to be a curse in disguise? Or have you forgotten that we live in a dualistic world?

If your wish is a hot summer, are you ready for a drought? If you pray for rain, will you accept responsibility for the floods? He who sows the wind must be ready to reap the whirlwind. The last of the legendary three wishes, you may recall, is the wish to undo the first two.

The biblical *caveat* has more solemn implications too. For as well as ensuring that you really know your own mind, you will also need to see that your vision is one which you have a *right* to create—one that will further the true destiny of humanity. You will need, in short, to know the universe's mind.

For the universe seems to have its own potential vision, its own archetypal blueprint for evolution. The process starts in the very stars themselves, the furnaces where hydrogen is transformed progressively into the whole gamut of the natural elements. It continues on planets such as Earth, where those elements become transformed into the compounds first of inorganic, then of organic chemistry. Then life itself takes up the story. The simplest cells become more complex, combine to form colonial animals. These in turn evolve to produce not only the colonial species such as the ants and bees, but also the eventual flowering of consciousness in humanity. The next step would logically involve the 'colonialisation' of that consciousness into a single world-mind—so that all men and women become what St Paul called the body of Christ on Earth. And of what follows we can have but the merest inkling.

The universe, in short, has a destiny to fulfil, and it falls to us, as the flowers of earthly evolution, first to discover that destiny and then to help fulfil it. There is a potential cosmic vision which it is our task to make actual, a blueprint for which we must supply the visionary bricks and mortar. And the universe will not be thwarted.

Attune your vision, then, to the continuing song of the universe and your purposes will prosper. But create a vision which conflicts with it—a selfish power-dream, perhaps, or some vision of evil—and you will create a dissonance, a conflict of powers, a cosmic imbalance whose inevitable resolution must destroy its own source. The fulfilment of your dream will turn out to be your own undoing. The universe will inevitably win. There is no future in resisting the flow.

Stay tuned to your friendly station.

The Genesis text also makes it plain that the light of your vision must be 'separated from darkness'. You need to be sure that the fulfilment of your vision will not be contaminated by any other, contradictory visions of your own making. Single-mindedness is essential. The medicine of the Creative Law is incompatible with other drugs. As Matthew's gospel puts it, 'It is better to enter into life with one eye (one vision) than to keep both eyes and be thrown into the fires of hell.' You will need to keep your vision not only cosmically-attuned, but also whole and single. Until its fulfilment it needs to be your *only* vision, and from that vision everything else will then flow.

Seek ye first the kingdom of God, and all the rest shall be added unto you.

*　　*　　*　　*　　*

Having conceived the initial vision and satisfied yourself of its rightness, whether by meditation or by reflective study of the world's great scriptures and religious traditions, you can now go on to the second stage (Day Two). The text describes it in terms of the division of the primeval waters and the separation of earth from heaven. The imagery is reminiscent of birth itself, and the meaning appears to be that the future birth of your vision must now be cosmically placed. Are you aiming to produce a spiritual or a physical, a symbolic or an actual event? At what level of manifestation are you aiming? You will need to make up your mind, and to concentrate on that aspect alone.

Now the vision must be sited (Day Three). The text speaks of the division of land and sea. You must now be quite precise about where you want your vision to materialise. You must imagine its fulfilment in its true spatial context—imagine it coming to life, imagine its results. The text speaks here of seed-bearing plants, and insists once again that you must see that those results are good—cosmically in tune.

The fourth stage is the stage of timing. The text speaks of the role of the sun and moon in dividing day from night (Day Four). You must now decide when you intend your vision to be fulfilled, and once again you must see that your timing is good.

49

This can be one of the more difficult stages of the process, since it is not always easy to see events in their true perspective and to time them correctly. Dispassion and lack of involvement—both of them traditionally regarded as trademarks of the enlightened individual—seem to be vital prerequisites for a clear perception of the ebb and flow of events. The imagery of the text seems to suggest that you should aim at a maximum accuracy of somewhere between a day and a month. Bear in mind that even Jesus of Nazareth declined to specify days or times in his eschatological predictions (see Matthew 24, for example). Bear in mind, too, that being in the right place at the right time seems to be one of the hallmarks of the initiate, as well as the apparent basis of many reported 'miracles'—the ultimate in manifested visions.

In short, your success in controlling stage four of the process seems likely to depend very heavily on how spiritually evolved you are.

And so we come to Day Five of the creation-account, which speaks of the making of the birds and fishes. You have sited your vision in space and time, as well as in its level of cosmic vibration. You have checked its rightness. Now you must allow it to take off, to gain in intensity. 'Be fruitful and increase', says the text. Give your imagination full rein.

Which brings us to stage six, the culminating stage of the process. For now you must people your vision, finally bring it to life. And among the 'living creatures' to which the text refers (Day Six) it is absolutely vital to imagine *yourself*—to 'create man in your own image'. Imagine yourself observing the final manifestation of your vision, ruling over its fulfilment. And above all see that it is 'very good'. Anticipate your joy, involve your deepest feelings in your imagined goal, for it is that strength of feeling that will finally catalyse the whole process.

Whereupon we reach the final stage, stage seven. You have completed your work. By dint of repeated visualisations you have succeeded in constructing the house of your vision. Now you must rest. Allow the Law of Creation to take its course. For this is the Seventh Day, the Sabbath.

All things come to those who wait.

* * * * *

Perhaps it is by using some such technique that we shall eventually learn to harness the enormous reserves of mental power that we never use and put them to the service of humanity's further evolution. It is a case of mind over matter—or even mind *through* matter. Perhaps the two are ultimately one—a fact which would help to explain the operation of the Law itself.

Certainly there is nothing occult or magic about it. Subconsciously you have used the Law of Creation all your life. You used it to create your present circumstances. You not only chose, but created who you are. In a very deep sense you are a figment of your own imagination. And the process goes on, for still you spend most of your days creating your tomorrows, and most of your nights finding out the consequences of what you have created.

The operation of the Law of Creation is not only well-attested; it is self-attested.

But if you have created yourself, what of the world around you? What of the universe itself? If the Law of Creation states that universe to be the manifestation of a vision, is it a dream in the mind of God, a work of pro-vidence, literally of 'fore-sight'? In that case, who is God? And who are you? Is there any difference? Can it be that we all are ultimately co-creators of the universe about us?

If so we have a heavy responsibility to bear. Few of us would care to suggest that everything is really for the best in the best of all possible worlds—at least in terms of human affairs. Relying on the purely subconscious operation of the Law of Creation we have come perilously close to losing our way. Blindly using the Law in the blatant service of our envy and greed, our pride and gluttony, our sloth, anger and lust, we are like children with a cosmic time-bomb. Or rather four-and-a-half thousand million cosmic time-bombs.

Thanks to the advent of the mass media the vision of whole nations can now be captured and manipulated in the space of a moment. The word 'television' is truly apt. No wonder the pace of change constantly increases. And as the problems of the whole world come crowding into our very living-rooms, we are naturally beset with anxieties and fears. Yet, by the Law of Creation, it is those very fears themselves that, multiplied and made even more vivid by the media, will inevitably produce what we most dread. It is the story of the sorcerer's apprentice all over again.

Perhaps it is time that we realised what we are doing. Perhaps it is time that we became fully conscious of the Law's operation. What we think and will and visualise today will surely come to pass tomorrow in an unholy cocktail of incompatible elements, a mixture that will almost certainly explode in our faces. In a remarkably literal sense, we may all be blown to Kingdom Come. Should we not be agreeing on what we *really* want, searching for that greater universal vision in which alone there is some future?

'I have a dream', proclaimed Martin Luther King, and his dream was the dream of seers and prophets all down the ages. The dream of a future golden age when people would embrace as brothers and sisters, when war and malice would be no more, when humanity would go forward to meet its greater destiny in further ages yet unborn.

That, too, is a vision. That, too, will therefore inevitably be fulfilled. It has already been created by those who have repeatedly prophesied it. It is their fault.

So, too, is the dark age, the river of fire, the time of hell on earth without which, say the ancient scriptural predictions, the New Age cannot be born. For that also is inevitable. The former dreams and their manifestations are incompatible with the universal vision. 'My thoughts are not your thoughts,' says the biblical Jehovah. The old must be destroyed before the new can take its place.

Things have to get worse before they get better.

The test of a prophet is not whether his or her predictions come true (for that, ultimately, will take care of itself) but whether those predictions accord with the march of cosmic evolution—whether the prophet is *right,* in other words, to help create the predicted events. In the cases I have mentioned time has ultimately to be the judge. But the general trend predicted by present-day seers for future events seems to accord well with the deepest and most respected revelations of the world's major religions*; they look right in the light of such knowledge as we have been able to achieve.

The true prophet, then, is an initiate, an enlightened being. It is out of that enlightenment that she or he then goes on to create a vision for humanity, a future for the universe.

So you may cheerfully blame the ancient seers for the bad times to come, as long as you also blame the financiers, the industrial bosses, the workers, the unions, the politicians, yourself—all those whose jarring vested interests have long since done more than enough to create the coming dark age without even the redeeming feature of a united vision of a brighter tomorrow.

That vision at least you must give the seers and prophets credit for.

And meanwhile there are some who, in New Age communities all

---

*Compare Carter, *Edgar Cayce on Prophecy* (Paperback Library, N.Y., 1968, available in U.K. from Adele Spero, 80 St. James Road, Surbiton, Surrey); Dixon, *My Life and Prophecies* (Muller, 1971); de Sabato, *Révélations* and *25 ans à vivre?* (Pensée Moderne, 1975/6).

over the world—communities such as that at Findhorn in Scotland—
are already seeking to plant the vision of that New Age firmly here on
earth*. To plant it, that it may grow and flower.

It is just as well. For where there is no vision the people perish.

*Compare Annett: *The Many Ways of Being* (Abacus/Turnstone, 1976); Hawken,
The Magic of Findhorn (Fontana, 1976).

7. WE WHO ARE
THE DEAD

But I say unto you, that ye resist not evil.
Jesus of Nazareth (Mt. 5:39)

You won't have long to wait. The bad times are here already. You don't have to be especially observant to realise that all is not well with our world.

Life is hell.

The expression is truly apt, almost literally true. For nothing, surely, could be clearer than that *this* is the place of suffering, the legendary outer darkness, the prison, the underworld, the biblical 'place of wailing and gnashing of teeth.' Hell is not some mythical, post-mortem place of torment, but a living, ever-present reality. Its dead, its tormented souls, are creatures of flesh and blood, not insubstantial shades. Ghosts have no teeth to gnash.

And so we are confronted with a realisation that is almost earth-shaking in its implications. A realisation that may yet shatter our whole view of ourselves, our whole system of values and beliefs.

It is we who are the dead.

Not that the idea is a new one. Far from it. It is an inevitable consequence of reincarnation-theory—for the fact that we are here now means, under the terms of the law of karma, that we have been here before, and that in the process we have condemned ourselves to a further round of mortality.

It is we who are the dead.

That is what is meant by being mortal. Through the visionary process we are self-condemned to an underworld, a hell, a Hades, a *sheol* of our own making. A hell whose inmates persist in imagining that they are mere names, or roles, or personalities, or souls. Hence, presumably, the Christian idea that we need to be saved, for how should we be saved from something into which we have never fallen in the first place?

As Jesus of Nazareth himself pointed out*, it was not for him to condemn anybody: they had already made a perfectly adequate job of it themselves.

Thus the problem of evil, the enigma of suffering over which Christians agonise so endlessly, is in reality no problem at all. As the Buddha was wise enough to realise, suffering is the chief characteristic of life on earth.

What else do you expect of hell?

*   *   *   *   *

At this point in the argument the traditional Christian faces severe difficulties. God, after all, is good. God is love. The Bible says so. How, then, could He have created an imperfect world that turns out to be a place of suffering? How could He have created something evil?

And so a special myth has to be invented. It's all the Devil's fault. Blame it on Satan, the Prince of Hell, whose only too willing subjects we have all become.

But in that case, who created the Devil?

Ah, comes the answer, Satan is really Lucifer. He is a dark angel who, even before time began, fell from heaven through his sin of pride. At which point you might find it difficult to avoid asking further embarrassing questions. Such as how either pride or Lucifer's capacity for it got into a supposedly perfect heaven in the first place.

Let alone the question of who created God.

But by this time your traditional Christian will already have beaten a hasty retreat behind a smokescreen of Sacred Mystery. God works in a mysterious way. He is eternal, infinite, unfathomable. You must not expect to understand Him. It's a question of believe it or not. And if not, then you die.

Which is all very well, except for one point.

The fact that you are dead already.

It is at this point that it starts to become apparent that, somewhere along the line, someone has been barking up the wrong tree. But which

*Jn. 3:18, 12:47-8.

tree? You've guessed it.

The tree of the knowledge of good and evil.

The basic weakness in the argument that I have just been outlining is that it subjects God to our own self-created duality, assigns Him to only one half of reality. Yet God is also supposed to be the ultimate reality itself, that reality which, by definition, cannot be a function of language or duality at all.

Certain things follow. There can be nothing that He (She? It?) is not. If He is love, then He is also hatred; if He is good, then He is also evil. He is His dark side (the Egyptians' *Set*) no less than His light side (the Egyptians' *Horus*). And if there is a Devil, a Satan, a Lucifer, then that too is no more than an aspect of His own Divine nature, an aspect, moreover, without which His lighter side, His 'shining countenance', cannot appear. 'Lucifer', paradoxically, means 'Light-bearer': he represents the primeval darkness, the gloomy background in the absence of which the heavenly light cannot be seen to shine. And so Christianity's all-righteous God and the Satanic embodiment of all evil turn out to be merely the two complementary aspects of a dualistic God-conception, the two sides of a single heavenly coin.

We Westerners, projecting our own psychic image upon the heavens, have managed to make even the ultimate reality seem two-faced.

But that is not the end of the argument. In fact it is only the beginning of it. It is the chink of light, the thin edge of the wedge, the key which may yet open the door to a new vision of reality, and thus through the inevitable effects of the Law of Creation to a new heaven and new earth.

For if it is obvious that we in the West have traditionally fashioned God in our own image, it is also clear that if we can succeed in remodelling that image we can hope to make a start on remodelling ourselves. The consequences of that achievement would be both profound and almost unimaginably far-reaching.

The world would be transformed.

*   *   *   *   *

As we have already seen, the world as we know it is essentially our own creation. If, then, life is hell it is we who have made it hellish. The world about us is the fruit of our own vision, and that vision has been created out of the stuff of our thoughts—thoughts which are in turn very largely a function of our language. But at the very basis of that language there lies, as we also saw earlier, a process of negation and discrimination. With it we divide reality into imagined polar opposites, carve our experience up into whole dictionaries of separate, watertight concepts. And so it is hardly surprising that our vision of the world should have conjured up a cacophony of jarring elements, a struggle between warring opposites in which it is almost inevitable that we shall be forced to take sides, even though those sides themselves are merely imaginary devices of our own invention.

So it is that we come to make the familiar distinctions betwen this and that, here and there, now and then, yours and mine. This might be excusable, but then we commit the unforgivable, the fatal mistake.

We divide good from bad.

It may seem harmless enough at first, but in no time at all the process becomes addictive. Soon we are applying it even to the largely neutral ideas just listed. That becomes preferable to this, there nicer than here, then better than now, yours superior to mine. Except where we are saddled with something for life, in which case mine is better than yours. We start to apply value-judgements to everybody and everything—and not least to ourselves.

Now it is important to be quite clear about what is involved at this point. It is nothing less than a rejection of half of reality. 'Good' means that which you (or others on your behalf) approve of, welcome, accept: 'bad' means its opposite—that which you disapprove of, dislike, reject. And never the twain shall meet.

You may regard as 'good' such abstractions as unselfishness and reasonableness, love and conjugal loyalty, cleanliness and order, peace, democracy and freedom. By the same token you may attach the label 'bad' to their opposites: greed and irrationality, hatred and lust, unwholesomeness and chaos, violence, dictatorial attitudes and the oppression of others. And were I to speak in favour of this latter group, you would possibly attach the label 'bad' to me as well.

Against other imagined evils you may react so strongly as to impose blanket taboos upon them. So great an aura of fear and aversion do they carry that you may find it difficult to discuss or even mention them. In this category you could perhaps place death (as opposed to life), disease (as opposed to health), and even such curious bedfellows as defecation, urination, nudity, sex and religion itself. And if, while reading the last sentence, you find yourself mentally cringing at the very words, you will have some idea of how much you have long since fallen prey to the spell!

Yet you need only reflect for a moment to realise that of all these supposed evils and unmentionables, of all these ideas from which you

57

would cut yourself off, each and every one is already a deep and ineradicable part of your own nature.

It is perfectly obvious that you can no more survive without defecating and urinating than you can do without eating or drinking. They are all parts of the same digestive process around which your body is built. 'Accepting' the ingestive aspects of that process and 'rejecting' the excretive ones may be curiously apt in a curious, symbolic way, but it's an odd attitude to take to reality. Especially when you are also expected to banish those 'rejected' activities to a hidden place or room, and even to avoid, or at any rate disguise, all reference to them. There is something curiously sick about the whole business; something rotten, and not only in the state of Denmark.

Just as there is about the question of sex. Here, once again, the process is one that you cannot avoid. You are the result of the sexual process, and even if you chose to avoid expressing it directly in your own life, you would still be unable to avoid the astonishingly varied urges which are its psychic side-effects. Yet sex itself must be screened from the light of day, all reference to it carefully veiled.

The state of affairs is no better where death, disease and nudity are concerned. Death and disease are as essential a part of you—who are a living creature, a biological process—as are birth and health. Nudity, too, is inevitable. Whether or not you now approve of the fact, naked you came into the world and at death, similarly, you will be revealed in all your nakedness. Even the clothes that you wear in deference to present social fashion serve only to cover up your nakedness, not to abolish it.

Similar considerations apply to our original list of 'baddies'—greed, hatred, violence and the rest . While you may reject such ideas as greed and irrationality, you would be foolish to deny their presence in the depths of your own psychic make-up: a century of psychological science has done more than enough to demonstrate that hatred and self-interest are universally active in the human subconscious. The most saintly folk are often the first to admit to 'unwholesome inner stirrings' and undisciplined mental chaos. And anyone who has not recognised innate tendencies to tyrannise and do violence to others—however veiled and subtly transmuted their actual expression—has been living in a brittle world of self-delusion, a fool's paradise.

And so if you reject evil you reject half of yourself. You approve of the rational aspect of yourself and disapprove of the irrational. You accept the conscious and reject the unconscious. You side with 'I' in an effort to subdue the unruly 'me'. Yet the attempt is always futile. It has to be—for the very reason that 'I' *am* 'me'.

Meanwhile you may be blissfully ignorant of this inner state of undeclared civil war. Your conditioned responses, your inherited sets of values, were drummed into you by your elders almost as soon as you learnt to speak, so that you may never consciously have experienced any other way of looking at things. Consequently you too easily assume that your present attitudes are the only possible ones, that everything is for the best, in your own world at least.

But your unconscious self knows otherwise. As time goes on, the urges that you have suppressed become ever more powerful and insistent, until eventually the conscious mind can no longer be sure of controlling them without taking a further, crucial step. It places an absolute taboo on them, denies their very existence within the psyche.

And sure enough they disappear.

But let someone suggest that they still exist—that you are still greedy or irrational, hateful or self-centred, tyrannical or aggressive—and see what happens. Often there is a sudden, almost apoplectic anger, a blind and irrational rage. And at once the truth is out. For that rage is an infallible symptom of the very suppression that I have just been describing.

Yet most of us are still undeterred. We screw down the lid of self-repression even further. The unconscious drive for self-expression builds up even more, the bottled-up psychic wine ferments. The banned ideas and tabooed concepts surface in dreams, bubble out in artistic fantasies, seek political, academic, sporting or spiritual outlets, or manifest themselves in oddities of behaviour that seem inexplicable to our startled conscious mind, the mind which had thought itself to be in sole control. And if these manifestations of the subconscious mind are themselves suppressed, worse ensues.

A psychosis.

The long-repressed urges seize power by force. The psyche is taken over by those very forces which its conscious part had thought banned and destroyed for ever, and the sufferer becomes incapable of surviving any longer within the framework of a predominantly rationalistic society.

It is we, in short, who are our own worst enemy.

Yet for the most part we do not recognise the fact. The inner enemy remains hidden, and being hidden it is not easily recognised. We do not know how or where it will strike next. Yet our symbol-obsessed psyche cannot resist giving it a face, assigning it a role. And so, unknowingly, we project that image upon the screen that is the world about us—an image which, magnified by our own fears, looms even larger than life. It becomes a demon, a malevolent cosmic force about to spring out upon us from behind every tree, or waiting in the darkness to waylay us. We see even our fellow human beings as possessed by it. Soon we are dividing the world into a malevolent 'out there'—in which the forces of darkness are watching our every move, awaiting their chance to pounce—and an 'in here' which corresponds to what we imagine to be our real self. Our inner drama is converted into an outer, cosmic one. The entire universe becomes caught up in an archetypal, imaginary Western of our own devising, the exclusive playground of cosmic goodies and baddies, with next to nothing in between.

In black and white, of course.

* * * * *

Since we are the writers and directors of this galactic spectacular—not to mention the stars of the production as well—we are not necessarily the best people to criticise either script or performance. Self-appraisal demands that we stand outside ourselves. The Universal Being itself apparently has the same problem—which seems to be why we are here in the first place. We are in dire need of some dispassionate Martian to put our strange antics into perspective.

'The more advanced inhabitants of Planet Gaia', the report to the Intergalactic Cultural Commision might run, 'consist of a kind of gelatinous bladder stiffened by a harder framework. This framework has extensions (one at each corner) for locomotion and for manipulating the environment. Another hard protuberance, containing a fuel-input and a remote-sensing array, serves as the creature's main control centre.

'The members of the ruling species (we have naturally dubbed them the 'Overlords') have developed a sophisticated system of communication based on the creation and reception of atmospheric pressure-waves. They use this system to relate themselves to each other and to the world around them. Unfortunately, however, they have long since blinded themselves with their own science. Not content with using their pressure-wave system to represent reality, they have apparently gone on to assume that it *is* reality. As a result, most of the Overlords are now in a serious state of self-delusion.

'It has, for example, become the custom for the Overlords to live together in large groups. This in turn has made it necessary for them to accept certain limitations on their freedom of action. Yet the creatures often respond to this need by denying the very existence of some of their most basic natural impulses—and this they do *simply by banning the signals of their communication-code which correspond to those impulses.*

'This is all very well, but naturally the creatures then tend to find it very difficult to cope effectively with those impulses—which are still very real, despite the fact that they have to deny their very existence. Reality keeps breaking free despite all their efforts. And so the Overlords have taken the whole process a stage further. They now frantically cover up every physical aspect of their existence which does not square with their agreed ideas on how things should be.

'The species' eventual terminal breakdown and re-absorption into the chemical environment, for example, is shrouded in an extraordinary veil of secrecy. The production of new members of the species is even more obsessively hidden. Dire sanctions are visited on any Overlords who, despite their conditioning, allow any aspect of that process to be seen. Most bizarre of all, perhaps, individuals are often actually forbidden to touch other members of the species—or even to allow themselves to be *seen* by them—except at their very extremities, or by special permission. Consequently the Overlords often drape several layers of fibrous wrappings about their gelatinous bladders, while often mutilating or removing the partial fibrous coating which grows on them naturally.

'Meanwhile the suppressed urges referred to earlier—which now often resurface in the form of anger, violence, envy and ill-will, for example—are still there, and sooner or later they have to be expresssed if the organism is not to become internally unbalanced. Denied expression within the home-group, they duly come out in the form of concerted attacks on *other* groups. Enormous technical resources are devoted to piercing small holes in the gelatinous bladders of members of these other groups, so allowing the vital fluids inside to leak out, or to damaging both them and their life-support equipment in even more disastrous ways. In pursuit of this aim they are quite prepared to lay waste large areas of their own planet if necessary—possibly even to destroy it entirely.

'The Overlords generally justify this extraordinary, aggressive behaviour by claiming, not unnaturally, that their opponents embody all the impulses which they themselves have sought to ban. Destroying their opponents, they seem to feel, will destroy these imagined evils too. Yet facts always prove otherwise. However many opponents they destroy, the evils refuse to go away. And so most of the Overlords have

61

taken to believing that evil is somehow inherent in the outside world itself (and even, as some believe, in the inner one too) as a kind of independent, living force. The result is a theory of the universe which sees the cosmos as somehow divided against itself—a good force whose loyal servants they try to be, and a bad force which it is somehow their duty to help defeat. But then, since their opponents are generally seen as the willing servants of the bad force, the mutual slaughter continues.

'And so the ruling species of Planet Gaia is currently in a dangerously sick state. Unwilling, for social reasons, to accept their own real nature in its entirety, the self-deluded Overlords would rather decimate their own species—even tear apart the very cosmos itself—than face up to their own inner reality. What they currently seem to need, therefore, is some kind of external "mirror"—independent observers such as ourselves capable of helping them to perceive their own state of delusion and to re-achieve a measure of inner integration. The danger is, of course, that we ourselves, as outsiders, may also become identified with those very powers of evil or forces of darkness which they most fear. Indeed, we are already portrayed in this way in some of their symbolic video-diversions. In which case. . .'

I need hardly go on. Hell our world may be, but if it is, then it is a hell of our own making, and most of the ills which make it hellish spring from our refusal to recognise the existence of our own dark side. We refuse to admit the presence within us of those perfectly natural and instinctive wishes and impulses which we have been taught to categorise as 'bad' (since the very word means 'unacceptable' or 'to be rejected'). Misusing the sacred visionary process, we project these banned impulses upon the world around us and turn others into their living symbols. We belittle the other sex, condemn our neighbours, reject other social classes, pronounce judgement on other political groups, ascribe all manner of devilry to other religions, accuse the universe itself of ranging its darkest forces against us. In the name of order and reasonableness we pit ourselves against imagined national foes, strain every muscle to wipe them from the face of the earth, proclaim our readiness to destroy our very planet if need be to prevent them from imposing their will on us.

And then we are surprised to find our world in turmoil.

But it is also at that point—the point which we have now reached in human history—that the real nature of the whole process starts to become clear. People who would rather destroy themselves than accept a modified life-ethos are dangerously sick. Humanity too, by the same token, is menaced by a collective psychosis of the most perilous kind, a sort of world-schizophrenia that is on the verge of becoming a planetary death-wish. Nothing could be more obvious than that all these forms of social rejection are typical forms of neurotic behaviour. They are merely the symbolic, external acts with which we try to objectivise and come to terms with our own inner conflicts.

The inexplicable behaviour of the other sex, the imagined misdeeds and personal oddities of our neighbours, the crimes of other social classes, the ideological and philosophical idiocies of other political and religious groups, the primal threats supposedly posed by other nations and races— each of these is the inevitable expression of basic impulses and attitudes which are common to all humanity, *including yourself.* The more violently you condemn the foibles and oddities of others—their tastes, their opinions, their alleged sexual peculiarities—the stronger and consequently more repressed you reveal those same tendencies to be in yourself.

As we judge, so we are.

* * * * *

And so, in the time-honoured manner of neurotics everywhere, we project the hidden aspects of ourselves onto outward phenomena, using these as our psychic tools—symbols which allow us, if not to come to terms with our inner urges, at least to express them and relieve the inner pressure for a while. But in the process we contrive to turn almost the whole of the physical world into a set of symbols for our own inner conflicts. While bitterly opposing all sorts of imagined foes 'out there' we remain blissfully unaware that the enemy is already within the gates, hidden among our own ranks, gnawing away at our very vitals. The warlike analogy is actually quite apt, for war itself, despite all its death and bloodshed, its vast technologies and its utter down-to-earthness, is in the same way a mere psychic mirage, a symbolic act.

Time was when the fact was recognised. The fate of nations could be settled by a combat of picked champions, or decided by the outcome of a pitched battle between small representative armies. The symbolic battle having been won or lost, the equally symbolic sceptre would pass to the victor. The faces of the rulers would change, but life itself would go on very much as before.

But now we take things much more seriously, and the symptoms have become much more grave. Reluctant to believe that we could have become so passionately involved in what is a mere symbol-game, we have managed to convince ourselves that what we see as external phenomena are reality itself. The symbols of war are taken literally.

'Destroying the enemy' has become a goal to be applied not merely to the enemy's symbols—the flag, the standard, the leader—but to the enemy in person. 'Kill or be killed' has become the physical order of the day. Total delusion has led to total war.

But with the final development of all the murderous weapons and titanic technologies necessary for Armageddon, the human neurosis whose progress we have been tracing has now reached the limit of its possibilities for self-expression. On this convergent and ever more crowded planet we can no longer afford to take it out on somebody else. As with the severely-disturbed mental patient, we have reached the point at which any further worsening of the symptoms must result in our own self-destruction. The point of psychosis has been reached.

The human soul, in short, is desperately ill. That illness, in keeping with current medical fashion, we have so far tried to treat simply by suppressing its symptoms. Unfortunately the result, as usual, has been a growing dependence on the various drugs and medicines taken, the production of further, more serious and less easily treatable symptoms, and a general deepening and complication of the case. The time has come for us to realise that, if humanity's psychic sickness is to be cured and its symptoms relieved, then our psyche itself must literally be made whole again.

* * * * *

Thus we need to turn once more to the age-old technologies—many of them almost buried now and half-forgotten under the accumulated debris of centuries of blind, rationalistic, language-based dogma—in an effort to restore that long-lost psychic wholeness. Once again we need the technologies formerly wielded by the ancient religions; technologies rediscovered by the pioneers of psychological science during the last hundred years or so of our own era.

Not that it will be easy. The widespread and well-known taboo on religious discussion makes us aware of the magnitude of the task, for it represents a deep-seated aversion to the possibility of real introspection, a real fear of what an in-depth examination of our psyche might reveal. It is as though we expect it to turn out to be a kind of Pandora's Box, out of which all manner of unnameable horrors will crawl forth to devour and lay waste our familiar world.

And perhaps there are good grounds for that assumption. Our whole culture and life-style, after all, are based on the workings of our reason. So, at least, we believe. Any resurgence of the irrational is something to be feared and resisted—not least because it pertains to the 'unknown'. Indeed, it is because this whole area of the human psyche is 'unknown' that the followers of Jung refer to it as the 'unconscious', those of Freud as the 'subconscious'.

Yet this aspect of ourselves is 'unknown' only because of our upbringing, which never allowed it to become conscious in the first place. Most of the urges and instincts from which we are so keen to dissociate ourselves were relegated to the dark dustbin of taboo and irrational subconscious fear at such an early age that we never had the chance to learn to handle them rationally. Small wonder if those urges subsequently come to be expressed—as expressed they eventually must be—in irrational form. Two horrendous world wars in our own century testify to the dangers of allowing our subconscious urges free and uncontrolled expression.

Yet as we are, so we behave. The fact that we have chosen to conceal from ourselves one part of what we are will not alter the fact. The truth will out, sooner or later.

Thus it is that the search for the true self, the quest for the re-achievement of psychic integration—and with it the achievement of full conscious mastery over our formerly subconscious urges—acquires in our own time a truly cosmic significance. Our very future hangs upon it.

The road onward lies inward.

And so your own quest for self-knowlege, your own attempt to answer the question 'Who am I?', your own struggle to illuminate even the deepest subconscious areas of your 'unknown' psyche with the light of full consciousness, is of vital importance. Literally so. For you are humanity, as humanity is you. And if you have still not learnt to escape from your self-created hell, your prison of duality, your iron mask of personality, then the reason is plain. It all goes back to the fact that, with the aid of your language, you are eating what the Bible describes as the fruit of the tree of knowledge of good and evil. The diet, as we have seen, is highly addictive. It sunders both your outer and inner worlds into irreconcilable opposites.

And it leads only to death.

What is the alternative? The symbolic biblical account once more gives the answer. It is the tree of life. Eat its fruit, states the tradition, and you will live forever, achieve immortality, become as God. And so the quest for that tree becomes of paramount importance.

But where is it to be found?

The answer in the text is equally clear. It is to be found in the middle of the garden, the Paradise Lost, the abode of eternal bliss, that is the centre of yourself.

Part II
Symbols of Destiny

Identification:
Advance and Be Recognised!

There is a traditional response to those who are depressed, sick at heart, inwardly torn apart:

'Pull yourself together!'

It seems excellent advice. Until you realise that it leaves two vital questions unanswered.

Who is the self that would be pulled together? And who is the you that would do the pulling?

If you cannot answer those questions, the advice is pointless. If you can, it is superfluous.

What separates the psyche into its two opposing halves, into 'I' and 'me', into 'you and 'yourself', is no more than a cloud of unknowing, a barrier of ignorance. Yet it is an iron curtain that is impervious to everyday words, proof against mere ideas.

Only our symbols are powerful enough to penetrate the mists of that other world, to translate ignorance into recognition. A wordless knowing that dissolves the barriers, mends the divisions, heals the wounds.

And makes all advice unnecessary.

8. ORDEAL AND INITIATION

Except a man be born again, he cannot see the kingdom of God.
Jesus of Nazareth (Jn. 3:3)

The picture that I have been painting is inevitably a gloomy one, and you may be tempted to assume from it that all is not as it should be with our world. But that would be to beg a great many questions.

It is one thing to establish that humanity has undergone some kind of 'fall'. It is another thing to deduce that we need to be rescued from the 'hell' that we have created for ourselves. And it is quite another to suggest that we ought never to have fallen into it in the first place.

We saw earlier how the unity that is the cosmos seems constantly to divide itself into a duality, or relativity, between whose poles eventually flashes the spark from which the fire of an even higher stage of cosmic evolution can arise. From thesis and antithesis an even greater synthesis ever springs. And it is we who alone can supply that cosmic antithesis. We are the vital tool in that primordial cyclic process, the catalyst evolved by the universe for that very purpose. We alone, you could say, are in a position to stand apart from ourselves and look at the universe 'from outside'. We alone can report what it looks like from 'hell'.

And we owe that position to our gift for creating symbols.

If we humans eventually came to lord it over the animal kingdom somewhere in the dim and distant past, it was not because we were bigger, or quicker, or stronger, nor because there were more of us, nor even primarily because we were more intelligent. We owe our

69

planetary lordship to a simple but effective technique, a gimmick, almost a sleight-of-hand.

The symbol-game.

Thanks to a highly-developed brain, we learned at a quite early stage in our prehistory to create and manipulate symbols for our ideas—those insubstantial, airy, but nevertheless devastating symbols that we now know as *language*. And it was from that dicovery that our whole subsequent development and civilisation sprang.

In the beginning, truly, was the word.

It was by using as symbols the sounds and sound-groupings of language that our primitive ancestors first embarked on the construction of a whole symbolic world of their own devising. Not only did they eat: they spoke about eating. Not only did they make love: they re-created the act in speech. Not only did they hunt: they sat down together and simulated in words the excitement of the chase. Thanks to the magic of language, no less than to that of their cave-art, they could now celebrate events, recall events, create events in advance.

And so, out of the mists and ethers of that new, symbolic world, they could go on to construct ideas and concepts that had never before seen the light of day. The visionary process could commence.

Put yourself in their place.

The universe has given you no specialised tools or weapons; your genes have never heard of the subdivision of labour; you do not breathe fire; your body-mechanism is totally ignorant of the wheel. If you can exercise a measure of telepathy, it was never designed to cope with the organisation of communal flint-knapping or metal-smelting. All you have is your brain, your senses, your hands and feet.

And your tongue.

But with that tongue you can now devise linguistic symbols; with those symbols you can start to build a new vision for yourself; and out of that vision you can go on to create a whole new order of existence.

That, in short, is how our now-familiar world duly came into manifestation. The overlordship of *homo sapiens* was established. The natural, exterior world was first kept at bay, then subdued. Civilisation could arise. Our modern world was born.

But that, as it happens, was not enough for our ancestors.

Perhaps it was inevitable. Perhaps somebody should have realised that if you give a child a bicycle it is liable to ride away on it. For that—or something rather like it—is just what now happened.

You can imagine the delight with which prehistoric people regarded their new-found powers of visionary symbolism. It was as if they had been given a magic wand. All at once it seemed that nothing was unobtainable if they but knew the right linguistic spell. And so you can hardly blame them for using language as a springboard for embarking on a further flight of sheer fancy.

For not content with modifying reality, with transforming the concrete world about them, those ancient pioneers of consciousness now became seduced—and not for the last time—by a mirage, a dream, an impossible ideal.

They would replace the real world entirely with an artificial world of their own devising.

Until now words had stood exclusively for concrete objects and events: they had represented concepts based directly on human sense-impressions. But now further words were to be added—linguistic symbols for a whole range of purely imaginary ideas, concepts which had no existence outside the human brain, mere words about words. In its long history the world had known a whole range of hideous monsters—but never had such abstractions as 'truth' or 'falsehood', 'good' or 'evil', 'reason' or 'intuition' squelched through the primeval swamps. Never had creatures such as 'progress' or 'stagnation', 'democracy' or 'tyranny', 'spirituality' or 'physicality' stalked the ancient hills. The primordial deeps had been entirely innocent of such vast conceptual leviathans as 'existence' and 'non-existence', 'consciousness' and 'unconsciousness'. And such ultimate horrors as 'quantum-mechanics' and 'tangentiality', 'transcendentalism' and 'cartesianism', 'revisionism' and 'antidiscrimination', 'instrumentation' and 'microminiaturisation' were yet to flap a reptilian wing, let alone take to the air.

But now all that was to change. The new dinosaurs of thought were let loose upon the earth. And so it is that the modern world now teems with such abstractions. Heavy-footed, they clump daily through our media, crash into our conversation, trample on our thought—and especially our social thought.

But then you will no doubt appreciate that abstractions such as these have their usefulness. They allow you to approach even practical problems via a new dimension of thought. They can help you bring off a veritable coup of conceptualisation, short-circuiting your inbuilt thought-processes via a kind of symbolic shorthand, a calculus of rationality. Rather like the knight in chess, they allow you to transform even everyday situations by means of a new and astonishing leap through the air of logical abstraction. At the conceptual level you may regret their vagueness and elephantine clumsiness, but without them you would be quite unable to handle the ideas in question. Indeed, because you would now have to explain each idea as you came to it, instead of merely naming it, your train of thought would be lucky ever to leave the station in the first place. There would be no science, no mathematics, no religions, no philosophies, no political institutions, no programmes of social welfare. Humankind would never have taken to the air, let alone set foot on the moon.

But there is a problem.

All the while your words still stand for concrete things—an objective reality that can be sensed and felt 'out there'—there is some hope for you. You are not running away from reality. If those words help you further to control and transform that 'outer world', then the results are there for everyone to see.

Historically, human societies and their technologies indubitably existed.

But now start talking in abstractions, and what happens? There is no longer any external reality to correspond to your words. The concrete universe lacks the means to bring to life your linguistic symbols, to manifest your inner vision. Your new concepts turn out to be mere thoughts about thoughts, images of the purely imaginary.

Yet for you those abstract concepts are quite real. They are no less a psychic reality than all your earlier symbolic concepts that were based on direct sense-impressions. They are not 'just psychological'. For you, *everything* is psychological. It is your psyche that experiences everything that you ever experience.

And so what are you to do? Believe in your senses and reject the new, abstract world that you have just created? Or believe instead in your symbols, which allow you to have your cake and eat it too?

Ever gluttons, our ancestors made the obvious choice.

Without so much as a white paper, discussion-document or international commission they plumped *en masse* for the world of symbols. For the arithmetic of reality they chose to substitute the algebra of their own thought. To have done otherwise would have been to deny half of reality as they now knew it.

The results, as we shall see, were to shake the very foundations of existence.

From now on, the world of concepts would lord it over the world of reality. Words would become more important than things. No longer could an object or an action be simply accepted as it was. It had to be labelled, fitted into a category drawn from the 'higher' world of abstract symbols. That is why young children ask, 'What's that?' or

'What are you doing?' They are not just being stupid. They know perfectly well what it is and what you are doing. They are not blind. What they are demanding—what they have been *conditioned* to demand by the society into which they have been born—is that you should supply them with a set of labels and categories, teach them where to fit their new experience into the framework of the illusion you are imposing on them. So it is that even external realities gradually come to be treated as mere symbols for an inner reality that we somehow feel to be more tangible and more relevant. Concrete sense-impressions of the world 'out there' are used as mere building-bricks to construct a whole house of inner illusion, a counterfeit world of our own devising.

In defence of that world no sacrifice is too great. To suppress the use of particular words laws must be passed. In defence of mere concepts wars must be fought.

The word and the image are all.

Nothing exists for which there is not a word. Conversely, behind every word there lurks a reality. So, at least, we fondly believe. If, then, there are words such as 'freedom', 'democracy' and 'progress', then these must be treated as real things.

Even though you might be hard put to it to point to the actual existence of any of them in practice.

And so such words must be defended and fought for. Especially against speakers of other languages, members of other linguistic faiths, devotees of different hierarchies of symbols from our own, whose very existence, it seems, threatens the stability of our own pattern of illusion, our frail structure of symbols, our house of cards.

The story of our money shows very clearly this process of self-delusion in action. Long since a mere token for reality, literally a paper currency of exchange, money's actual worth is nowadays next to nothing. And yet we persist in confusing price with value. We persist in treating money as if it were real. The old, particularly, complain ceaselessly about rising prices, obsessively converting new currencies into their former equivalents—as though the latter were some kind of yardstick of real worth. In the case of the old *poor* it is perhaps understandable: but the old *rich* do it as well.

Even our governments have become obsessed with the problem, turning the battle against what they call 'inflation' into a semi-religious crusade. To defeat it they impose draconian price-freezes, credit-squeezes and wage-policies—or, alternatively, treat monetarism as a god. They are even prepared to call international conferences to discuss the issue, and to put at risk their own very survival in monetary feuds with clamouring trades unions.

Yet, in the developed world at least, there is little or no real inflation.

The value of bread is the value of bread is the value of bread. And in terms of most other vital commodities it stays substantially the same. So does the value both of those other commodities and of labour itself.

It is not values that keep increasing, but prices. The problem, if problem it is, is merely that more paper is needed, that our monetary symbols are constantly being devalued. That is the real disaster.

For the symbol has become our god. And to devalue your god is always sacrilege.

*   *   *   *   *

So it is that we now live almost entirely in a world of our own devising—a world of insubstantial symbols and airy images, disembodied ghosts flitting about a misty dreamworld behind which loom only very vaguely the shapes and contours of objective reality. Orpheus has finally entered Hades, the underworld and abode of the dead. The son of man has descended into hell.

Mere myths, admittedly. But the ancient myths, too, are part of that dreamworld, and an important part at that. Along with our dreams, they are one of our chief ways of expressing the inner, archetypal processes that are forever at work in the depths of our psyche. They are one of the vehicles whereby we reveal ourselves to ourselves.

And it is some such revelation that we need today, perhaps as never before.

For humanity, it must by now be quite obvious, has long since reached the point where it has finally lost sight of itself. We are truly lost souls. So intent are we on the symbol-game that we now take it for reality itself. We have committed ourselves to a basic mutation of consciousness, and if we fail to realise the fact it could eventually prove disastrous.

Which is where our myths come in.

The myth of the descent into hell is a very ancient one, and provided that you don't either take it literally or treat it as a 'mere fairy-story', it can reveal a valuable truth. Even fairy-stories, you will recall, can have a useful role to play. In this case, the lesson is that even gods have to die, to descend into the underworld, to lose themselves. But it is not a once and for all affair. If they die, proclaims the myth, then it is only to be reborn; if they descend into the earth, it is only the better to rise again. The doctrine of reincarnation proclaims the same vital message. To find your true self you must first lose yourself.

It is the myth of perpetual initiation.

At the present moment, as we have already seen, it is our symbols that have become gods, and we, consequently, who are the dead. Unless we want the story to end there, we now have to write its next instalment. Our present symbols must die. And with their death we in turn may yet become as gods.

* * * * *

How the myth of initiation arose nobody knows for certain. It may have come from a deep, intuitive realisation in the early human pysche; or equally it may have been derived from nature herself.

Perhaps, indeed, the two are ultimately one and the same.

If, after all, you are a primitive, you are aware of the cycles of nature in a way that modern city-dwellers are not. Your life revolves around the daily death and rebirth of the sun; your seasons are geared to the moon's monthly decay and renewal; your agriculture and food-gathering reflects the annual rhythm of heat and cold, of seedtime and harvest.

Now one thing particularly seems to have struck the ancients about the various natural cycles. Far from wishing that they would suddenly stop, they seem to have realised that there is nothing more constant about the universe than the fact of eternal change. The Greek Heraclitus and the ancient Chinese authors of the *I Ching* clearly realised the same thing. And from it there followed the obvious conclusion that the universe was not a thing or a state, but a process; not a noun, but a verb. Existence was not static, but dynamic—a constant, never-ending flux from which all life, power and energy ultimately derived.

It was actually *essential* that the sun should rise and set, that the moon should wax and wane, that the seasons should revolve. Therein lay their very life. Consequently, from the earliest times, ceremonies and rituals were devised the world over to 'assist' and promote the process. In practical terms they might do little to help the universe on its way, but they certainly helped people on theirs.

Because, from this realisation in turn, there arose a very acute and pertinent observation. If the sun and the moon and the seed were to be reborn, it followed that *they must first die*. Such was the nature of the cycle. Death, in short, was an essential prelude to life. And there was no point in wishing otherwise.

But if that was the way of nature, the destiny of the universe, then

75

surely human beings too, as part of that universe, must undergo similar cycles of death and rebirth? Not only in their outer, but also in their inner life. If the life of the universe was not linear but cyclic in character, then the inner human processes must take a similarly cyclic form. In particular the continuing struggle towards the full light of consciousness—that evolutionary process for which the universe seems deliberately to have bred *homo sapiens*—must involve a continual process of death and renewal, of darkness and light, of losing and finding, of hide-and-seek.

And so a myth duly arose to reflect this fact—the myth of initiation. Orpheus, as we have seen, must descend into the underworld, Christ into hell. Adam and Eve must be cast out of Paradise. Daniel must pass through the lion's den, his companions through the burning fiery furnace. Jesus, like Osiris, Adonis, Tammuz and a host of other middle-eastern corn-gods before him, must first die before he can be resurrected. But the myth, remember, is only a reflection of a much deeper, fundamental truth.

Like the seed itself, which must 'perish' in the earth before it can sprout anew; like the Hebrew day, starting at sunset, which must pass through the long darkness before attaining the light; like the drowning St Peter who must be helped up by his Master from the engulfing waters; like the candidate for baptism who must likewise undergo ritual drowning before rising again to the kingdom of the spirit—like all of these, it seems, humanity itself has undergone a fall into the dark underworld of delusion. And from it, eventually, we too are to emerge victorious.

Such at least is the almost universal religious tradition. The most ancient scriptures proclaim it again and again. The former mystery-rites—still preserved in part in the Church's Easter ritual—were to make of it an annual celebration. Forsaking the familiar world of light, the candidate for initiation must be prepared to abandon all that is most dear. Submitted to the most fearsome of ordeals in the darkness of the 'lower world', the postulant must be prepared to suffer mental torments, to bear the destruction of the most cherished ideas and beliefs, even to let go of sanity itself. Then must follow the 'little death'—the three-day period of almost cataleptic trance, reportedly in a symbolic 'tomb'. Only then could he or she rise again, as it were from the dead, in the form of the fully-enlightened initiate, the twice-born, the resplendent bearer of total wholeness and of ultimate human self-knowledge.

Whence, of course, the story of the first Easter.

But that initiation, likewise, is only a symbol—a symbol for the greater initiation, the experience of 'hell', the baptism of fire into which humanity itself has long since plunged. Nor does it stop with us. The whole process is only the tip of the cosmic iceberg. For when we humans abandon reality for the world of symbols—forsaking what is there for what we think is there—we are merely acting on behalf of the universe itself. And it is 'lost' humankind—living and moving as we now do in a separate, symbolic universe of our own devising—that is alone capable, so far as we know, of looking back at the real universe 'from outside'. We are the cosmic antithesis, reality's mirror—and are thus destined to be the collective begetter of the next great synthesis. Our 'fall', far from being a disaster—literally a derangement of the stars—actually turns out to be the universe's salvation.

Humanity's present state of illusion is nothing less than the universe's own initiation-sleep.

For the eye eventually opens. The human eye, which is the universe's window on itself. As we become truly conscious the universe becomes self-conscious. And as that self-consciousness expands to take in all possible phenomena as an interrelated whole, fully aware both of the 'in-here' and of the 'out-there', the very universe itself must eventually be transmuted into the pure, undifferentiated consciousness, the total field of blissful awareness which, in reality, it always was.

As it was in the beginning.

And so the universe will have re-attained its primal state, though at a higher level of the spiral. A new cycle can begin. A cycle destined, perhaps, to produce even more advanced stages of cosmic consciousness.

But one of the preconditions for that achievement—that fusion of knower and known into a simple knowing—is that we human beings, who had thought ourselves to be individual egos or 'I's, should come to realise that we are really no more than *eyes.* The eyes of a greater, cosmic 'I'. The difference, admittedly, is only a matter of spelling, but then you could say that it is 'spell-ing' that lies at the root of the whole problem in the first place. For a 'spell' is a story, a relating, which in due course transforms itself into a piece of magic. Similarly it is by our use of language that we spin the long yarn, the grand fiction, and out of it weave the all-enveloping veil of human illusion—the 'spell', the magic enchantment, under which we have been slumbering now these many millennia.

The wheel of becoming. The magic roundabout.

It is we humans who, through our language and thought, divide reality into discrete 'things' and so create the fictitious alienation of 'this' from 'that', of 'self' from 'other'. It is we who relate the old, old story and, by relating, create relativity. Even in etymology, *things* are a function of *think*ing. Even in the New Testament, it is the *Logos,* or Word, through which every-thing is created out of no-thing. It is above all via language that we sunder the cosmic unity into a pathological duality. And so it is perhaps through keeping silent that we are most likely to regain the unity that is at once our origin and our goal.

The wordless stillness of true meditation. The courage simply to be. Now.

9. THOU ART THAT

We are such stuff as dreams are made on.
William Shakespeare: *The Tempest*, Act IV, Scene 1

Cheer up, then. Things aren't really as bad as they seem. Humanity is no mere terrestrial fall-guy. We are nothing less than the agents of the universe itself, its postulants at the altar of cosmic evolution. And if we are to fulfil that awesome role, it is literally vital that we should undergo the archetypal process of initiation—that process which demands that we must first die in order to rise again.

So do not bemoan our 'fall' into the world of symbols, our lapse into dualistic illusion, our entry into the mythical underworld. It is an inevitable consequence of terrestrial evolution, an inseparable aspect of ourselves. And in any case it is no use fighting what has already taken place. We are no longer in Eden. To return to the archetypal Garden of Delights, the world of unconscious bliss, would be to regress, not to progress. If we have become creatures of illusion, slaves of the almighty symbol, then it as such that we have to act. We must use our very weakness, like the pearl-diving prince, as our tool of redemption. For better or for worse we have committed ourselves to the great ordeal, and it is too late now to withdraw from it. Only by passing through the torments of our own self-created hell are we likely to come out again on the other side—strengthened, and with our consciousness purified and totally transformed.

If we now seem to be surrounded by the darkest night, then perhaps it is a sign that the dawn itself cannot be far off. And if so, the time has already come for us to start the process of self-revival by taking stock of ourselves and recognising ourselves as we really are. Self-awareness is now of the essence.

But this is where our long-standing addiction to the world of symbols starts to pose major problems for us—problems whose roots lie far back in the past.

How did it all come about? Could a more detailed look at the process that we have already sketched in outline suggest some clues to possible action, provide a key to unlock the door of our self-delusion?

It seems worth a try, at least.

* * * * *

We have already seen how, as a result of our early ancestors' invention of linguistic symbols, they suddenly became able to act *en masse,* to tackle difficulties in concert, to bring hitherto unimagined power to bear on the problems of basic survival. For the first time, perhaps, what could be described as a 'group-will' could develop—a will that would have at its command almost unlimited numbers of human hands and feet.

But there was an additional, unintended by-product.

If language had at last permitted group action, it had also permitted group living.

And so the first primitive tribes came together, each based on the use of a particular tongue. Together their members constructed shelter for themselves, assembled their dwellings into larger and larger groups. The labour of the community could be increasingly subdivided, specialist skills developed, the food supply augmented and enriched by new techniques of plant and animal husbandry. And, perhaps most significant of all, those early ancestors of ours could create a breathing-space for themselves.

For almost the first time they acquired leisure, gained time to think.

Perhaps that was when the first abstract concepts arose. Perhaps that was when our forebears first started to turn their attention from what was to what *should* be. For as their early communities, now adequately fed and protected at last, grew and expanded out of all known proportion, new problems started to loom up with almost startling suddenness. Problems of social administration and relationships, of squaring individual liberty with social constraint.

As a member of an isolated family-group in the middle of nowhere, you are as free as the wind. In the case of your hunting, the more aggressive you are the better. In the case of your food-gathering, the more efficient you are at taking whatever goodies present themselves to your eyes, the better you and your family will live. In the case of your love-making, the freer rein you give to your sexual urges, the more assured your posterity will be.

But now all that had changed. Within the community, at least, the aggressive instinct now had to be curbed. The instinct for individual freedom of action had to be subordinated to the need for communal unity of purpose. Where the concept of property arose, the natural impulse simply to take whatever was needed, wherever and whenever it presented itself, had to be stifled. Where the idea arose that a woman was, similarly, a piece of sexual property, even the natural sex-urge—one of the most basic and powerful instincts of the animal world—had to be brought under control.

The prospect was daunting. The task was one for which nothing in our ancestors' natural make-up had really prepared them. Apart from the colonial ants and bees—among whom such things as free will, personal greed and indiscriminate lust were apparently unknown in the first place—nature provided no model to imitate, offered no concrete assurance in practical fact that the thing could be achieved at all.

And so they fell back upon the only world that *could* offer assurance, that could provide a model of what they were trying to achieve. The inner world of symbols.

And it was at that point that those ancient precursors of ours took a step that was to prove of truly epic importance for humanity. They created what may well have been the first consciously-conceived myth.

The myth of good and evil.

In all probability they never realised what they were starting. After all, what is there so special, you may ask, about rejecting a small number of behavioural ideas and banning them from your mind? It is merely a matter of practical convenience.

So, indeed, it may seem.

But consider what now happened. Murder, assault, lawlessness, theft and unbridled fornication had, for various reasons, become undesirable. They must therefore be banned, outlawed, destroyed forever. Reality, in other words, must be changed—and there were perfectly good models, you will recall, for doing that. Language had worked before, and language could do it again.

It was quite simple. If some aspect of reality had to be rejected, all you had to do was invent a word meaning 'undesirable'. Then glue it to the word standing for what you wanted to reject, put it about that the two are now one, teach it to the children and—hey presto!—rejected that concept would duly be.

And so there arose the new mental concept of 'bad' or 'evil'. For the first time in the history of the universe, perhaps, there were evil deeds, bad thoughts. And worst of all, bad people.

But our forebears, it seems, were not too skilled in philosophy. They had not heard of dualism. They had not yet come across the concept of polarity. How could they? They had not yet invented it. Even though by their very use of language they were already demonstrating it every day.

And so they failed to realise that, by labelling one part of their conceptual world 'evil', they were, literally by the same token, labelling the rest of it 'good'. They failed to realise that, by dividing the world of inner reality into two opposing camps in this way, they were in effect splitting the human psyche right down the middle. And they failed to realise that, by embarking on the slippery slope of value-judgements, they had sown the seeds of an inner disease that would eventually destroy their inner wholeness and consign humanity to the fires and fevers of hell.

It was indeed in eating the fruit of the tree of knowledge of good and evil that we humans underwent our initial 'fall'.

For consider what now resulted.

Among living adults, it is true, the new myth probably proved relatively harmless. They, after all, had personal experience of what it was all about. It was a known quantity, capable of being seen and understood in its proper perspective.

But if human society and its newly-acquired values were to survive in their existing form, then the myth must be passed on to future generations. The young must be indoctrinated. As new words were learnt, new concepts acquired, each must be 'painted in its true colours'. Murder was a bogey; assault, lawlessness and theft were evil; fornication a crime.

Yet what was an infant of a few years old to make of it all? The child was too weak to commit murder, even if the impulse ever occurred to it. Fornication was something completely beyond its ken. Only lawlessness, theft and assault were even marginally within its grasp. And its efforts to commit them were almost laughably impotent. What, then, could these have to do with the great 'evil' concepts against which the grown-ups continually warned in such ominous tones?

What indeed? And yet the fact remained—the child had been warned against them. Therefore they must exist. They were real concepts, real constituents of its growing inner world; real aspects, therefore, of itself. And they must be rejected. The child's whole relationship with the surrounding adults depended on it—their love, their approval, the vital need for security.

And so rejected those concepts duly were. *What* they were, however, was not at all clear to the child. And for that very reason they now started to loom even larger than life. Murder became an ogre, the banned sexual urges loathsome monsters lurking in the darkness of the unknown lands of life. Before long they would even start to surface in dreams as symbolic images of the night. From simple concepts to be rejected as 'evil' they were in due course to develop into threatening, living entities to be feared and shunned. The natural reaction was to pretend that they didn't exist at all, to erase their very symbols from the paradigm of the inner world.

And so humanity's game of hide-and-seek commenced. Our ancient ancestors had rejected part of themselves, denied its very claim to existence.

* * * * *

A thing that is hidden is, by definition, unseen. It is removed, however temporarily, from the light of day. And so it all too easily becomes associated with the 'things of darkness'. The fact that the 'hidden' aspects of human nature tend to surface involuntarily in dreams, at dead of night, reinforces the association. And so, inevitably, the now-hidden urges would in due course come to be seen as 'dark' urges. Both the inner and the outer 'unknowns'—those vast areas of external reality and inner experience on which the light of full consciousness never shone—became fused into a single world of 'darkness'. The whole world of the unconscious and of the occult ('that which is hidden') became merged, confused, impartially identified with the powers of darkness, black deeds, black mischief.

Yet the world of the unconscious is not hidden because it is dark. It is dark because it is hidden.

And it was in forgetting this basic fact that our early ancestors put the final seal on the process of self-alienation which was to lead, eventually, to our present planetary psychosis.

The point is, of course, that urges of the type we have just mentioned—the impulses that early human society tried to control by means of linguistic and conceptual taboos—are in fact instincts of the most primal and basic kind. The power-drive, the freedom-instinct, the squirrel-complex, the sex-urge—all these are essential, and morally quite neutral, aspects of our genetic inheritance. And they have to be expressed.

Somehow, somewhere.

And so our forebears took yet another step into the engulfing mists of their world of symbols, added yet another tier to their tottering tower of illusion.

They invented the technique of projection.

*　*　*　*　*

The unconscious is not just some incidental, inferior, insubstantial shadow of the conscious mind. On the contrary, it comprises by far the major component of our psyche. Primitive it may be; pre-rational and pre-linguistic it certainly is. But it contains within itself the seeds of all our instinctive behaviour, all the accumulated animal wisdom of the race, and a whole range of psychic powers that most of us have scarcely heard of, or at best refuse to believe in. And sometimes it seems to have ways of perceiving (who can say?) the very nature of humanity's ultimate destiny.

The unconscious, in short, is a powerful, primal entity in its own right, a veritable tiger prowling amidst the howling forests of your inner night. It has a will of its own. It refuses to be thwarted. And it is none the less powerful and dangerous for being ignored.

And so you and I have an inner communication-problem. For you are your unconscious, no less than your conscious mind. If, then, you are to achieve the power and the glory that derive from total psychic wholeness—if, in short, you are to be finally healed of your inner sickness—your conscious mind needs to speak to the unconscious, the unconscious to your conscious mind.

In the case of your conscious mind, there is no problem. It can order its experience, formulate its thoughts, express them with the help of language. And the unconscious, ever alert despite its misleading name, can take it all in, process it through dreams and assimilate it for future reference.

It never forgets a thing.

But the unconscious itself, as we have seen, exists at a deeper level altogether. Representing as it does a pre-rational and pre-linguistic form of consciousness, it cannot read or write. Language as we know it is, at best, an inadequate vehicle for it. And so it has to devise a language of its own.

The result is a remarkable piece of compensation-therapy.

The workings of the unconscious are, as we have seen, almost wholly instinctive and intuitive. Consequently they are basically no different for you than for me, for the Arab than for the Eskimo, or indeed for modern people than for Stone Age folk. More veiled and repressed they may often be today, but they are none the less there for all that. For convenience, psychologists have divided these unconscious activities into a series of basic instincts, a gallery of psychic behaviour-patterns, to which the great Carl Gustav Jung gave the name 'archetypes'. His term for them seems as good as any.

But how do we know about them? How, in other words, does the unconscious put these archetypes across to the conscious mind?

Basically, it puts on a film-show. It writes a whole scenario around its ideas, drags in objects and scenes from your own familiar world to act as props and scenery, turns your own friends and acquaintances into its actors and actresses, engages you yourself as the principal star. It composes and performs its own quadraphonic film-music, produces a cacophony of unheard-of sound-effects, employs a whole range of flashback and superimposition techniques, creates 4-D impressions as yet unknown to cinematography, and presents the whole thing in an astonishing mixture of black-and-white and full colour. Then it craftily waits for the board of film-censors to fall asleep before finally giving you the full, uncertificated treatment.

If the unconscious feels a particular film to be important enough to you, it will put on regular performances. Other shows you will only see once. Some will delight you, others frighten you, occasional ones terrify you out of your wits. You may even become so scared that you refuse to watch any more. You may deny, even to yourself, that you ever go to this particular cinema. But you still do. You have to. It is a command performance.

And it takes place every night of your life.

It is through your dreams, in short, that the unconscious speaks to your conscious mind, clothing its ideas in symbols mined from the world around you. Consequently, little or no dialogue needs to take place. A picture, they say, is worth a thousand words. Moreover, dreamers of all nationalities see substantially the same dreams. The instincts of the unconscious are common to us all. The themes, therefore, are universal. Dubbing is all but unnecessary. Only the actors and the scenery are changed.

The international film-festival is a continuous, nightly performance.

And so we all get used to certain, archetypal stories. They are recounted the world over. They are tales that have been known since the dawn of time. Consequently they are reflected, too, in our most ancient myths.

The unconscious, then, for the benefit of our psychic development, takes the whole world as we know it, and instinctively turns it into a set of symbols for our own inner dialogue.

*　　*　　*　　*　　*

Which is all very well as long as we are content to confine the process to our own inner cinema. The trouble starts when, succumbing to projection-mania, we begin to apply the same technique to our understanding of the outer world itself. Not content with turning the whole of reality into a mere set of night-time symbols, we start to carry the process over into our waking hours as well. The world 'out there' becomes one big, open-air film-show.

For what happens next is that we start to use the same technique to project onto the world around us all the symptoms of our own inner sickness. Soon, what we see outside us is no longer what is there, but what we think is there. The real world becomes a mere cinema-screen illuminated by our unconscious minds, a cardboard Disneyland animated by our inner thoughts.

There is an ancient tradition that we see the world outside us by virtue of the light that emanates from our own eyes. In psychological terms it is not so very wide of the mark.

So it is that we come to believe in a host of nonsensical propositions. Among them, the idea that all evil is the fault of somebody else, all injustice due to Them. Indeed, we go on to divide the whole world symbolically into black and white, paint the whole of reality in the colours of our own minds.

Imagine, then, how it must have struck the white peoples of a few centuries ago when they discovered that there were large areas of the globe whose inhabitants were, if not always black, at least a darker shade of pale. What a godsend! All evil could now be subconsciously laid at their door—be it murder, violence, theft, lawlessness or uncontrolled sexuality. *Especially* uncontrolled sexuality. There were 'savages'—literally 'wild ones'—the very embodiment of everything that we 'civilised' folk had rejected for the sake of communal peace and quiet at home. Therefore their societies must be destroyed. Their blackness of body and soul must be concealed, if not washed clean. They must be clothed in white, taught white values and lifestyles, converted to white religion, trained to worship a Jesus whose very skin had been bleached by reverent tradition from near-black to shining white.

And if, in spite of everything, evil still refused to go away, then it merely served to confirm an ancient suspicion—a psychological projection on a truly cosmic scale. The universe, it seemed, was under the spell of some dark, cosmic being—a prince of evil whom even the resplendent light of Godhead could defeat only with difficulty, and even then only at some indeterminate date in the future.

All of which we can now see, not as a true reflection of the world 'out there', but as a mighty inner myth of humanity itself—a drama in which the very powers of the universe have been turned into mere symbolic actors. The saga that scrawls itself across the starry heavens in archetypal graffiti is no more than a projection of our own ancient, inner struggle. The symbolic odyssey in which we would involve the whole cosmos is no more than a reflection of our own psychic pilgrimage.

A pilgrimage which, like all pilgrimages and odysseys and initiations that have ever been, must end back where it began.

* * * * *

And so it is possible to start interpreting the myth, to decode the archetypal message as it wells up from the depths of the collective unconscious and sprays itself indiscriminately upon the world about us via the aerosol of projection.

If, after all, you have imposed on the heavens an all-righteous God, fount of all light and power and goodness, and in the presence of whom no evil can bear to exist, then it is perfectly clear what that God really is. He is your own conscious mind, unable to tolerate any threat to its tyrannical rule over your kingdom of illusion.

If, similarly, you have set up Lucifer as Lord of Darkness and banished him from before the face of God because, in his pride, he has revolted against the divine light, there is another fairly safe conclusion to be drawn.

Lucifer is none other than your unconscious mind.

He stands not merely for those instinctive urges which you have been forced by society to reject, but also for all those other aspects of your inner and outer life which you have never got around to making sense of in the first place. That, no doubt, is why pioneering ventures into the unknown—whether scientific, spiritual, social or moral—are so often lambasted by religious establishments the world over as 'of the devil.'

The God of the ancient myth, in other words, corresponds largely to the powers of human reason and will. The other face of God—the darker, more 'occult' and mysterious aspect—is not so often acknowledged or allowed for. You will find reflections of it in Hindu and Taoist thinking, in the startling perceptions of Zen Buddhism, in the dreamlike writings of the early Gnostics and the Christian mystics, in the highly original tales of the Sufis and the stories of the Jewish Hasidim, even in the mysterious rituals of traditional Roman Catholicism and the Eastern Orthodox Church.

But otherwise it is the devil who traditionally stands for the darker and less easily understood aspect of the human psyche—our feelings and hunches, our instincts and animal appetites, even our bodies themselves. Hence the ancient Christian prayer which craves salvation from 'the world, the flesh and the devil'.

Almost as if all three were one and the same.

* * * * *

And what of Lucifer's 'fall'? That, too, it must now be pretty clear, is merely a reflection of your own experience. Which is presumably why the Bible speaks of humanity, too, as having fallen.

No doubt you will recall the famous biblical creation-account (and what else should a creation-account be but an explanation of how it came about that the world got into its present state in the first place?). Actually, the book of Genesis offers us not one account, but two. The first of these (chapter one) traces the creation of the world from the very beginning to the creation of man and woman. It is the second (chapters two and three) that describes the curious episode of the 'fall'.

Adam ('man'), it seems, was originally a complete and self-sufficient being in his own right. Living in full and direct contact both with the world around him and with the Cosmic Being itself, he had no need of 'others'. He realised, in other words, that only he was, that only I AM. That, presumably, is why he lived in a garden called Eden (which means 'delights').

At length, however, he was invited to give names to the creatures around him. The invitation seemed too good to resist. The result was the invention of language. And it was shortly after that crucial event that he fell into a deep sleep, during which Eve ('life') was taken out of him and fashioned into a separate being.

His wife. His *alter ego*. His 'other half'. Even, as some persist in saying, his 'better half'.

The common figures of speech are even more revealing than we might suspect.

For what had really happened was that rational humanity, entranced and bemused by the activities of the conscious mind, had lost contact with its own 'feminine' aspect—that deeper, intuitive nature which was its true link with the rest of life. With the advent of language, the conscious mind had become divided from the unconscious.

Of course, reunion was still possible. In terms of the story, there was still the sex-act. But now even that was to be overshadowed. Guilt would intervene. The onset of the 'fall' was to mark the beginning of the death of love.

The kissing would have to stop.

For in the middle of the garden, it seems, there were two trees. One was the tree of life, the other the tree of the knowledge of good and evil. This second tree was forbidden to humanity. Its fruit, if eaten, would prove deadly. It is not difficult to see why. 'Knowing good from evil'—thinking of reality as divided into 'good' and 'bad'—is a sure recipe for cutting yourself off, both from your own deeper self and from the world around you. Swallow that idea, and you're as good as dead, as far as reality is concerned.

Which no doubt is why the text says as much.

Adam, however, was unconvinced. Tabooing anything, after all, is a sure way of making it seem more attractive, as anybody with experience of bringing up young children will know. And so the fruit of the forbidden tree duly proved altogether too tempting. Indeed, the fact that the Creator had seen fit to ban it in the first place leads us to a curious if unfamiliar conclusion.

Either the Creator was a very bad psychologist, or He actually *intended* the forbidden fruit to be eaten—with all that that entailed.

He realised, in other words, that some kind of 'fall' was necessary for humanity's further evolution, that some kind of 'death' was needed if His new protégé were fully to come to life.

One step backwards now must subsequently lead to two steps forward.

For 'the Creator', of course, you may cheerfully read 'the universe'. For how should the Creator be separated from His creation? It was the universe, you could say, that arranged for its human agent to 'lose its way', to descend into the depths of night, to enter Hades. It was the universe that, sensing the need for a new initiation, came up with the evolutionary process which produced, in us, the achievement of consciousness.

And the 'fall' was its inevitable result.

* * * * *

According to the story it was all the serpent's fault. The serpent, which here stands for our innate drive towards developing consciousness. Working through Eve (the unconscious), it made Adam (who now, of course, stands merely for our conscious mind) an irresistible offer. By eating the forbidden fruit of the tree of the knowledge of good and evil, he could become a god, master in a world of his own creation. A world of mere symbols, maybe, but a world for all that.

And so, as we have seen, it proved to be.

But there was a snag. For no sooner had the conscious mind swallowed that symbolic fruit than it fell prey to the almighty value-judgement. The oneness of the cosmos was divided into 'good' and 'evil'. Duality had struck.

And not merely 'out there'.

For, in the story, our ancient progenitors suddenly become aware that they are naked and vulnerable. And since there is nobody but themselves to be afraid of, the real nature of that vulnerability is quite clear. The two halves of the human psyche—'Adam' and 'Eve', conscious and unconscious—have now become liable to injure (in Latin, *vulnerare*) each other.

The human unconscious can no longer fully accept the trickster-like convolutions, the seductive lies, of the conscious mind. The conscious mind, for its part, cannot bear to be reminded of the disparities between the real world and its own private world of illusion.

And so the symbolic fig-leaf must be put on. A veil must be drawn across the face of reality. Humankind must conceal itself from itself. And in that same moment the great gulf is sunk between 'heaven' and 'hell'.

Which is why the ancient motto 'Man, know thyself' may yet hold the key to bridging it again.

So our mythical ancestors are duly expelled from Eden, forsake their primal garden of delights. The age of agriculture begins. The first civilisations arise. And as the mists of time conceal the picture from our gaze, the symbolic scene traditionally shifts to a hill called Golgotha. The first Adam has initiated the myth: the 'Last Adam' —Christ—it seems, must now complete it.

For if we humans wish to be saved from the hell we ourselves have created, we must now be prepared to sacrifice ourselves, giving ourselves up to the powers of darkness and deliberately entering the underworld. We must learn, in other words, to acknowledge and accept our own unconscious mind. Only then shall we be able once again to see our deeper nature for what it is. By bringing that nature into the light of full consciousness we shall finally obviate the need to control the urges of the unconscious at all—since that unconscious will no longer exist as such. It will have risen from the dead, broken out of the tomb, emerged into the light of conscious day.

And it is in that moment that the son of man will discover that he is the heir to a new dispensation, the lord of a new kingdom. The kingdom of God. The kingdom of total consciousness.

*　　*　　*　　*　　*

So it is that we, unlike Lucifer, are destined to recover from our 'fall'. For we are higher than the angels—even, in the eastern traditions, than the gods themselves. We are more real, that is, than the mere projections of our minds. Having served their purpose, the projections can be discarded.

And it is now more than ever important that they should be.
In its proper time and place projection is a useful technique, a helpful compensation for inner conflict. Without it we should not have evolved to our present level of consciousness. The danger arises only when we start to take it too seriously—when we begin to treat our inner symbols as reality and the outer world as a further set of symbols for what is going on inside our minds.

Project your inner symbols upon the 'outer' world and you create a vision. That vision in turn duly becomes reality—at least for you. And so events start to arrange themselves to reflect your own inner state. When you are inwardly confused, everything seems to go wrong: when you feel at peace with yourself, everything seems to go right. Whatever your assumptions and prejudices, the world 'out there' continually supplies 'omens' to back them up. Your psychological hang-ups even become reflected in physical diseases and disorders. You 'cannot face up to' what you must do today, and so you awake with tired eyes or a headache. You are continually 'eaten up' (perhaps without even knowing it) with suppressed rage, or jealousy, or frustration, and so fall prey to cancer. You 'cannot stand' a particular state of affairs, and so almost any passing virus will obligingly lay you low.

And of course you can always blame the germs and microbes 'out there', when it is really yourself who are to blame. Germs, after all, are no respecters of persons. We are all crawling with them. But not all of us suffer from colds, or 'flu, or infections of skin or gut. Those of us who do have simply invited them in.

Jung's term covering this general phenomenon of 'inside-out' and 'outside-in' was 'synchronicity'—the idea that everything that happens in the universe is somehow a direct function of everything else. Quantum-physicists, on the other hand, tend to refer to 'bootstrap-theory'—the idea that the whole universe consists of nothing but pure interrelationship—which amounts to much the same thing. Hindus and Buddhists, meanwhile, prefer to explain our illusions of reality in terms of 'karma'—the universal law of cause-and-effect. Whatever you call it, however, one thing must by now be plain.

Whatever seems to you to be happening 'out there', *you yourself have largely created it*. Thanks to the technique of projection and the Law of Creation, it is merely a reflection of your own inner state.

Thou art that.

And your psychic pigeons duly come home to roost.

If, then, you project all evil upon the blacks 'out there', is it any surprise that they eventually start to infiltrate your own heartlands? Not merely as menial workers, but as teachers, doctors, priests. Who knows? We may yet have a black President of the United States, even—in a symbolic somersault of the first order—a black Pope.

Again, if you brand the communists of the Eastern Bloc 'out there' as your worst enemy, is it all that astonishing when your own society starts to fall prey to left-wing subversion from within?

It's no good—you can't run away from yourself. The world that you see 'out there' is no more than a mirror of your own inner world. And on a convergent planet you are bound to finish up by looking yourself in the face.

And being horrified by what you see.

The consequent reaction, almost inevitably, tends to be a violent one. Not only do we find ourselves menaced by a flood-tide of unbearable inner neurosis—a flood-tide which we are currently struggling to hold back behind a tottering dam of pills and drugs, entertainments and intoxicants. We are also poised to destroy the very planet on which we live in an apoplectic frenzy of self-rejection. Our outer world, like our inner world, is split into opposing factions. East is sundered from West, North from South. Socialists and capitalists, haves and have-nots, blacks and whites find themselves split apart by a great divide. Yet that divide is no more than a projection of the impenetrable iron curtain within the mind of man.

That split—whether inner or outer—must be healed if the human race is to survive. As Jesus of Nazareth so clearly realised, nobody can serve two masters.

And so a two-pronged attack now seems to be called for. In the psychic realm we humans need to learn to recognise and accept ourselves as we really are, instead of as we think we ought to be. Adam must return to Eve, the conscious mind must return to the embrace of the unconscious. The kissing must recommence, love be restored, for only then will our lost Paradise be regained. And meanwhile, in the outer, social sphere—the realm of our projected symptoms—we must make every effort to close up the divisions and heal the wounds, lest they turn septic and destroy us before the inner cure has had a chance to take effect.

Thus, curiously enough, it is in the *outer* realm that the first aid needs to be applied. For by operating on our psychic projections we can actually operate on ourselves. To a major extent those projections *are* ourselves. Our symbols, in other words, can yet serve as our lifebuoy, our means of self-transformation.

Transform 'God' and you transform yourself. Transform the heavens and you transform the world. As above, so below.

Traditionally, the instrument of humanity's salvation is expected to be some future Messiah-figure. Religions the world over subscribe to the belief. The Latter Christ, the Buddha Maitreya, Vishnu as Kalki. Even the Little Green Men from space and the hierarchies of Himalayan Masters are only variations on the act. But to take such beliefs literally is, once again, to confuse symbol with fact, myth with reality. The Messiah will not come. Not at any rate, from 'out there'. Extra-terrestrials there may well be, but the biblical being 'coming in the clouds of heaven with great power and glory' is nothing more or less than conscious humanity itself—a humanity that has at last faced up to the 'powers of darkness' in its own unconscious and, by making peace with them, carried away the victory.

And so it is by drawing new and unimagined power from as-yet largely unsuspected dimensions of the psyche that the true son of man, archetype of the entire race, will eventually establish a mighty kingdom over a new heaven and new earth. In scriptural terms the instrument of his victory will be the sceptre that he carries in his right hand. That sceptre is of course the instrument, or tool, with which he holds sway over reality. And so there can be little doubt what that tool is.

It is the very symbol itself.

Those who are saved are likewise marked out by a symbol. It is a sign upon their foreheads corresponding, in Christian terminology, to the 'name of Jesus', the symbol of his *gnosis* or revelation.

Possibly you could identify this sign with the early Christian *vesica piscis,* or secret fish-sign, which was traditionally formed by the overlapping of two circles:

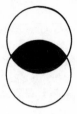

Certainly if the upper circle here stands for the conscious mind and the lower for the unconscious, the symbol is an apt one. For the 'fish' itself—the *single* fish which appears in conjunction with the sign of Aquarius, not the two separate fishes of the present age of Pisces—would then represent the eventual merging of the 'known' and 'unknown' parts of the psyche into a single, 'total' consciousness.

Which, of course, is entirely as it should be.

Or perhaps you feel more drawn to the ancient Star of David. For this, too, was traditionally regarded, by the Jews at least, as the 'sign of the Messiah':

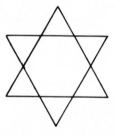

Here it is the upward-pointing triangle of Jehovah (the conscious mind)

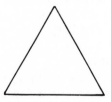

and the downward-pointing triangle of Satan (the unconscious)

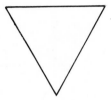

which are fused into a single, six-pointed star, celestial symbol of
human completeness. Fused, it should be said, in terms of the geometry
of a single circle.

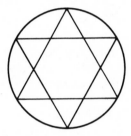

Which, once again, is entirely as it should be.

You may even prefer the Christian cross, which for many centuries
now has been the messianic sign uppermost in the western mind. For
most of that time, of course, we have disfigured it with the image of a
tortured corpse. That fact is itself perhaps a revealing one, indicating
humanity's own inner condition. But remove the corpse, take down
the image of the crucified, and you soon start to see the symbol for
what it is—a vertical line (representing the eternal, or spiritual) and a
horizontal line (representing the temporal, or physical) converging into
a single, non-dimensional point of nowness:

Originally, the cross had arms of equal length. It too, in other words, was geometrically a function of a single circle:

So that once again the messianic symbol stands for ultimate human synthesis and wholeness.

And before it, relates the tradition, every knee shall bow.

The symbol, then, may yet supply us with our lifeboat. It was the symbol, you could say, that through language and the technique of projection got us into our present mess. And now it is the symbol that has to get us out of it again. For the two processes—'fall' and 'redemption', death and life, delusion and enlightenment—are in reality not two, but one: a single, cyclic process of initiation which now has to take us one stage further towards our destiny.

And in that process the symbol must remain the vital catalyst.

With its aid the cosmic mirror of separation, created by our thought and language all those long millennia ago, must now be broken. It is for some new symbol to reunite the 'above' with the 'below', 'God' with 'Satan', the 'out there' with the 'in here', you with me, humanity with itself.

But then what else should the cure be for dia-bolism—'throwing apart'—if not sym-bolism—'throwing together'?

The quest for wholeness is of the essence. And in that quest the symbol will reign supreme. What form it will take remains to be seen. What myth has power enough to rescue us from our inner sickness and restore life and harmony to our stricken 'silent planet' has yet to be discovered.

But never was there greater need for some saving symbol of wholeness.

10. THE TURN
OF THE TIDE

There's nothing either good or bad but
thinking makes it so.
William Shakespeare: *Hamlet,* Act II, Scene 2

The symbol, then, is our tool *par excellence.* It was with it that our ancestors first constructed their all-enveloping house of illusion, with it that we who have inherited that house still maintain and extend it from time to time in response to our growing needs. And in theory we could also use it to break down the door and finally escape altogether.

Unfortunately, however, we more often use the symbol as a ball and chain. And in more senses than one. For, having knocked down the walls of our prison with it, we promptly use it to shackle our own feet.

Consider what happens, even today.

Our foremost thinkers are currently engaged in trying to push back the frontiers of human perception and imagination. At one end of the spectrum of magnitude, the astrophysicists tell us of horrific 'black holes' in interstellar space—'fallen' stars of such immense density that they can drag whole galaxies down with them into ultimate darkness as they collapse inwards at an ever-increasing rate under the pull of their own gravity. What is supposed to happen then is uncertain, except that those particular galaxies will never be heard of again.

Such, you could say, is one possible view of the universe's ultimate future.

As for its ultimate origin, other astrophysicists claim still to detect the lingering echoes of its very beginning—a 'big bang' of stupendous proportions in which a 'primeval atom' of almost infinite mass and density exploded to produce, in the course of time, our present, allegedly

97

expanding universe.

'Big bang' and 'black hole', then, are (we are told) the alpha and omega of existence as we know it, and it is tempting to conclude that the matter has at last been settled for good and all.

We know where we have come from, and we know where we are going.

Unfortunately, however, things are not quite that simple. Substitute 'God' for 'big bang' and 'Satan' for 'black hole' in the above account and you will soon see what I mean. Both pairs of concepts are still unknowns. Both are no more than speculations. The change of terminology still brings us no nearer to discovering either what caused the 'beginning' or what will ensue from the 'end'. What the scientists have really produced is not so much a new scheme of things as a new set of names for a very old scheme of things indeed.

We are faced, in fact, not with a new reality, but merely with a new kit of symbols. And, as has happened before, the universe will obligingly supply us with evidence to back up that symbolic view just so long as we do not grow tired of it.

At which point some worrying new evidence will, as usual, crop up to discredit the theory.

And so, in perhaps fifty years from now—perhaps considerably less—it will seem just as old-fashioned and superstitious to speak of ultimate big bangs and black holes as it now is to believe in gods and demons.

Perhaps, by then, the increasingly popular 'oscillating universe' theory will have obviated the need either for a big bang origin or for a black hole conclusion. Perhaps the one will merely come to be seen as the alternative aspect of the other. Perhaps we shall come to think of both in terms of a single cosmic gusher.

But then that view would not be a new one either. It would merely be the ancient Hindu concept of the 'days and nights of Brahma', of the universal outbreath and inbreath, expressed in different terms—an unbelievably old idea clothed, once again, in new symbols.

The case of the 'anti-universe' theory is perhaps an even more revealing one.

Impressed by the evident polarity and balance of the whole of existence, scientific theorists have long postulated that somehow, somewhere, there must exist a negative equivalent for every positive particle in our universe, and vice versa. Otherwise, it is argued, the universe could never have arisen in the first place. Every action, you will remember, has an equal and opposite reaction, and the universe is

98

nothing if not action and reaction. Consequently the sum total of cosmic matter and anti-matter, as of cosmic energy, should equal zero*.

And yet our own universe seems to provide precious little evidence to back up the theory. There seem to be about as many natural anti-particles in the universe as there are crocodiles at the North Pole.

The conclusion, therefore, is obvious. We are looking in the wrong place. It is less a case of somehow and somewhere, as of another how and another where entirely. Not to mention another when. In short, there has to be a separate anti-universe, a mirror of our own, in which everything as we know it, including time, is turned topsy-turvy and back to front. By our very nature we can never hope to detect it, but it is there, wherever it is, for all that.

And perhaps it even includes, among other anti-things, an anti-you and an anti-me.

It may all sound highly scientific, if rather startling. But whether the theory's proponents would still think so if they realised what they had really done is open to question. For in fact what they have come up with is an almost exact description of the shamanic 'underworld' which was already familiar to the tribes of northern Eurasia in prehistoric times.

In this supposed 'world of the spirits', too, everything was reversed. Time went backwards, the old grew younger every day. Which is why the dead were not only buried in the position of the foetus which, through reincarnation, they must once again become; they were also provided with a variety of upside-down pots and pans for their long journey**. It was always the prime characteristic of the underworld, of *sheol,* of hell, in other words, to be topsy-turvy. The ancient ceremonies of witchcraft testify again and again to the fact—the upside-down cross, the reversed Lord's Prayer, the counterfeit Black Mass celebrated by a defrocked priest.

All of which sheds a great deal of light on the real nature of our present topsy-turvy world.

And so the process of symbolic substitution continues. Humanity's self-induced illusion persists. In the case of the hypothetical anti-universe, what was once a mere primitive superstition has come to be

*Compare Tryon, E.P.: 'Is the Universe a Vacuum Fluctuation?' in *Nature,* No. 246, 1973.

**Compare Eliade, M.: *Shamanism: Archaic Techniques of Ecstasy* (Routledge,1964)

regarded as a serious scientific theory, simply because it has been proposed by people in white coats, printed in scientific journals and—most important of all—expressed in terms of a new set of symbols.

*　*　*　*　*

The same process is in evidence at the other end of the cosmic scale of magnitude, too—in the sphere of microphysics. Here, the specialists are engaged in a frenzy of investigation into the sub- and sub-sub-particles of atoms. Atoms which, if you please, were once, by definition, held to constitute the ultimate constituents of matter. Then, of course, it was discovered that the atom really consisted of smaller particles, and these smaller particles of yet smaller particles . . .

And so it came about that we are today subjected to a flurry of speculation about such things as neutrinos, antineutrinos and quarks. For it is really quarks, it has now been revealed, that are the very bedrock of matter*. And what, one wonders, will *they* turn out to consist of?

But once again, as it happens, somebody seems to have got there before us. The speculations of the microphysicists are suspiciously similar to those celebrated medieval theories on the question of how many angels could dance on the head of a pin. The alleged properties of microparticles are now said to include such denizens of Fairyland as 'charm' and 'strangeness'. Only the symbols have changed. And it becomes increasingly obvious that what the scientists are really talking about is the inside of their own heads.

For the universe, as the researchers in question are often the first to admit, does not really divide itself into particles at all. It is not a thing, nor even a series of things, but a process—a single, ever-active process comprising an infinite number of sub-processes. It is a verb, not a noun.

Verbum—the Word.

And in trying to understand it, despite all our imagined progress, we have still not succeeded in pressing any further forward than the back of our own eyeballs.

The symbol remains supreme.

*　*　*　*　*

How then do you break out of the vicious circle? If you escape from one prison, only to find that you have surrounded it with another, what

---

Daily Telegraph Science Correspondent, 29/1/77.

can you do about it? For that is what our search for reality, our attempt to return to the original experience of universal wholeness, seems to amount to. It is, to quote a Churchillian phrase, a riddle, wrapped in a mystery, inside an enigma.

The answer seems to lie in realising just how the prison of illusion got there in the first place. It didn't just grow. It had to be built. And it was built, as we have already seen, by people using symbols—in this case, words—as their tools. That was how we humans first carved up the universe, then sundered ourselves from it, and finally contrived to split even our own psyche apart.

But it is at this point that the outline of a possible way out of the problem starts to appear. For if our scientific attempts to escape the ancient symbols have not so far met with much success, then it seems quite likely that the opposite approach might well produce better results. If, in other words, we originally used symbols to build our house of illusion, then we can deliberately use symbols to *un*build it too. Not, in this case, the divisive symbols of language, but the natural, healing symbols of the unconscious.

It may have been our ancestors who started the ball rolling in the first place, who invented the symbolic equipment with which humanity plays its game of illusion. But now it is *our* turn to play.

And we can change the rules.

And so a gleam of light starts to shine amid the darkness. The symbol itself can indeed become the medicine of the soul.

Perhaps it is worth remembering that the original Greek *symbolon* was a broken coin—a coin whose two perfectly-fitting halves were kept and treasured by two parting friends. It stood for the union which had once been and might one day be again.

A token of wholeness, no less.

*   *   *   *   *

The way in which symbols operate on our psyche is still not properly understood (which, of course, is merely another way of saying that we have so far found it difficult to explain the process in terms of other symbols). But that they can have a pronounced healing-effect is now beyond all reasonable doubt. The fact has been repeatedly observed and documented by psychologists and psychiatrists. Whether through dreams, myths or rituals, patients of all kinds continually find themselves healed, reintegrated, rejuvenated not only in mind, but also in body, thanks only to being made aware of the symbols that continually surface within their own psyches*.

Why it should be so is, of course, by no means easy to grasp. But that is no reason to deny *that* it is so. You don't deny yourself the benefits of sunlight merely because you cannot decide satisfactorily whether it consists of waves or particles. You don't refuse to make use of solar heating—whether directly or indirectly—merely because you cannot explain satisfactorily how energy is transmitted to us through empty space. You don't fly off the handle, so to speak, merely because nobody has so far managed to explain convincingly what gravity is or exactly how it works. The fact that you are able to read this book, that your blood-temperature is around thirty-seven degrees centigrade, and that you are not stuck to the ceiling or hurtling off into space, you would presumably attribute, if asked, to 'light', 'heat' and 'gravity'—all three of which are mere symbolic terms for realities that nobody can fully grasp, still less explain.

Yet you don't let that fact prevent you from getting on with the business of living.

So it is, too, with healing. Traditionally, medical cures were applied simply because they worked. No questions were asked. Since modern science has appeared on the scene, it is true, there have been sporadic attempts to discredit 'cures' that could not be explained rationally in terms of existing knowledge. But that was in the days when it was assumed that we already knew everything there was to be known—or very nearly so. Now, however, things have changed. The more we know, the more we become aware of our ignorance. And so a more pragmatic approach is already being applied, in medicine as elsewhere.

If the Indians of the Amazon basin assure us that an extract from cinchona bark can cure malaria, or if their North American cousins claim that an infusion of willow bark will ease aches and pains and relieve rheumatism, we no longer dismiss such claims as primitive superstition merely because we cannot at present trace all the causal connections.

We conduct clinical trials.

If the claims prove justified, we gratefully accept the advice. If we can, we then synthesize the product, feeling, perhaps, that this helps to make the natural cure more 'scientific'. And finally we invent scientific-sounding names for the products in question and call them quinine and aspirin.

Such are the marvels of modern science.

*Compare Jung, C.G.: *Man and His Symbols* (Aldus, 1964).

Again, medical experts were at one time quick to condemn as ignorant quackery the old witches' brews concocted from lichens and fungi, complete with their ninefold magical incantations and their stipulations about stirring with a wooden, not metal, spoon. How, it was asked, could such weird activities possibly have anything to do with the nitty-gritty of curing diseases? It has taken us years of scientific research to realise that some of the concoctions in question were a primitive form of antibiotic, the ninefold spell a means of timing the preparation, the wooden spoon a means of avoiding deleterious chemical reactions between spoon and ingredients.

Meanwhile in no form of medical treatment can the psychic element be entirely ruled out. Many a case is cured either wholly or partly by suggestion. Even word-magic has a supporting role to play. You may tell the doctor that you have a worrying rash on your skin. He responds by telling you that you have dermatitis. There is an almost immediate feeling of relief. Identification, you feel, is already half-way to cure. Yet all the doctor has done has been to tell you in Greek what you yourself have already told him in English.

Certainly there is more truth than meets the eye in the well-known observation that doctors cannot heal patients—they can only help patients heal themselves. In this process a psychic element may well be present. But to say 'It's just psychological' is to miss the point entirely. As we have already seen, *everything* is psychological *by definition.* It is only with our psyche that we can experience anything at all. And if the disease is cured, then the disease is cured. Precisely how it came about is of no great importance after the event.

So it is too, with the medicine of the psyche. The evidence shows quite conclusively that it works. It is more than ever apparent that, through the use of mere symbols, the human unconscious can and does effect cures. Total and unqualified cures, both mental and physical. And not only with the aid of trained psychotherapists. For the psyche has constantly been performing such miracles of self-healing, largely through the medium of its dreams, ever since the dawn of human history, without so much as a by-your-leave from the goddess Reason. (Perhaps it is significant that our illnesses so often seem to disappear *overnight,* rather than during the day.)

And so the legendary elixir of life is not 'just symbolic'. In large measure it is the symbol itself.

As we saw earlier, we humans have, both individually and collectively, a psychic re-integration to undergo, an inner split to be healed. Otherwise destruction both psychic and physical stares us in the face.

And since the disease was symbol-induced in the first place, it is through symbols that we are going to have to cure it again. The symbol, in short, has to provide humanity with a vision of healing—a prototype, or blueprint, which reality itself can then bring into manifestation.

Such, after all, is the Law of Creation.

*   *   *   *   *

And so what are the auguries? Are such symbols already surfacing out of the depths of the collective unconscious? And if so, where would we expect to find them?

Where else but 'out there'? For that is where we constantly project the contents of our unconscious. It is in the outer world, if anywhere, that we should expect to find some signs of a healing impetus, a move towards re-integration, if the human race is to have any future. It is our outward, everyday acts and attitudes that should give us a clue as to what is really happening deep within our psyche.

And, curiously enough, there are already signs of hope. Already, in numerous 'outward' spheres, the barriers are starting to come down. Among the young, particularly, distinctions of colour, creed, race and sex are coming to be seen as increasingly irrelevant. War is anathema, party politics seen as a mere refinement of gang-warfare. Even the citadels of the political establishments seem less secure than they might once have been in the face of the gathering tide. Already, anti-racist and anti-sexist legislation (however unenforceable) is finding its way onto the statute-books. 'Anti-discrimination' is the catchword of the moment. And it is from this development especially that we may draw some hope.

Not, of course, that all ills can be cured by legislation. But the willingness at least to initiate and pass it suggests an inner, psychic change which may yet pave the way for a whole revolution of consciousness.

*   *   *   *   *

Time was when discrimination was of the essence in western society. Male must be distinguished rigidly from female, good from bad, white from black, fellow-countryman from foreigner, civilised from primitive, Christian from heathen, rich from poor, educated from ignorant, polite from rude.

And, not least, God from Satan.

And it went without saying that God was on the side of male, good, white and fellow-countryman. The civilised, the Christian, the rich, the

104

educated and polite had right on their side almost as a matter of course.

You might think that was why the very structure of society reflected this set of assumptions. But in reality the assumptions were merely reflecting the structure of the society that produced them. They were the projections of social humanity.

And so, in the west at any rate, it was the man, not the woman, who reserved to himself the decision-making role. It was he who could build and explore, colonise and go to war, found religions and take over the reins of government. The woman, for her part, was left locked up at home—sometimes literally so, in a chastity-belt. 'Kinder, Küche, Kirche' (children, kitchen, church) was the old Germanic view of her proper place. In the case of kitchen and church she was safely imprisoned within man-built walls. In the case of the children, she was shackled to them rather as a keeper is bound to the animals at the zoo. She was totally dependent, totally immobile. For her, there was no escape.

Of course this, too, was only a projection of the inner state of the human psyche at the time. The conscious, rational mind was rampant. The unconscious, irrational, and therefore 'dangerous' part of the psyche therefore had to be suppressed. And so the symbolic play duly had to be acted out for real, with man in the role of the conscious mind and woman in that of the unconscious.

The same process of separation and suppression applied, too, in the other spheres I have listed.

Because 'good' must be separated from 'bad', vast prisons had to be set up to house those who seemed to embody badness. The sick must similarly be hidden from the sight of the healthy, the insane shut away in mad-houses, the penniless safely immured in the workhouse, the debtor in jail.

'For their own benefit', of course. But even more for the benefit of those more fortunate ones who stayed outside.

It was the same with race, colour, religion and culture, especially where all four coincided. Pity, then, the black peoples, together with their brown, red and yellow counterparts. All were alike fair game.

The blacks especially.

For, as we have seen, the blacks had the special misfortune to fulfil an urgent psychological need in the whites.

The need for a scapegoat.

And so they could be slaughtered, colonised, 'civilised', converted, enslaved. First as mere curiosities, and later as a source of cheap labour, they could even be deported from their homelands—significantly described as 'The Dark Continent'—to serve their white masters.

But, once there, they must be kept separate. The servants must not be fraternised with. They must be kept in their place.

And their place, except when 'on duty', was strictly in their own quarters.

Which was all very well, except for one thing. People breed. Since the blacks were no exception, their numbers grew. As they did so, the magnitude of their plight became ever more obvious. Eventually it could no longer be ignored. And so an anti-slavery movement set in. Measures were put in hand to free the blacks. At last they could live where they wished, take up any job they pleased.

But it was all a mirage. They could live where they wished, certainly, but only so long as it was not in neighbourhoods where their former masters wished to settle. They could take up any job they pleased so long as it was one to which no self-respecting white would stoop.

In practice, then, freedom of habitation and employment meant living in slum ghettos and performing menial and degrading tasks fo the meagrest of wages. Which was little better than their former plight in a new disguise.

If not worse.

For where, previously, they had been forced into that position, now they had the privilege of choosing between it and starvation.

*   *   *   *   *

And so the process of separation went on unabated in western society. From womb to tomb, the rich must be kept separate from the poor, the educated from the ignorant, the rulers from the ruled. Behind the high walls of public school and ancient university the distinctions must be preserved among children and adolescents. In adult life, whether in country residence, inns of court, officer's mess or church pew, the privileged could pursue their separate course through life virtually untainted by contact with the lower classes.

And even in death the relics of the ruling caste must be kept demurely screened from the common gaze, entombed behind iron railings or in family-vaults where they were safe from the prying eyes and fingers of the profane.

Of course the time came when this situation, too, came to be seen as the human scandal it was. Democratic forces were at work. And so the educational system, in particular, had to be transformed. Yet the new state-controlled systems turned out to be mere copies of the old.

In Britain, for example, there was still one education for the rich and another for the poor. And if scholarships and bursaries allowed small numbers of lower-class children to enter the academies of the élite—the so-called grammar schools, most of which were still closely modelled on the earlier fee-paying establishments—it was only so as to help swell its numbers.

The basic social distinction, the dichotomy between ruler and ruled, remained inviolate.

Not that the idea of élitism lacked its usefulness. The rise of every historical high civilisation has been based explicitly on the concept. It is the educated 'high-flyers' who have always set the pace in society. It has been their intellectual vigour, their new ideas, their insatiable appetite for life and experience, that have brought about the rise and triumph of every major society throughout history.

And so it has been of the essence to isolate and give special attention to this élite. Capitalist and communist countries alike have recognised the fact. For all stood to benefit. In terms of privilege and human rights it might smell of injustice, yet in terms of usefulness it could be regarded as not only desirable, but even natural. Plato's concept of aristocracy—of 'government by the best'—is no more than a human reflection of the insect-world's cult of the queen bee. A reverse it may be, in broader human terms, but to it we owe the rise of the very civilisation of which we are members, the development of the very consciousness with which we now choose to criticise it.

And so the private educational system of the élite continues to flourish even today, if under a new disguise. It may have been largely taken over by the state, but the result has been not to destroy its élitist nature, but merely to substitute public subsidy for private finance.

The élite has actually managed to get its continued élitism paid for out of the public purse.

The fact has not escaped the attention of egalitarians. New pressures have been applied, the system further reorganised into larger, 'comprehensive' schools. Yet even here the curriculum continues to reflect the original élitist aims. It is still conceived largely in terms of success and failure.

For 'success' read academic attainments leading to professional and administrative roles. For 'failure' read lack of worthwhile pass-certificates at external examinations and eventual consignment to the menial occupations reserved for the ruled and the underdog.

The truly democratic concept of educating each child strictly according to its age, ability and aptitude, and then simply certificating the results in all areas of human activity, has still scarcely got off the ground, despite the lip-service paid to it in the 1944 British Education

Act.

And so in education, too, discrimination continues to rule.

*   *   *   *   *

But it is in the sphere of religion and morality that the western tradition of rigid discrimination has always been at its strongest. Perhaps that is not too surprising. Christianity, after all, has always taught that what is not of God is necessarily of the Devil. Consequently the object of its worship has traditionally been dualism, rather than the Absolute or the One God—and dualism, as we have already seen, is little more than diabolism ('throwing-apart') in a different guise. Is it any surprise, then, that the resulting effects on the human psyche have been so catastrophic?

For Christianity's constant message has been 'Believe or die'. Believe, that is, that the mere physical death of a historical Jewish rabbi can somehow preserve the life of your soul, here and now. Or fail to believe, and be condemned to spend an eternity in the unspeakable torments of hell.

Whatever the proposition may have lacked in logic it more than made up for in effect. Westerners, in their efforts to believe in such an apparent absurdity, in due course became obsessed with dark and unreasoning fears, riddled through and through with sordid feelings of imagined guilt. Faced with the awful prospect of eternal damnation, they had only one course of action left open to them. They must strain every muscle and fibre of their being to wipe all trace of evil from the face of the earth.

And so, in the spiritual sphere, any religion which did not proclaim by name the Christians' own God must be attacked and destroyed. That the real godhead might have more symbolic names than one, or even none at all, scarcely seems to have occurred to anybody. Crusades must be mounted, witches and heretics burnt at the stake, the native theocratic cultures of unexplored continents shattered, their achievements expunged from the planetary record. Nobody was safe who did not accept the literal truth of every word of the scriptures. Nobody could feel secure who did not admit that the mere linguistic symbols of current dogma were eternal reality itself.

As if they ever could be!

Meanwhile, still hot and bloody from this nightmare of religious self-delusion, westerners had long since turned their fury on their inner selves as well. And not merely on those relatively harmless peccadilloes once known as the Seven Deadly Sins. Under the influence of the more

puritanical brand of Christianity, they turned with astonishing fero-
city on the natural functions of their own bodies. If only they could
overcome the flesh, they seem to have thought, then perhaps by that
same token they would have achieved victory over both world and
Devil as well.

At all events, what the body normally expelled physically, the mind
now turned with increasing fervour to expelling psychically.

One out, all out.

So it came about that in most Western societies the human reproduc-
tive and excretory functions were not merely rejected as somehow
'evil'. They were in due course banned entirely from conversation,
hidden from view, treated as if they did not exist. To the concept
'polite' was opposed not merely 'rude', but downright 'disgusting'.
The natural functions of ordinary people were degraded into mere
'dirt' and 'filth'. With the waters of the fountain of linguistic symbolism they must therefore be washed clean away.

But it was at this point that the game of symbolic self-deception at
last started to come unstuck.

* * * * *

Using external phenomena as symbols for your projected inner illusion
is all very well while those phenomena continue to do as you tell them.
Having projected the unwelcome aspects of your unconscious onto the
female sex, you can lock away your womenfolk. By the same token,
you can imprison social offenders, consign coloured immigrants and
native populations to ghettos and reservations, condemn the working-
classes to slum accommodation and squalid jobs. You can even banish
the 'dark aspect' of God to an imaginary hell. And to those who reject
your particular religious symbols you can deny entry into the equally
imaginary heaven that you have created for your own delight.

For what must be rejected in time must certainly be rejected in eternity.

But when it comes to rejecting your own natural functions it is a
very different matter. True, you can project that rejection upon others.
You can plead indecency as a motive for punishing those who
camouflage their nakedness insufficiently. You can persecute as sexual
perverts those who express urges that you yourself have felt able to stifle. You can even prosecute those who indulge those natural urges that
you have *not* felt moved to stifle, merely on the grounds of having done
so too openly.

But when it comes to your *own* natural functions, you find that they

109

have an amazing tendency to refuse to go away. Even if you banish them to a special hidden room, or lock the door and turn out the light, you still cannot go out and leave them behind. You cannot even project them onto others. They simply refuse to accept defeat.

So it is that as soon as we try to turn the weapon of symbolic projection on our own bodies we learn a painful lesson—the lesson that ultimately we cannot run away from ourselves.

* * * * *

Not that this stops us trying. Even as our consciousness slowly begins to adjust to the realisation that there is no future in rejecting one half of reality, our army of linguistic symbols manages to fight a spirited rearguard action, a losing battle though it may be.

And it is this battle that we can observe today in our use of what I describe as 'disguise-words'.

It is no great surprise, of course, to find that the classic example of this phenomenon is the long-running saga of the lavatorial symbol. What the original term for 'lavatory' was—if there ever was one—is anybody's guess. Certainly it was not the word 'lavatory', which is merely a disguise-word dating from monastic times, and literally meaning 'wash-place'. 'The back', 'the bog' and the 'privy'; 'toilet', 'loo', 'water-closet', 'W.C.', 'little room', 'throne-room', 'bathroom' 'cloakroom', 'convenience', 'ablutions', 'gents', 'ladies', 'powder-room' and latterly, so help us, 'rest-room'—there is not one designation for it that is not in reality some kind of disguise-word invented to avoid having to refer to the real nature of the place.

As for what goes on there and the human organs that perform it, these too are usually disguised in polite circles. In this case the substitute-words used include a range of biological technical terms drawn mainly from Latin. These are felt to be relatively 'dispassionate' and 'scientific', and so they have not yet become associated with the guilt-feelings that the more familiar words too easily evoke.

But the days of such terms are numbered. Sooner or later they will come to be felt as meaning what they in fact mean. And then, if the reigning taboos still hold sway, a whole range of new terms will have to be invented to avoid breaking them. That of course, is why we have the whole resplendent succession of terms for 'lavatory'. No sooner has one word succeeded in taking over the role of current lavatorial symbol than it must be jettisoned in favour of another, as we frantically substitute symbol after symbol in our efforts to retain a slippery grasp on our fading world of illusion.

The greater the guilt-feelings, it seems, the greater the rate of linguistic change. Which prompts me to formulate what I make bold to call Lemesurier's Law: *The rate of substitution of disguise-words is directly proportional to the degree of social guilt felt about the topic in question.*

If I am right, then, we have only to look around us at those ideas for which we are continually inventing new disguise-words to discover which aspects of the world around us we find most difficult to accept—and, by extension, which aspects of ourselves we are still intent on rejecting. Our disguise-words can serve as a useful index to the state of our inner neurosis.

*   *   *   *   *

Now the sheer richness of vocabulary which we have accumulated over the course of time to describe the lavatory and the associated human functions and organs should make it amply clear that, for modern speakers of English at least, the human excretory functions are high on the list of 'rejected' phenomena. So, too, are the sexual functions. Nor is either fact very surprising, in view of the influence of puritan Christian thought in the two areas in question.

But these are not the only areas where Lemesurier's Law applies. Such camouflage-techniques are nowadays being used on an increasing scale in the sphere of social discrimination too. According to Lemesurier's Law, this fact ought to indicate a growing sense of social guilt about its continued existence, which in turn ought to mean that the days of social discrimination are numbered. Not merely as a fact of government policy; nor even as an aspect of political fashion; but actually among people at large. For it is people—you and I—not governments or political pressure-groups, who fashion our language.

And so this new development, if development it is, can only be a sign of hope.

Even in the early years of our own century, for example, it was still perfectly respectable, even in polite circles, to refer to 'old men' and 'old women', to 'dunces' and 'dimwits', to 'lunatics' and 'congenital idiots', to 'dwarves' and 'cripples', to 'heathens' and 'wogs', to 'niggers' and 'savages', to 'tramps', 'gipsies' and 'paupers'. People could still be described as 'deaf', children as 'scruffy urchins', corpses as 'dead'. There were still 'rat-catchers' and 'pedlars', 'sewage-workers' and 'road-sweepers'. There were 'labour exchanges' and 'reformatories'. You could still describe people and their actions as 'bad'.

And the Devil was alive and well and living in the East End.

But now all that has changed. Where previously age and misfortune were things that happened only to other people and could therefore be shut away, or at least kept decently out of sight; where previously the 'wogs' and all their imagined savagery could be kept safely at bay on the other side of the water; where society's menial tasks could be allocated to nonentities and 'unpersons', kept underground (like the dead) or performed at hours when the upper classes were safely tucked up in bed; where the 'bad' could be condemned, ostracised and locked away, and the Devil consigned to a convenient hell well out of sight of your own anticipated seat among the angels—where, in short, you could look down on anything and anybody who reminded you of the less 'nice' aspects of existence, and even pretend that they didn't exist, it gradually began to be felt that this was somehow an unfair and unrealistic attitude to take.

Which, of course, it was.

Quite why this change of attitude took place is anybody's guess. You could attribute it to the rise of socialism and the social services. You could blame the social mixing brought about by two World Wars, and the consequent discrediting of former ideals and values. You could even explain it in terms of an eventual bursting of love and healing compassion out of the self-defeating straitjacket of dualistic religious dogma. Perhaps it was all of them at once.

But whatever it was, there seems to have been a change for the better as far as social attitudes were concerned. No longer could you just 'reject' other people. They were there, and you were there, and you might as well get used to the fact. You couldn't even justify looking down on them, now that your own lofty pedestal of moral superiority had been shown to be so insecure. The old could not help being old. The unintelligent were not, after all, to blame for their lack of intelligence. The blacks couldn't even be held responsible for their unfortunate pigmental affliction.

Of course, even this attitude still left much to be desired. Who, after all, is to say that age is a scourge any more than youth? If lack of intelligence is a catastrophe, what of a superabundance of it? How can blackness of skin be regarded as a kind of disability, when the black actually possesses additional pigmentation that the white European lacks?

Or should 'normality'—that fictitious average that nobody in fact ever attains—be regarded as the sole desirable state?

There was a saving grace, however. At least pity had entered the picture, where previously there had been little but fear and hate. All these 'unfortunates' now came to be seen as mere victims of circumstance, pathetic playthings of a malignant and incomprehensible fate. They must be helped, encouraged, compensated—if possible, 'normalised'. Who could tell? If everybody pulled his full weight, perhaps the dark and unwanted side of life could eventually be persuaded to go away entirely, and a new social utopia be founded.

Inspired by this ideal, social and political movements, and even national governments, started to commit themselves to massive programmes of social welfare—programmes of which we today are the beneficiaries. We should do well, then, to be grateful.

But at the same time we should take care not to forget what all this reform was *really* about. Basically what it amounted to was a face-lifting job on a set of social projections. What the reformers were really trying to change, had they but known it, was their own inner nature. They were attempting to wash clean humanity's own 'dark side' through sheer sweat, toil and sacrifice—a magnificent commitment to what the Hindus traditionally refer to as *karma yoga*. And if, so far, it was only the *projections* of that inner darkness that were starting to be disinfected and restored to the light of day, it was still a start.

At least we westerners had started to get to work on our social image.

But of course this was still tackling only the periphery of the problem. If old people could now be accepted, old age itself still could not. Low intelligence, madness, deformity, paganism, foreignness, vagrancy, poverty, idleness, delinquency, private squalor and death were still intolerable ideas. The concept, if not the fact, of menial employment still aroused almost unbearable guilt-feelings. The very existence of 'evil', whether inner or outer, still had to be denied. And this in turn meant that the concepts in question had to be tabooed.

But how?

The answer is a familiar one. You simply taboo the words that stand for them. Whereupon you are faced with the usual set of problems. The old, the unintelligent, the mad, the deformed, the dead, are still there. The poor, as Jesus of Nazareth himself observed, are always with us. They simply will not go away. And neither, therefore, will your gallery of supposed evils. Yet you are constantly going to have to refer to them if you are to carry out your programmes of social reform. How, then, do you go about it? How can you talk about the people you are trying to help if you have tabooed the very words for their various afflictions?

Answer—you invent new words. In short, you invoke Lemesurier's

Law all over again.

And so in Britain old men and women duly became first 'old gentlemen' and 'old ladies' (in an effort to compensate for their senility through apparent social promotion), then 'old people' (when the attempt failed), then 'old-age pensioners' (to suggest the just reward for their sheer powers of endurance) and finally 'senior citizens' (to offset their final attainment, in practice, of total lack of social status). In school, the younger 'dunces' and 'dimwits' became in turn 'backward', 'educationally subnormal', 'educationally deprived', 'remedials' and at length, with touchingly misplaced optimism, 'slow learners'. Their older counterparts became first 'young citizens' (note the parallel with their grandparents), then 'the Newsom group' (all the while nobody knew what Newsom's report was about) and eventually 'ROSLA pupils' (all the while nobody knew what ROSLA meant). 'Lunatics' and 'idiots' were successively reclassified as 'mental cases', 'psychotics' and 'mentally disturbed', then awarded a variety of increasingly abstruse diagnostic labels drawn from psychology. 'Dwarves' became 'small people'; 'cripples' were transformed into 'disabled'. The 'heathen' were converted into 'pagans' and then—as the influence of Christianity steadily waned—into 'followers of other faiths' or, more specifically, 'Buddhists', 'Hindus', 'Muslims' and so on.

As the pre-eminent virtues of Britishness likewise started to become less self-evident, 'wogs' first became 'foreigners', and then were allocated more or less objectively to their various nationalities. Among whites, 'niggers' were deprived of their Latin description to become successively 'negroes' (the same word in Spanish), 'darkies' (almost the same word in English), 'coloured people', 'Commonwealth citizens' (note the clear parallel with the elderly) and latterly simply 'immigrants'. As in the cases of the aged and the unintelligent, the number of different terms used here within a comparatively short time suggests the presence of particularly strong guilt-feelings that such people should exist at all. But the blacks themselves for the most part naturally suffered no guilt-feelings about being themselves, and so they resolutely persisted in calling themselves 'blacks', even going so far as to coin the splendid slogan 'Black is beautiful'.

Meanwhile foreign 'savages' had in turn become 'natives', then 'aboriginals' and 'indigenous peoples', while their homelands progressed from 'uncivilised lands', via 'underdeveloped countries' into 'developing nations'. Nearer home, 'tramps' came to be described by the law as 'vagrants' and by themselves as 'men of the road'. 'Gipsies' were transformed into 'travelling-folk' and (their own word) 'Romanies'. 'Paupers' became, first, simply 'poor' and then 'socially-deprived'; the 'deaf', 'hard of hearing'; 'scruffy urchins', 'deprived children'. The 'dead' were upgraded to the 'deceased', then sentimentalised into the 'dear departed', the 'loved ones' who had merely 'passed on'. 'Rat-catchers' acquired new jobs, first as 'rodent operators' and then as 'pest control officers'; 'pedlars' as 'commercial travellers' and 'travelling salesmen'; 'sewage workers' as 'sanitary department employees', 'dustmen' as 'refuse collectors', 'road-sweepers' as 'cleansing department employees' or even plain 'council workmen'. Even farmers were heard to re-classify themselves as 'food production consultants' and milkmen as 'dairy operatives', while small businessmen were universally re-appointed 'company-directors'.

At the same time even the word 'bad' itself started to go out of vogue. It was as if the self-appointed guardians of public morals had started to lose the courage of their convictions. It you *had* to reject an idea or a person, you now had to make up your mind just what you meant. If you suspected deliberate evil intent, then 'evil' was the word to use. If it was merely a case of accidental misfortune, then you could apply such social value-judgements as 'immoral' or 'obscene'. Otherwise you were better off remaining outwardly as dispassionate as possible. Things were just 'unfortunate' or 'regrettable' or, if you were a newspaper reporter, 'horrific', or 'shocking'. As for people, their behaviour was at worst merely 'permissive' or 'uninhibited'.

Unless, that is, you were a judge or magistrate.

In time, of course, all these disguise-words will come to mean exactly the same as the words they originally replaced. Whether they in turn will then have to be replaced will depend on whether we have by then learnt to accept the seamier and less pleasant side of life as a necessary and inevitable part of existence. If we have, then it will bode well for the next step in our rediscovery of ourselves. For it will mark our first step towards accepting our own 'dark' side—our first step, in short, towards the achievement of 'total' consciousness.

* * * * *

But the battle is not over yet. The signs are not universally encouraging. Too much still seems to depend not merely on how far you can avoid referring to the socially 'tabooed' concepts, but on how far you can cover up their manifestations too.

Admittedly, you can minimise the effects of low intelligence by abolishing examinations and lowering academic standards. You can

115

drug the mentally ill. You can cover up minor physical deformities in a multitude of ways. You can as easily turn a blind eye to paganism as you can to Christianity. You can ignore foreigners, so long as they stay at home. You can even discriminate positively in favour of the blacks.

You can subsidise the poor and re-house the slum-dwellers. You can give hearing-aids to the semi-deaf, re-clothe the children and take them into official care. You can invent previously unnecessary jobs to absorb the unemployed. You can refuse to recognise or curb delinquents. You can pay menial workers more than yourself and provide them with uniforms or clean overalls. You can abolish evil by ceasing to believe in good, and dethrone the Devil by sacking God.

All these, indeed, we are in the process of doing.

And in our progressive abolition of the dichotomy between good and evil, between God and Devil, there is a definite ray of hope for the future healing of our inner, psychic split. Even if, during the period of transition between self-acceptance and eventual self-control, the blurring of basic principles must result in the temporary destruction of society as we know it.

Yet in those areas where we still find it difficult to mask the symptoms with harmless cosmetics, we are still showing a disturbing reluctance to accept reality as it is.

Unable to hide the inroads of age, we still shut away our old people in institutions that bear the ironic name of 'homes'. Unable to conceal the blackness of the blacks, many whites still deny them social advancement, and regard the arrival of black neighbours as a blot on the neighbourhood. Even femininity we are still unable to accept as a fully-fledged force in our society. And so not only must women be referred to as mere 'persons'; they must claim men's supposed rights, dress in men's clothes—almost never the reverse. So pervasive is the anti-feminine tradition that even women themselves fall prey to it. 'Housewifery' is a heresy, motherhood a crime.

And meanwhile solemn legislation is passed to decree non-differentiation between blacks and whites, between men and women—almost as though colour and sex could somehow be abolished by Act of Parliament, or the human psyche itself restored to wholeness by government edict.

And so, while there are signs, even here, of a shift in the right direction—or at least of a growing awareness that such a shift is urgently needed—our psychic disease remains in need of some more potent medicine. By at least starting to operate on the symptoms of our outward projections, we seem to reveal a dim awareness that it is through

116

our symbols that we need to start tackling the problem. We are already working at the periphery.

But time is short. In our efforts to reach the heart of the matter, the source of the infection, we need to discover for ourselves some more powerful symbol of wholeness for humanity at large than a mere blurring of our projected distinctions and value-judgements.

And it is in the world of dreams and myths that we may yet discover that healing talisman.

11. THE SYMBOLS AT YOUR DOOR

Life is a dream . . . we sleeping wake and waking sleep.

Montaigne: *Essays,* Bk.II

Humanity—the sick man of Planet Earth.

It is an apt description of our present predicament. And if the human race as a whole can be compared to a person who is ill, then it may be that we can gain some clues as to what to do about it by observing how the individual human psyche itself sets about the task. For the process is now well-documented. And one fact particularly emerges from all the data.

The psyche knows best what is good for it.

Basically, the doctor of your psyche is the Jungians' unconscious, the Freudians' subconscious. Actually, of course, it belongs neither to the Jungians nor to the Freudians, but to you.

Or rather, *you* belong to *it.*

And it takes that responsibility very seriously.

Constantly it takes upon itself the role of your inner healer. Seemingly affronted by your inner split, the psychic dichotomy between conscious and unconscious, it seeks to tackle the problem on two fronts. First, it tries to alleviate the symptoms by applying emergency first-aid in the form of a kind of compensation-therapy. And second, it undertakes the whole business of finding and applying a suitable cure.

And it does both through the medium of dreams.

We have already seen something of the process in action. With the aid of your dreams, the unconscious constantly presents to your conscious mind—that part of your psyche that has become divorced from reality through its addiction to the world of linguistic symbols—a whole series of images and inner movies. They are designed to remind you of what you are too anxious to forget, to show you how you are consequently damaging youself, and to advise you how best to put matters right.

You would do well, then, to take account of your dreams.

Do not assume, however, that the message always comes across in the form of normal language. It hardly ever does. Indeed, when you realise that it is 'normal language' that is actually the nigger in your psychic woodpile (how revealing of the whole problem the expression is!) perhaps that fact is not very surprising.

Yet the language of your dreams is still one of symbols. No language, after all, can be anything else. And the symbols, for their part, are still your old, familiar ones. They have to be, for otherwise they would mean nothing to you. Nevertheless those familiar symbols—images, pictures, feelings, experiences, even actual words—are used in ways that are totally unknown to your conscious mind, totally foreign to its nice, neat, logical habits. That is why dream-events seem so confused and contradictory, why your normal concepts of space and time are turned topsy-turvy, why your neat, conventional assumptions as to which ideas go with which often go completely by the board.

But that doesn't mean that your dreams have no meaning. Far from it.

True, it may be difficult to translate them into normal language. That is to be expected. But then linguistic explanations are not themselves an index of meaning. They are merely a way of expressing that meaning in other symbols. If Jung himself were to translate your dreams into his Swiss German, you would not necessarily be any nearer to understanding them. For it is understanding, not language, that is the heart of the matter.

And your conscious mind, it seems, is perfectly capable of disengaging for itself the meaning of your dreams, given only one proviso.

That you give it the chance to think about them.

'Fair enough,' you may say, 'but supposing I don't dream?'

As it happens, the supposition is no more than that. Everybody dreams. A person who is prevented from dreaming, who is woken up every time the tell-tale rapid eye movements occur in sleep, eventually suffers as a result. The fact that you cannot *recall* your dreams is neither here nor there. Unaided, you probably cannot recall what cars you saw parked in the street last time you went to the supermarket, or describe the clothes of the people who were in there at the time. You cannot now recall every maths problem you ever did at school, or everything that happened to you between the ages of nought and two—still less your experiences in the womb, and even before that, in earlier lives maybe. Yet all those experiences are still there in your mind. You may not recall them, but you have remembered them. They have all had their effect. They have helped to make you what you are.

And the same applies to your dreams.

But there is a problem. Long-term memory is a function of the unconscious, not the conscious mind. And during sleep, too, you are by definition unconscious. So how is the vital information to get across to your waking consciousness? What is the point of dreaming if you cannot consciously recall what you have dreamt?

This, in fact, is the nub of the problem. Recall is essential. If a dream is disturbing enough to wake you up, or if you manage to recall your last dream before awaking, then you will certainly benefit from that dream. For now your conscious mind can get to grips with its symbols and start to act upon their message. Otherwise the value of dreaming is less certain.

So how are you to assist the process of recall?

Conscious effort seems to be the answer. If you regularly make a point of trying to remember your dreams on awaking—and any later will almost certainly be too late—you will find in time that you will gradually be able to recall more and more of them.

But merely recalling them is not enough. The next vital step is to put them into words. The first words that come to you are invariably the best. Since your dreams are nearly always about you as you are now, at this moment, it helps to use the present tense, rather than the past, in your description. 'I am standing in this shop, waiting to buy a boa constrictor . . . ' or whatever. And often you will find that the everyday idioms that come to your mind first contain vital clues to the real meaning you are looking for.

As we have already seen, however, it is not meaning in terms of words that is of the essence, but understanding. And that understanding can best be brought about by re-creating and reactivating your dreams in as many ways as possible.

The medicine of the psyche needs to be thoroughly rubbed in.

And so, having recalled your dreams and at least fixed them in your memory by expressing them in words, you must now re-express them in other ways too.

For a start you could write them down, or tell them to somebody else. You could draw them or paint them. Best of all, you could, where permissible, act them out.

It is almost always beneficial to treat your dreams in this way, and your unconscious tends to react to the experience by coming up with even more dreams the next night. When they are ploughed back in, the benefits are multiplied a hundredfold.

And so the process of self-healing gets under way.

* * * * *

'Interpreting' your dreams, however, is not of the essence. Certainly there is no ready-made key to dream-interpretation with every symbol having a fixed and constant meaning. Despite much folklore to this effect, dreams just do not work like that. Your dream-code is not a public, agreed language, but a purely internal one, private to you alone.

It is your own unconscious that allocates meanings to your symbols, and nobody else can tell you what those meanings are.

Only if you keep having a dream of a particularly disturbing kind—one which causes you acute anxiety as to what it bodes for you and your psychic welfare, or even for your future—might it be worth enlisting the services of a professional analyst or psychotherapist. Only where there are signs of real psychic disturbance is such external aid essential. And even the expert can do no more than help you decode your dream-messages for yourself.

The only person who can interpret your dreams, in short, is you. Which, of course, is manifestly as it should be.

* * * * *

Not that dreams are the only medium through which you carry on that continuing dialogue with your deeper self. In your day-dreams and fantasies, or through such arts as painting, music or poetry, such crafts as pottery or sculpture, the symbols of the unconscious will constantly surface within you, given the chance.

Go collecting pebbles on the beach and your symbols will jump up at you out of the stones. Take up photography, and as though by magic they will appear before you on film. Do nothing but stare at the clouds or the stars, the cracks in the ceiling or the glow of the embers, and your symbols will still be there, staring you in the face. Wherever you go, they are forever there before you. You can no more escape them than you can dispense with your own shadow.

Which is appropriate. For it is from your 'shadow', your 'darker self', that they constantly proceed.

Do not assume from this, however, that your symbols are to be found only in the relatively abstract world of visual impressions. They can take a form as solid as a brick wall. Even your physical body is a mere musical instrument for the unconscious to play its ceaseless tunes upon. It speaks to you through your illnesses and accidents, through your joys and enthusiasms, your triumphs and your despairs. And even the everyday situations in which your body finds itself—or unwittingly places itself—are little more than a continuing sermon from the deeper you. To this extent everything that happens to you is psychosomatic or psychogenic. To this extent we are all accident-prone.

There are few, perhaps no, coincidences.

Watch, then, your dreams and fantasies. Give yourself opportunities for artistic expression. Study the results. Constantly observe everything that happens to you. Note how the bad things all tend to come together, how the good things often happen all at once. Take note of your good days and your bad days and see how they correspond to your inner states of mind. When you are ill, or suffer some accident, ask yourself what that experience is saying to you. Did you need the holiday? Did you need time to take stock? Has the moment come to change jobs, to move house, to abandon old ways of thought, to look for a new meaning in life?

Be continually aware, and you will have life more abundantly.

Remember, too, that you are not alone. Others have their own symbolic lives to live out. The people around you are constantly manifesting their own inner symbols, and you too can benefit from observing them. It is actually important for you to listen to their experiences—their illnesses, their family-problems, their worries, their alleged maltreatment by others—and to give them the benefit of yours.

That is why we are programmed to do just that.

Put two human beings together in a room, and in no time at all the immemorial process will start up. The mouths will open, the tongues start to clack to and fro. Putting out their feelers of atmospheric vibration, the two psyches will begin to prod and probe each other, establish links, exchange information. It is an instinct that no force in the world can resist. Even where prisoners are placed in solitary confinement it is not long before communication sets in. Anything that can register a pattern will convey the message. Tapping on a wall or a pipe. Shadows on a window. The rhythm of footsteps. Patterns of stones in a court-yard. Using visual signs, the instinct to communicate will transcend even the silence of a Trappist monastery.

The psyche is forever in search of symbols to read. And the symbols of others can be as valid as your own.

That is why the novelist writes novels and the public reads them. That is why story-telling is so vital to us in our infant years. Why else should programmes supposedly portraying 'everyday life' achieve the highest radio and television ratings? Why else should the most sordid newspaper disclosures of people's private lives find so avid a readership? If the gossip columns are so attractive, lurid films such good box-office draws, it is largely because people find lurking within them the symbols of their own unconscious.

Again, to an outsider it may well seem that the obsessive chattering of children in school, or the gossiping of men in bars and women on street-corners, is just so much hot air. Nobody, after all, seems to act on what is said; it never seems to lead to anything. And yet all this apparently pointless communication has real effects—effects which are none the less important for being hidden. The whole thing is merely the daylight equivalent of your own nightly inner dialogue, the external counterpart of that observation and retelling of dreams that is so vital for the continuing evolution of your own psyche. And the speaker benefits, possibly even more than the listener.

It is more blessed to give than to receive.

And so, next time you are waiting to be served at the corner shop and fuming because the little old lady in front of you is telling the shop-assistant at length about her illnesses and problems, the doings of the neighbours, the achievements of her long-departed sons and daughters, and perhaps even what happened on the telly last night—spare a thought. The shop-assistant may not need to hear it all, but the old lady certainly needs to tell it. Her psyche will fall sick if she does not. And she may have nobody else to tell it to.

All of us need to converse. We need both to speak and to hear what others have to say. And the more stressful our lives become, the more we need to seek further symbols in the world outside ourselves. The time comes when the events of our own lives are insufficient by themselves to meet our psychic needs, and we have to start living the lives of others too. Hence the nightly television soap-operas, the long-running radio serials about fictitious doctors' wives or non-existent agricultural communities. To the addict, there is not one of them that does not soon assume a psychic reality almost as great as that of life itself. Consequently, when one of the characters 'dies', it is a real disaster. If two of them are 'married', it is a cause for national rejoicing. There are cards and letters and gifts and flowers.

Replacing the ancient religious rituals, it is the media that nowadays regulate the festivals of the universal psyche.

Take care, then, to stand back from yourself and watch your inner movie project itself upon the outer screen of everyday life. For you stand to benefit considerably from an attitude of mind that is truly meditative—or, as the Buddhists would call it, truly 'mindful'. By observing what you think and say and do, as well as what is being thought and said and done by others around you, you make it easier for yourself to fulfil your psychic potential. Your conscious mind will learn from your unconscious, adjust its own attitudes, modify its behaviour and, by remaining in contact with that deeper self, help to compensate for—and eventually heal—your inner split.

'Watch and pray,' commanded the departing Jesus. And if what he meant was 'observe and meditate', then there was much good psychological sense in what he had to say.

Be alert, then, for the signals of your unconscious. That, indeed, is what is meant by being intuitive. For intuitions are the very stuff of the language of the unconscious, and whoever denies them, or who claims to have no time for them, is heading—like the person who cannot bear consciously to accept his or her dream-life—for acute inner conflicts and psychic problems.

We are truly such stuff as dreams are made on.

And we are all in the same boat.

For we are all 'members of one body'—members, that is, of a single human race. Humanity, too, is sick—and sick of the self-same sickness that you and I are suffering from. It is a psychic sickness that is currently tearing humanity apart, and one for which, consequently, the self-same psychic remedy is likely to prove the cure.

Self-observation. The reading of the symbols. The breaking of the dream.

*   *   *   *   *

Your dreams are of course your own affair, and consequently their language is private to you alone. It is not for others to meddle with your inner dialogue. Yet at a deeper level we all share the same mental needs, the same psychic stresses and strains. So that it is not too surprising to find that we also share, as Jung demonstrated, certain common dream-patterns, or 'archetypes'—common not merely to certain types and races, but to the human race as a whole. Just as we have inherited a number of physical instincts, so a whole series of psychic instincts—what Jung called the 'collective unconscious'—have long since become part of the genetic inheritance of *homo sapiens*.

The resulting psychic behaviour-patterns are constantly at work within us, influencing our behaviour, moulding our characters, modifying our cultures, giving shape and direction to our very civilisations. And not content with impinging on our daytime activities, they continually surface at night, too. By clothing those patterns in dream-images drawn from the world about us, the unconscious seeks constantly to make us aware of what you and I are really driving at. We are given a nightly chance to stand back from ourselves and see things in their true perspective. As we enter the land of sleep, we are brought to the very gate of self-knowledge.

And all we have to do—did we but know it—is to open it.

Now the chief purpose of all this activity, as we have already seen, is to compensate for humanity's inner split, to heal your own psychic dichotomy. It is a vital therapy which you can ill afford to do without. That is one reason why you need your sleep. Your unconscious and conscious minds need the chance to adjust their relationship in the light of what you have learnt during the day. The whole thing needs to be re-run, re-permutated, re-assessed. That is why a baby, who is learning all the time, has to sleep so much, and why an old person who has long since stopped learning needs to sleep so little.

We sleep, perchance to dream.

The psyche's aim is personal wholeness, a re-integrated you. But that quest cannot be fulfilled all at once. Like every journey, it has to be tackled one step at a time. At each stage of your psychic pilgrimage there are different needs, different problems to be overcome. And so the inner treatment, too, tends to come in clearly marked stages. At one point you will be nudged towards a particular goal by one set of psychic instincts. Then, as that goal is achieved, another archetype will set in, and you will bear off willy-nilly in search of your next objective. The process is repeated throughout life until, if circumstances have been favourable and your conscious mind has responded well, you will find yourself in sight of your final goal—the biblical 'Heavenly City' or 'New Jerusalem' that represents your achievement of total consciousness and wholeness.

And this inner educational programme works quite automatically.

*　*　*　*　*

When you were quite young, for example, there was undoubtedly a strong 'heroic' element in your dreams. Across the land of Nod there marched a whole series of death-defying, larger-than-life figures, dauntlessly overcoming superhuman odds to become the saviours of their peoples. Most of them, of course, were you in disguise. And what your unconscious was doing by throwing up these images was invoking the *hero-archetype*.

The function of this psychic pattern is to foster the growth of a separate conscious mind out of the original wholeness of the infant psyche. The conscious mind, you could say, is a kind of emissary sent out by the psyche to learn about the outside world through practical experience, subsequently reporting back what it has learned to its unconscious counterpart. But if that process is to take place, then the conscious mind has to be encouraged to assert itself, to stand on its own feet, to take risks, to develop self-confidence. And so the hero-archetype arises to show the way and offer encouragement.

So far, so good.

Unfortunately, however, the conscious mind generally takes the process too far. Not content with standing on its own two feet, it goes on to declare UDI. Diplomatic relations having been all but broken off, the unconscious is in danger of losing control of its agent altogether.

As our modern world knows from bitter experience.

And so the unconscious activates a new psychic behaviour-pattern—the *archetype of initiation*.

You have probably had dreams displaying this particular archetype on various occasions since the age of puberty. You will certainly have more before you die. The 'mid-life crisis' at around the age of forty tends to be particularly fruitful of such dreams. Basically their theme is voluntary submission to a power greater than yourself, followed by a new start. Self-sacrifice figures largely in them, as does a whole series of initiatory themes ranging from marriage at the one extreme to death and resurrection at the other.

Here you could say that the 'maternal', unconscious part of your psyche is recalling the child of consciousness to the womb. Alternatively, in terms of our diplomatic analogy, it is 'recalling the conscious mind for consultation'. The roving ambassador, having exceeded his terms of reference, must be shown his place, cut back down to size. Then he (for the conscious mind is traditionally symbolised, as we saw earlier, in masculine terms) must be given fresh instructions and sent back into the world again. He may resent and resist that recall. He may even regard it as a personal disaster. Yet he will be all the more effective for his brief holiday. Refreshed and recuperated, and with a renewed sense of purpose, he will be able to penetrate even further than before into the unknown lands of experience.

Until, that is, he once again goes too far.

This process of dispatch and recall goes on repeatedly throughout your life. You have a whole series of initiations to undergo. Each time your conscious mind returns to its roots, then sets out again with renewed vigour, leaving the unconscious much enriched by the fresh experience it has collected. That is how the being that is your psyche continually grows and develops. It is a constant process of action and reaction between your unconscious and conscious minds.

Of thesis and antithesis.

But then a curious thing happens. The further afield the psychic emissary travels, the more he starts to realise that things are getting not stranger but more familiar to him. Even the farthest corners of the globe start to seem almost like home. For, quite unknown to him, he is about to complete the circumnavigation. What is needed now is a last burst of courage, sufficient to carry him through the final, one-way journey.

Your conscious mind, in other words, starts to realise that it is not really exploring new worlds at all, but merely the same old world from which it originally started out. The worlds of consciousness and unconsciousness turn out to be not two worlds, but one. In attempting to delve into the world 'out there', you eventually discover that you are really delving into the world 'in here'.

For between them, ultimately, there is not a jot of difference.

And it is when the time has come for this realisation to dawn that the next great archetype sets in—the *archetype of transcendence*. Now the dream-images are full of snakes and birds, of fishes and humans who can fly. In short, the time has come to 'take off'. Your conscious mind has burst through its self-imposed chains of dogmatic rationalism. Now you must learn to accept that 'there are more things in heaven and earth than are dreamt of in your philosophy.'

You must learn to accept. Period.

The moment has come, no longer to broaden your horizons, but to break through them completely. Follow your intuitions now, and they will lead you clean across the frontiers of the possible into a strange land that, paradoxically, you will find that you already know like the back of your hand.

For you will have come home.

Circumnavigating the globe of experience, the envoy of consciousness has rediscovered his own homeland. For the first time now, he sees it as a stranger sees it—in other words, as it really is. His thoughts, for the first time, are 'home thoughts from abroad'. As never before, therefore, he fully appreciates that homeland. He is Glad To Be Back. His wandering days are done.

The Prodigal Son has returned.

And that is the moment for the last great archetype to arise—the *archetype of the Self*. This pattern may clothe itself in any one of a multitude of dream-images. It may appear as a magic crystal or as a curious sacred stone. It may adopt the image of a circle, often inscribed within a square or subdivided into four. Frequently it takes on the shape of an almost godlike wild beast, much like Blake's celebrated

> Tiger, tiger, burning bright
> Amid the forests of the night.

But that is not the end of the shapes it can assume. Pursue it, and the archetype may turn into a venerable guru-figure of your own sex. The image of some famous world-leader may even be called in to eke out the resources of your imagination. Or it may descend upon you in the guise of a mythical super-person, a godlike being who, it seems, has been since before the world began.

In whatever form, the appearance of this archetype speaks to you of the archetypal human nature of which you are merely an individual expression. According to the image chosen, your dreams may stress that nature's stone-like changelessness, its resilience, its uncomplaining acceptance of itself and its role in nature; they may emphasise the almost circular wholeness and symmetry of the essential 'you'; they may bring to your attention the fact that, as an animal—albeit the most lordly of animals—it is your instincts that lie at the basis of your psyche, instincts that will not lightly be gainsaid; or they may elect to remind you that human nature is a great deal bigger than you are, and that beside it your own tiny will necessarily pales into insignificance.

Whatever the image, however, the coming of the archetype of the Self brings with it the possibility of a miracle. For it represents the final reunion of your conscious mind with the unconscious that it originally left behind. Formerly imprisoned within the womb of that unconscious, its one thought had been to get out, to escape, to reject its origins. Of its 'mother', consequently, it knew virtually nothing—only the dark walls of the enclosing womb. It was like a person trying to gather what the earth looks like by gazing up at the sky.

But now all that is about to change. Rediscovering its ancient homeland, your conscious mind sees its 'maternal' unconscious as it really is for the first time—no longer as a mother, but as a bride. The great wedding duly takes place within your psyche. Conscious and unconscious are re-united. In biblical parlance, they 'know' each other. They become one body, one mind. One Self.

Or should it be 'oneself'?

And so the former country of the blind becomes, for you, the kingdom of light. For the eventual child of the union can only be pure and total consciousness.

* * * * *

Such is the archetypal saga which we all have to undergo. Such is the internal epic which the archetypes continually prod us into undertaking. It is a long journey, and for many its ultimate goal is probably unattainable in a single lifetime.

But that is not because life itself is too short. Nor is it because the archetypes don't try hard enough.

It is because, too often, we refuse to listen, decline to act.

Unlike our more 'primitive' cousins, we are too prone to dismiss our dreams, to scorn our intuitions, to override our hunches. This is even truer of most men than it is of most women—for in today's 'developed' world it is generally men who tend to pride themselves on being 'rational' and 'sensible', women who most often pay due and reverent attention to the deeper aspects of human nature.

And it is the men who dominate that world.

Small wonder, then, that society itself should be unbalanced in favour of the rational. Small wonder that society as a whole should pay too little regard to the archetypes that continually surface within it.

And small wonder, consequently, that modern humanity itself should be stuck in an impasse, threatened with self-destruction, and in dire peril of failing totally to keep faith with its destiny.

The rediscovery of the archetypal quest for the Self is now, it seems, of unprecedented importance for the very survival of our species. We are four-and-a-half thousand million human beings in search of a soul.

And so on the world stage, no less than in the tiny television-studio of your own psyche, the cure for humanity's present sickness needs to be sought within the magic cave of the archetypes. It is there that we can hope to find diagnosis, prognosis and cure all rolled up in one.

If, that is, the cure doesn't find *us* first.

For there can be little doubt about it. We do not create and cause the archetypes. It is they that create and cause us. Or should it be they *who* create and cause us? For the archetypes are the gods, no less than your own personal demon; the *Zeitgeist*, or spirit of the age, no less than your own personal mood of the moment. It is they that constantly mould our art and literature, speak through our music and dreams. Regardless of our best intentions, they stride across the arena of world-history, as well as dictating much of what happens in our humdrum,

129

everyday lives. Not only that—they stand fixed forever in our ancient myths, and continually stir into new life in our deepest religious mysteries.

They are the most vital of instincts, the very mainspring of the whole life and activity of *genus homo*.

But perhaps you are unconvinced. Perhaps it is less than obvious to you that the major themes of your private dream-world are not only shared by everybody else, but constantly acted out for real in the concrete world around you. Perhaps it seems to you altogether too fantastic a proposition that those same archetypes, those same essential patterns of thought, were already hard at work in the collective human psyche even before the dawn of civilisation.

And perhaps you are not at all anxious to defer in your turn to what, in fact, are nothing less than the ancient gods in their new, 'psychological' disguise.

But since, whether we like it or not, you and I are eventually going to have to do just that, it is my duty to demonstrate what I mean.

12. THE CAVE OF THE ARCHETYPES

And the end of all our exploring
Will be to arrive where we started
And know the place for the first time.
T.S Eliot: *Little Gidding*

If you are familiar with the human race's ancient hero-myths, you will already know that they tend to share certain common elements.

Again and again they tell of a boy of humble but often miraculous birth who, at an early age, performs some feat of superhuman strength. Having proved himself in this way, he rises to a position of prominence, and eventually becomes the saviour of his race or tribe by defeating some kind of monster or common enemy.

In due course, however, the hero's success goes to his head and he over-reaches himself. Succumbing to overweening personal pride, he is betrayed, or forced to sacrifice himself, and is eventually killed.

This theme represents the *hero-archetype*—the first of our great, transformative psychic instincts—in perhaps its purest form. It is likely that you yourself have experienced various aspects of it in your own dreams. But it is not of course limited to the world of dreams. In the sphere of myth it can be traced in the legends of numerous of the Greek gods and heroes—not least those of Hercules and Theseus. The Irish likewise have their mighty Cuchulain, who magnificently displays the myth in all its aspects. His Central American counterpart and—astonishingly—namesake is the Mayan Kukulcan, who subsequently becomes the Aztecs' Quetzalcoatl. (Both, you may recall, appeared from the eastern ocean and subsequently returned there, just as Cuchulain sailed *westwards* to the Blessed Isles before returning home

131

again.) The legendary British King Arthur and the Anglo-Saxons' Beowulf also reflect the theme.

In the Bible, too, we find elements of the hero-myth already present in the story of Adam, the legendary 'first man'. Moses the law-giver and Samson the strong-man in their turn carry on aspects of the tradition. And so it is no surprise when we subsequently find all its elements present in the Christ-myth itself.

A miraculous virgin-birth, a prodigious display of knowledge in the Temple at the age of twelve (not to mention various apocryphal miracles, such as the infusing of life into clay birds), the assumption of the mantle of the Jewish Saviour and King-Messiah, the apparently rash provocation of the Jewish authorities and the consequent betrayal and death—in all of these events we find the typical, archetypal hero-myth either deliberately acted out or attributed to the man Jesus after his death.

Not that it is necessarily a matter of either/or. Fashionable it may be to assume that most of the ancient myths are merely fabulous, invented stories subsequently woven around the lives and deeds of long-since forgotten heroes.

But fashion is not necessarily fact.

The hero-myth, in particular, is often acted out, consciously or otherwise, in actual flesh and blood. Considerable chunks of it can be found without any difficulty, for example, in the lives of Alexander the Great and Julius Caesar. In the Middle Ages, Richard the Lion-Heart, Henry the Fifth of England and Joan of Arc all fell victim to its spell. Even in our own days, the lives of Mussolini, Hitler, Churchill and John Kennedy have all deferred in some degree to its unchanging paradigm. Napoleon was perhaps its outstanding example.

It is the myth that underlies and supports every dynamic leader and dictator.

And so today the motif of the hero continues to thread its way through the shadowy borderland between history and legend wherever either offers the chance of deeds of heroism. The days of the Wild West produced their Davy Crockett and a whole galaxy of larger-than-life heroes—ready-made stars around which the film-industry, the novelists and the producers of children's comics could go on to weave a whole universe of make-believe. War, espionage, crime and political intrigue continually offer further opportunities for hero-figures both real and imaginary to emerge. The pop-scene too throws up a whole succession of ready-made heroes to worship. And whether seven-league-booted, stetsoned, space-suited or merely slightly larger than life, they still stride nightly, in the person of the dreamer, through the swirling dreamworlds of millions of human beings right across our planet.

Including, perhaps, your own.

But bear in mind that, if they do so, it is not merely to provide entertainment. As the case of many a real-life hero will confirm, it is truly a matter of life and death. For the hero is none other than a symbol for the conscious mind. Arising out of the undifferentiated consciousness of childhood, it must progressively free itself from the 'darkness' of the unconscious until it has fashioned a role for itself in the outside world, and attained in the inner world a position of apparently unrivalled power. The monster from the deep, the demon in the forgotten attic, the ghost in the deserted East Wing, the dragon in its cave, the wolf in the forest—such are the 'black', archetypal symbols with which we represent the 'dark', unconscious powers that our conscious mind must conquer before its independence can be gained.

Hence, of course, the primal and disturbing dread, the sheer animal fear, which such images conjure up in us whenever we re-encounter them in children's story, thriller or horror-movie.

But pride, as they say, precedes a fall. And the myth, too, carries a stern warning of what will happen if the process is taken too far.

If you allow the new-found power of your conscious mind to go to your head, then your heart will inevitably take its revenge. Perhaps literally so. Having torn itself away from its unconscious roots, the conscious mind will be in danger of sickening and dying for lack of nourishment. The 'dark powers' that you had thought vanquished will stage a violent resurgence, undermine your efforts, threaten you from within. Unless your conscious mind is prepared to sacrifice its principles and come to terms with those inner powers—giving up, at least for a while, its dreams of empire—the wolves of the unconscious will pursue you, tear at you, drag you down from your flying steed of rationalism and ultimately devour you.

And so the hero-archetype, activated in its due time, offers us both encouragement and a lesson. To the youngster immersed in children's adventure-story or war-comic, to the teenager worshipping the current pop-idol, it fulfils an inner need appropriate to the stage they have reached in their psychic development. But if this attitude is prolonged too far into adult life their inner child will never grow up, and their future psychic health will be threatened.

Perhaps that is why pop-stars, like childhood itself, are essentially evanescent.

In time, then, the need for a new archetype arises. The myth of the Christ-hero, too, bears witness to that need. The celebrated final entry of Jesus on an ass into Jerusalem marks the beginning of a transmutation of the hero-myth—a gradual change, almost imperceptible at first, to the *archetype of initiation.*

* * * * *

To discover the typical features of the initiation-archetype we need look no further than the initiation-ceremonies still performed today by primitive tribes. Like the initiation-rites of the ancient mystery-religions, they present a clear and unmistakable pattern. Typically, this involves some kind of 'rite of submission' (generally in the form of an 'ordeal' or trial of strength), a period of confinement, and a final liberation. From all of which it must by now be fairly obvious that the whole thing is really a rite of death and renewal. Its various stages correspond, in fact, to conception, gestation in the womb, and eventual emergence into the light of day. Consequently it bears a close relationship to the ancient myth of the Great Mother, or Earth Goddess, based as this is on the annual death and rebirth of nature herself.

The initiation-rite has always had a vital role to play in the life of primitive societies. It is the means whereby the almost mature adolescent is freed from the control of his or her parents and turned into a fully-fledged 'child of the tribe'. To permit this to take place, a new 'actor' has to take over the parental role within the psyche. The candidate must die to one set of 'parents' (the natural mother and father) and be reborn to another (the tribe itself). And so a new parental symbol has to be supplied. Often this takes the form of some tribal totem—a special, sacred plant or animal. The process is by no means confined to primitive tribes. Modern states, too, have their totemic plants and animals, as well as their various symbolic flag-substitutes. The English have their rose, the Scots their thistle, the Welsh their leek and daffodil. Remember too, the British lion, the American bald eagle, the Russian bear, the Chinese dragon. To the service of such tribal symbols young patriots, on finally leaving home, have traditionally been expected to re-dedicate their lives.

And so the rite of rebirth is duly enacted. In its purest form, the candidate first undergoes a ritual ordeal or trial of strength to test both fitness and maturity for this 'rite of passage'. Then a symbolic 'death' must follow. The candidate is removed from everyday life, sometimes taken far out into the bush, sometimes hidden in a special, dark hut, where initiation takes place into the secrets and mysteries of the adult tribe. Finally, after this period of 'gestation', the 'new-born' initiate is brought triumphantly back into the daily life of the village as a fully-fledged adult, ready to start a fresh role in society.

Even in our own society, the initiation-archetype still dies hard. The traditional British public-school system, for example, still defers to it almost literally, complete with 'ordeal' (the Common Entrance Examination), removal from the parental influence, period of instruction, and final emergence as an adult member of the 'tribe'. So does the Christian rite of confirmation. To a lesser degree, too, we still find it reflected in our various systems of school-leaving examinations.

But young people themselves often attach much greater initiatory significance to the all-important driving-test. This displays most of the essential ingredients of the rite in particularly vivid form, if in slightly jumbled sequence—instruction, removal by a stranger, confinement in the 'womb' of the test-car, trial or ordeal, and final, triumphant return with the pass-certificate, symbol both of liberation from the parental nest and of the final and all-important freedom of the road.

Somehow, it seems, the inbuilt psychic instincts even of modern youngsters enable them to sense, without being told, the need for their attainment of adulthood to be marked by some kind of 'rite of passage'. And instinctively they come to regard as truly significant the one which reflects most vividly the basic pattern that I have already outlined.

The archetype of initiation is ever active within the human psyche.

That, no doubt, is why it still surfaces today in such a plethora of different forms. 'Ordeals' and 'initiation-ceremonies' without number still mark the entry of newcomers to a myriad secret sects and societies. Scouts and guides, students and servicemen, freemasons and Knights of the Garter, doctors and judges, congress-members and presidents—all must alike act out the archetype 'for real'.

And not least the candidate for Christian baptism.

Constantly the theme bestrides the pages both of history and of fiction—from childhood tales of capture by, and escape from, the wicked witch and the gargantuan ogre; through stirring epics of adventure among pirates, smugglers, professional criminals, political enemies and demonic madmen, via the current craze for prisoner-of-war stories both real and imaginary; even to such sobre realities as the Maoist doctrine of perpetual revolution.

Always it is the hero, whether individual or collective, who is captured, imprisoned and finally liberated. Always, in other words, it is the formerly unbridled conscious mind, threatened by its own very achievements, that must dare to re-descend into the hidden depths of the psyche in order to seek renewal and eventually gain an even greater freedom.

You may of course feel that I am exaggerating. You may doubt the effectiveness of the initiation-archetype. You may be reluctant to accept that a mere symbolic 'return to the womb' could produce any practical renewal, any actual restoration of life and vigour. And yet the very history of nations bears constant witness to the power of the ancient process. Those seventeenth-century pioneers, refugees from their European homelands, who chose to die to their former lives and start up anew in the North American colonies, were eventually to produce an explosion of energy and creativity such as the world has rarely seen. Out of that symbolic womb a very·Hercules was to spring. Out of the Pilgrim Fathers' acceptance of the archetype of initiation the modern United States of America would be born.

The process continues even today. For still it is first- and second-generation Americans who produce most of that society's cultural effervescence and pioneering vigour. The modern state of Israel provides an even more vivid example of the same initiation-phenomenon.

Again, the two chief 'losers' of the Second World War were undoubtedly Germany and Japan. Having committed themselves utterly and totally to the pattern of the hero-archetype, both went on to suffer the inevitable hero's fate. Both, in short, over-reached themselves.

But long before Germany's final collapse, German public opinion had come to regard that collapse as inevitable, as just, even desirable. The leaders might continue to rant and rave in the old heroic manner, but the German soul was already committed to a new archetype—that of initiation. In Japan, meanwhile, it was the leadership itself that almost eagerly accepted defeat and bowed to the inevitability of the new dispensation.

In both cases, 'death' duly followed. Both societies had already been physically laid waste. Now their very structures were dismantled, their reigning social attitudes and philosophies crumbled into dust. For the inhabitants of those countries a whole world had come to an end, and a new one must come to birth.

Today, only a few decades later, we can see the equally inevitable result. The two 'losers', Germany and Japan, are now by far the richest nations in Western Europe and the Far East respectively. Their cities, often rebuilt from scratch, are resplendent with new buildings and modern facilities. Their industries flourish, even threatening to overwhelm the rest of the world, thanks largely to the introduction of entirely new patterns of industrial thinking. Their people display a vigour and an ingenuity which few of their competitors can hope to match. And meanwhile the supposedly 'victorious' nations, unwilling to abandon their own former attitudes and patterns of thought, sink ever deeper into economic and social problems of their own devising. Britain, in particular, is currently regarded as the 'sick man of Europe'.

One might be tempted to suggest, in fact, that the best way to win a war, thanks to the archetype of initiation, is to lose it.

Were it not that the ancient Chinese *Tao Te Ching*, well over two thousand years ago, had as good as suggested it already.

This, then, was the self-same archetype that the ancient religions sought to activate in candidates for admission to their mysteries. Their initiation-ceremonies were rites of death and rebirth designed to bestow on the candidate new life and unimagined power. Often the 'new-born' initiate took on a new name in reflection of the fact. The newly baptised convert to Christianity received what we still call a 'Christian name'. The monk, no less than the Pope, still acquires a new identity on taking up his new status.

And even the bride traditionally adopts her husband's name, in recognition of the fact that marriage, too, is a rite of death and renewal, of new beginnings, and thus of initiation.

It is no surprise, then, to find that the ancient tribal shamans and medicine-men universally submitted themselves to special initiation-rites in order to gain access to their nether-world of gods and spirits. In Egypt and Tibet alike, the initiation-rite was as vital to the postulant seeking access to the Higher Knowledge as it was to the dead seeking entry into the after-life. And even the ancient corn- and vegetation-gods—reflecting the seasonal initiation-cycle of nature—similarly had to undergo a perpetual cycle of suffering, death and resurrection. The Greek Adonis, the Babylonian Tammuz and the Egyptian Osiris must annually be sacrificed and laid in the tomb, if their triumphant new-year rebirth was to be assured.

And so, once again, the Christ-myth in due course takes up the ancient psychic theme. At the critical point where the 'divine' hero is in danger of falling prey to Lucifer's own sin of pride and lust for power, he voluntarily defers to the need for a new archetype. Laying his head on the altar of human evolution, he accepts his own torture and death. Laid in the tomb that is also the cosmic egg, the womb of the Earth-Mother, he too brings off an Easter resurrection.

A new dispensation is inaugurated, a new phase of human development begun.

And yet the great task is still not complete. To use his own words, the son of man has still not ascended to the Father. It still remains for humanity to be re-united with the true source of its being.

And so the dream changes once again. A new symbol must accede to the throne of consciousness—*the archetype of transcendence.*

* * * * *

Whether in dreams, myths or everyday events, the transcendence-theme generally appears in one of two principal forms. At its lowest level it often involves the conquering of some higher element—the creature that emerges from the sea onto the dry land, the climbing snake, the fish that flies, the human being who takes to the air.

At a higher, and often more 'spiritual' level, it tends to appear in the form of a lonely and difficult journey through an inhospitable environment to some distant goal, followed by an eventual, triumphant return.

In both forms, then, the underlying theme is one of release, and so we can see the myth of transcendence as supplying the ultimate fulfilment of the earlier process of initiation.

It was in response to this archetype, then, that Homer's Odysseus—whether real or purely legendary—must set out on his celebrated wanderings. Jason, too, must embark on his quest for the Golden Fleece. Heroes without number must journey to foreign lands, do battle against unimaginable odds, and at long last return in triumph to their homelands, rendered all but immortal by the experience.

The motif is reflected in religious pilgrimages of all kinds. It was taken up historically, and on a mass scale, in the great medieval Crusades against the Muslim 'infidels'. It is the ultimate myth of all transcendental religions.

But, once again, there are secular applications too. Inspired by the same theme, Marco Polo must set out across the burning deserts in quest of unknown lands. Embarking in frail boats, St Brendan, Madoc, Leif Eriksson, Columbus, Magellan, Drake and Cook must all set sail in search of new worlds. The great explorers, the Livingstones and Stanleys, must open up the 'dark', unknown continents. Shackleton, Amundsen and Scott must attempt to conquer the poles, Hillary and Tensing the snows of Everest. And in their illustrious footsteps, first in a trickle, then in an ever-growing stream, the amateur adventurers, the tourists and holidaymakers too must all eventually follow.

Until at length our present-day world offers us almost nowhere else to go.

And so, having all but exhausted the horizontal possibilities, we launch out into the vertical. We explore the depths of the sea, blast off for the planets. Alternatively, we explore new dimensions of the old, familiar problems. We sail the ocean single-handed, circumnavigate the globe without stopping, then the 'wrong way', backwards, sideways, upside-down . . . anything, so long as it involves some kind of perilous journey and triumphant return. Our craze for breaking records is merely a new form of the ancient myth which ever and anon obliges us (split infinitive notwithstanding) 'to boldly go where no man has gone before'.

And all the time the experience is gradually strengthening us, preparing us for an even more perilous journey. The journey to the centre of the Self. For that is the essence of our next initiation.

And if we run out of practical challenges we can always fall back on fictional ones. With Robinson Crusoe, Jim Hawkins, Tom Sawyer, Wu Ch'Êng-Ên's *Monkey* and even Alice we can embark on a whole range of adventures before returning home again. Tolkien's hobbits, Adams's rabbits of *Watership Down* and Richard Bach's appropriately-named *Jonathan Livingston Seagull* strike powerful chords in the modern psyche as they undertake their various odysseys. With the great science-fictionists, not to mention the crew of the starship *Enterprise,* we can undertake epic, missionary voyages across the depths of space. The theme starts to acquire a lofty, almost religious intensity—always a sure sign that a society's vital myth has been touched upon.

Meanwhile—unlike the space-travellers, or even the legendary Three Kings of the Nativity-traditions—the migrating Israelites and Bunyan's celebrated Pilgrim decline to make the return trip. Both have their reasons for modifying the myth. For both see their distant destination as their real 'home'.

As we saw earlier, however, the theme of the perilous journey is not the only way in which the archetype of transcendence expresses itself. It also takes on such images as the flight of birds and the emergence of amphibious and subterranean creatures from the deep. Both themes continually express themselves, both mythically and in purely practical terms, throughout history.

So it is that the ancient shamans, even as far back as the Stone Age, immemorially adopted the guise of a bird to assist their wanderings in the nether world and their subsequent return with news of the beyond. The fact is memorialised in the cave-art of their day. The very name of the Aztecs' Quetzalcoatl—'feathered serpent'—symbolises the transcending of the physical world which has been associated with 'winged serpents' almost throughout history. In the biblical account, too, it is the tree-climbing serpent that first tempts humanity to taste the supposedly liberating fruit of the knowledge of good and evil.

Again, it was the amphibious creature Oannes—successor of the Sumerians' fish-man, Ea—who traditionally emerged from the sea to bestow on the Babylonians all their ancient wisdom. And meanwhile the unfortunate prophet Jonah, in the process of learning the painful lesson that you should never cry wolf, similarly emerges from the great fish's belly onto the dry land. His feat, you could say, is a direct, if somewhat farcical reflection of the Israelites' crossing of the Red Sea to reach the Holy Mountain, and of their fording of the Jordan to reach the promised land. All four events express the archetypal theme of liberation. So, too, does the Christian rite of baptism, in which the candidate emerges from the waters in full expectation of enlightenment by the Holy Spirit.

And even the risen Christ himself, emerging from the subterranean tomb, must duly complete the archetypal cycle by winging his way to heaven.

Yet the theme of transcendence, even in this form, is not confined to mere ritual and mythology. Without so much as a sidelong glance at the Greek Icarus or the later Peter Pan, humanity has dreamed for centuries of taking to the air and leaving earth behind. And so, first through the technique of ballooning, and later through direct observation and imitation of the birds, those dreams have duly been fulfilled.

The early gliding-experiments of researchers such as Lilienthal were in due course to lead, via a process of painful trial and error, to the Wright brothers' first successful demonstration of powered flight in December, 1903. And so, through the efforts of a whole succession of heroes, the archetype of aviation literally took off. As Blériot, Alcock and Brown, Lindbergh, Amy Johnson and all the other pioneers of flight in turn acted out their heroic dreams of transcendence and liberation—duly aped in their own way by all the world's private pilots and hang-gliding enthusiasts—human consciousness progressively learnt to liberate itself from the shackles of inherited dogma as to what was possible and what was not.

Until, with the eventual penetration of interstellar space, the archetypal themes of bird, fish and perilous journey became fused into a single, mighty saga, a planetary Jonathan-Livingston-Seagull theme magnified to the nth degree. To the acting out of that theme humanity came increasingly to devote its finest skills, its greatest riches, its supreme mental efforts. For, guided by the fictional foreshadowings of writers such as Verne, Wells, Clarke and Asimov, we humans had long since come to see the achievement of escape from earth and gravity as the fulfilment of our most ancient dreams.

Which, in a remarkably true sense, it was.

Yet hero and dragon-slayer, initiate and explorer, fish-man and bird-man are all one. Again and again their myths and motifs intertwine. Constantly reflected in our dreams, our mythology, our history, our fiction, our religious beliefs and even our social trends and ideals, they represent nothing more or less than humankind itself. They are symbols for the cyclic process of self-renewal that our conscious mind must continually undergo as it lays its gifts of acquired knowledge and experience before the 'maternal' unconscious and then departs again. But not, of course, before it has had bestowed upon it in turn all the renewed vigour and refreshment which must flow from such an integrative encounter.

*   *   *   *   *

And so the ground is prepared for the eventual coming of the last archetype—the *archetype of the Self*. It, too, is an archetype with which you are thoroughly familiar—if not through your own dream-life, then at least through the waking dreams of others. All those ancient religious promises of 'second comings' are nothing less than anticipations of this culminating psychic event. The Buddha Maitreya, the Hindus' Vishnu in his incarnation as Kalki, the Zoroastrian Shaushyant, the returning Quetzalcoatl of the Aztecs, the Christian 'son of man coming with the clouds of heaven'—all are merely yourself in disguise. Yourself made whole, restored and brought to life again.

Yourself that has at last come to your Self.

The event is one of almost magical transformation. Perhaps, indeed, 'transfiguration' would be a better word for it. It brings with it the release of almost inconceivable psychic powers. And so the dream-images through which the archetype expresses itself similarly have a magical, almost godlike quality about them. They send a thrill of excitement through you, a shudder of awe and recognition—or rather of Self-recognition. For their appearance signifies an inner event of overwhelming power and significance.

Deep within the dark tomb of your psyche, the being that is the deeper you has been slumbering ever since the dawn of time—*your* time—patiently awaiting its day of resurrection. Now it stirs into life. Soon it will burst from the tomb in a blaze of unimaginable glory. And the transformed being that is the real you will at last step forth once more into the sunlight.

But, as usual, your world of dreams is constantly reflected in the world 'out there'. And so any human figure who seems to embody that once and future promise of wholeness takes on the magic aura of the archetype. Saints and divines, kings and statesmen, artists and musicians, major scientists, even actors and sports-personalities—all can alike exude an aura of greatness, a true charisma, the feeling that they have somehow transcended the condition of ordinary mortals. Somehow, we feel, they don't make them like that any more.

And yet they do. They keep on doing so.

Lao Tsu and Pythagoras, Michelangelo and da Vinci, Shakespeare and Dickens, Mozart and Beethoven, Newton and Einstein, Lenin and Mao Tse-Tung, Van Gogh and Picasso, Freud and Jung, Gandhi and Pope John XXIII, Churchill and Kennedy, Grace and Bradman, Cobb and Pelé, Liszt and Paganini, Melba and Caruso, Pavlova and Bernhardt—all were once no more significant or immortal than you yourself. Yet now they bestride our cultural horizons like colossi from another world. And in their eventual passing we see the fading of a promise, the loss of a power and wholeness such as mortals can never hope to see again.

But that is because we appreciate their greatness only after they are dead or past their prime. Greatness, like the Kingdom of Heaven, seems to be an exclusively post-mortem affair. Yet, did you but know it, similar potentialities also lie dormant within yourself, only awaiting their chance to break out. And it is your own attainment of psychic wholeness that will eventually unlock the doors and release the shackles —the same attainment of wholeness that is reflected in the world-wide longing for larger-than-life saviours from 'out there'.

At least, then, the auguries are good. The human psyche is still active on its quest for the long-lost wholeness of the Self. Otherwise the Messianic dream, the belief in greatness, would have faded long ago.

And so other images of the archetype, too, continually come to the surface within and around us. National emblems and team-mascots apart, the quest for the 'godlike animal' still finds its reflection in the physical world. No longer is it merely a matter of the search for Moby Dick or the saga of the big-game hunter. True, there was always an element of holy awe present in those few moments before you saw the whites of the eyes and feverishly pressed the trigger. But now killing and stuffing the lordly quarry has become unfashionable. Today it must be preserved and memorialised in other ways. Kept alive in a sacred precinct, it must be worshipped from afar. And so, in safari-park and wild-life film, no less than through the efforts of the Greenpeace Movement, the great creatures of the wild still survive to excite in us an almost religious awe—again a sure sign that a mighty archetype is close at hand.

The power of the archetype still shows itself, too, in the magic of the sacred stone. You can see it in the Muslims' devotion to the famous Black Stone of Mecca, in the Hindus' reverence for the sacred *lingam*, no less than in the ancient Greeks' awe of the *omphalos*, or navel of the world. 'Phallic' you may think their symbolism to be, but then a phallus is itself only a symbol. And moreover, in that case, you would have to explain the modern fascination with ancient standing-stones in exactly the same light.

Which would be a pity.

For that would be to reduce the great symbols of the human psyche to mere sexual baubles—almost as if human beings were a function of sex, instead of the other way around. For if sex is to be regarded as our *summum bonum*, then it is also likely to prove the summit of our achievement.

I reproduce, therefore I am.

Which is a far cry from the attitude of those who toiled for decades to build that other well-known sexual symbol, the Great Pyramid of Giza. This colossal edifice, a truly awesome monument to the human psyche, not only represents the ultimate in archetypal sacred stones. It also ties in, via its semi-crystalline form, with the 'magic crystal' aspect of the archetype of the Self. And certainly the power of this image is far from spent. Indeed, in the current craze for 'pyramid power' and all its various adjuncts, we merely see one tiny aspect of the mushrooming crystal-based technology that has given rise to our modern world of transistors, lasers and microprocessors. The reign of the crystal, whether for good or evil, has barely begun.

Om mani padme hum! Hail to the jewel in the lotus!

And meanwhile the ancient stone-circles of Stonehenge and Avebury still survive, now attracting far more interest than they have done for centuries past. In the process they make the link between stone and subdivided circle, which represents the remaining form of this archetype. But of this theme we shall have more to say anon.

Suffice it to say for the present, then, that the rediscovery of the Self represents the ultimate purpose of the human psyche, the goal of our striving, the top of the ladder of our inner evolution. And perhaps of our outer evolution, too.

Truly the fulfilment of our dreams.

You may be lucky. You may achieve that goal during your present lifetime. Statistically, however, it is far more likely that you won't. Certainly its attainment by humankind as a whole still lies some centuries or even millennia in the future. And so what has to concern us here and now is the more immediate question of what to do next—the next rung on the ladder. And the answer, it must by now be abundantly clear, revolves around the continuing initiatory process.

It is initiation, in other words—the periodic return to the psychic 'womb' and the subsequent rebirth to a new and greater freedom—that lies at the heart of the whole process of our inner development.

The hero-phase simply prepares the ground for that encounter. The transcendence-phase represents its inevitable sequel, as our consciousness sets out for a new round of experience, culminating in a further homecoming and initiation. The biblical story of the Prodigal Son is nothing less than a solemn allegory of the human psyche itself.

But then the process of perpetual initiation within the human psyche is essentially the same process of thesis, antithesis and synthesis that we have already seen to be at work in the process of terrestrial evolution. Indeed, it seems to underlie the very unfolding of the cosmos itself. The 'unconscious' universe produces in us the consciousness with which it can view itself 'from outside': the earth produces the consciousness which now threatens to destroy it. And both developments must eventually result in a new synthesis, a new wholeness, a new cosmic order entirely.

Or else in annihilation.

In all these forms, then, we can observe the initiatory process, analyse it, watch it in slow motion. In the light of our new-found knowledge, we can then apply our conclusions to history, trace out the phases of our collective psychic development, and so use them as tools to understand the nature of our present crisis. Above all, perhaps, we can take full heed of the world-wide dream that we are currently acting out in stark reality.

And it is now more than ever vital that we should.

For the observing and representing of that dream seems to be the sole guarantee of human posterity. It alone can once more set in train the healing-process universally applied by the individual psyche to itself. It alone, consequently, can hope to cure the present sickness of humanity.

It is time for us to know ourselves.

13. RHYTHMS OF BEING

For each age is a dream that is dying
Or one that is coming to birth.

Arthur William Edgar O'Shaughnessy: *Ode*

We are at the end of an era. In almost every sense the fact becomes daily more obvious—physically, morally, psychologically and spiritually—to the point where it is scarcely a matter for controversy any more. And it is increasingly clear that, unless we are prepared to put an end to the old dispensation, the old dispensation will put an end to us.

Such is the brutal truth which today stares humanity in the face. Sick, tired and torn asunder both inwardly and outwardly, we have reached the end of the road.

And so the time has come for us to look, first for some friendly hostelry to spend the night, and then for a new road to follow. We need a road-sign. A sign that we can read and understand. A sign that we are then prepared to follow.

And that sign, as usual, the human psyche itself can be trusted to provide.

We have already taken a close look at the psychic development of the typical individual. We have detailed the inner process in which you yourself are continually involved. We have seen how your psyche throws up a whole series of archetypal images, each designed to take you one stage further along your path of inner evolution. Repeatedly, it seems, your concious mind is recalled to the 'womb' of the unconscious, and is then sent out into the world again refreshed and reinvigorated.

Throughout life, initiation must succeed initiation. Until eventually the point is reached where your conscious mind, penetrating even further into the wastelands of its self-created hell, at last comes out again on the other side.

And finds the 'maternal' unconscious waiting for it there with open arms.

Such is the inner process of the individual. Such, too, it now seems certain, is the process of humanity itself.

For humanity, too, has always had its common dream. To discover it, you do not need to analyse statistically the dreams of men and women all over the planet—possible though that may be. For those dreams, as we saw in the previous chapter, constantly surface in quite concrete form and, once fixed, remain for posterity. By unearthing the legacy of the past—its arts and sciences, its history and thought—we can trace the self-same procession of the archetypes as arises within the individual human being. And so we can follow in detail the successive phases of the psychic evolution of humanity as a whole.

Similarly, by studying our modern world in the same light, we can assess the present stage of its inner malady, and so hope to learn not only what we can do about it, but exactly where we go from here.

And knowing where we are going, there is perhaps a better chance that we shall eventually arrive.

What, then, are the 'signs of the times'? What prime theme is the collective unconscious currently beaming at us through those waking dreams that are our art and literature, our modern myths and obsessions, our current history and everyday life?

Consider the possibilities.

* * * * *

The first of the great transforming archetypes to arise in the mind of the young child is, as we saw earlier, the motif of the all-conquering hero. How far, then, does the hero-theme qualify for the title of dominant myth of our age?

Certainly the hero is still alive and well and living in children's comics. But then that is as it should be. The hero-myth is above all appropriate to the early years of life.

Yet what of the adult world? Here, it is true, the hero still flourishes in Westerns and war-films. But then both are set firmly in the past. Scarcely ever do their themes concern the *present-day* frontiers of civilisation, *modern* savages or *contemporary* wars. Somehow it all seems to be a reversion to childhood—as addicts are often the first to

146

admit.

And meanwhile, the heroes of the various television crime-series and medical soap-operas are themselves increasingly portrayed in a down-to-earth, everyday, fallible light. The role of Tarzan or James Bond is seen to be a piece of self-indulgent and self-satirising wishful-thinking, a daydream that has little do to with the humdrum reality from which it affords a welcome if temporary release.

Walter Mitty Rules OK.

The hero, in short, is increasingly felt to be an anachronism in our world. The single-minded idealism and enthusiastic violence that are the trade-marks of the breed have come to be regarded as threats to the delicate balance of our social order. The hero is little more than a bull in the terrestrial china-shop. Anxious above all to maintain global law and order—longing, in short, for a bit of peace and quiet—we seem to feel that we have somehow grown out of that sort of thing.

On the world-stage, consequently, the former patriot has degenerated into a mere nationalist, the political idealist into a dangerous extremist, the single-minded political leader into a fanatic and megalomaniac. That, at least, is how we have come to see them. We prefer our leaders and overlords to be quiet, faceless people. If we must have fictional heroes, then we would far rather that they were unreal, hairy-footed hobbits, or rabbits, or even harmless seagulls.

Anything, so long as they pose no real threat to our inner security.

The era of the hero-myth, in short, is over. In one sense at least, humankind has come of age. And so we need to consider the next two main contenders for the current title of ruling myth.

The themes of initiation and transcendence.

*   *   *   *   *

Conventionally, we have seen, the theme of initiation involves some kind of ordeal or trial of strength, a 'death' or period of confinement, and a final liberation. The theme of transcendence takes the process a stage further, as the new-born initiate of human consciousness penetrates into further dimensions of awareness. The process, you will recall, is often symbolised by the emergent denizens of the underworld, the flight of birds or a journey into the unknown. But the two themes constantly intertwine. The one arises from the other and subsequently leads back to it again. Deciding which of them applies to our present circumstances is thus unlikely to be easy.

Nevertheless certain observations are possible. We have already seen, for example, that, in a remarkably literal sense, we are the dead.

147

Dead to the light of full consciousness, which we started to shut out as long ago as the founding of our first civilisations. We are confined in the womb of our own self-delusion, buried in the self-dug grave of our own symbolism, imprisoned in the hell of our own rationalistic and self-alienating dogma. We are in the midst, in other words, of an initiation-process, and in this respect, at least, we are now due for a rebirth.

And certainly there are already signs that such an event is imminent.

Through our study of language we are already aware of the extent to which we use it to mask the real world and create a 'reality' of our own devising. Through our study of psychology we have come to realise that we are neither our conscious minds, nor a mere function of the world created by their symbols—not, in short, who we think we are, but something much deeper and more mysterious altogether. Through our study both of microphysics and of astronomy we are increasingly realising our congenital inability to grasp or understand the nature of physical reality at all. And through our study of religion it has long been apparent that we can never 'understand' reality for the simple reason that we *are* reality.

And so our thought and philosophy are already starting to take account of our 'deadness'. Our advanced thinkers are already proposing new paradigms of consciousness. Our psychic researchers and innovators are revealing and elaborating an ever more rich array of transcendent psychospiritual technologies*. Our idealistic young are committing themselves to new, alternative, communal lifestyles dedicated to laying the foundations of a future New Age of total consciousness and cosmic wholeness**.

In terms of the broadest possible overview, then, we humans have reached the end of stage two of the adventure of consciousness. Starting out as the unbridled, nomadic heroes who were our primitive forebears, we have gone on to commit ourselves to the ordeal and 'death' of self-alienation for the sake of our own social evolution. That process is virtually complete. Now, therefore, we must break out of our self-imposed prison if we are not to suffocate in the womb of human consciousness. The transcendent stork of rebirth is at hand. The baby is overdue.

Yet we have so far refused, by and large, to recognise even the fact of

---

*Compare Annett: *The Many Ways of Being* (Abacus/Turnstone, 1976).
**Compare Saunders: *Alternative England and Wales* (N. Saunders, 1975).

our 'death'. Like the traditional 'ghost', we persist in imagining that we are fully alive. The hero that is rational humanity still refuses to admit that it has over-reached itself and taken a nasty fall.

It is 1812 all over again, without even the saving grace of a later Overture.

And yet there is no denying the fact. Before any new birth can take place, our present mode of consciousness—our present 'sense of I'—has to pluck up sufficient courage to take Death by the hand and welcome him as an old familiar friend. We must agree to go through with the initiation that we ourselves have started. Otherwise Death himself may break into the house when we least expect it and take us in the night.

The unknown night of our present illusion.

It is no use delaying, for the longer we do, the more cataclysmic the experience is likely to be. Death has good reason for his haste, for already the messengers of the new, transcendent tomorrow are knocking at the door.

*　　*　　*　　*　　*

But other rhythms, too, can be observed in the pattern of human history. The evolution of civilisation, it has often been observed, seems to fall naturally into a series of 'ages', each of which lasts some two thousand years. And these ages, it is further suggested, are directly reflected in the twelve 2160-year 'months' of the astrological Great Year—the cycle of the equinoctial procession.

Our race's whole development, in other words, seems to resonate, as do the earth's climates and sea-levels, to an astronomical cycle whose period is some twenty-six thousand years.

The astrological proposition may seem fantastic. The climatic link is far from illogical, however. And if the stars help you to depict and time the stages of the wider ecological cycle, who are you to spurn their aid? That, at any rate, seems to have been the view of the ancients. And so they projected onto the circling heavens a series of symbols, a whole celestial zoo. To each sign of the zodiac they then allotted one of the twelve ages of the cycle.

To every age a sign.

Between 4,000 and 2,000 BC, for example, the earth's slow, precessional gyration brought the sun of the spring equinox into the sign of Taurus. The symbolism of the age of the Bull duly demanded the undertaking of massive physical projects in the service of humanity's spiritual development—the great Egyptian pyramids, the megaliths of the European Atlantic seaboard: for, as I have suggested in my book *Gospel of the Stars**, this must be an era for sowing the spiritual seed.

In the furrow ploughed by the Cosmic Ox.

Then, during the next two thousand years, the ensuing age of the Ram would usher in a new order—an era during which the great leaders and initiates must cultivate and nurture that sprouting seed in the hearts of their peoples. These they must therefore discipline and control—by force if necessary—like wise shepherds guiding and guarding their lambs. Abraham and Moses, Zoroaster and Lao Tsu, Confucius, the Buddha and Pythagoras all duly ministered to the concept.

But that age, too, must be superseded. The seed must become a mature plant, the lambs attain adulthood, the children come of age.

And so Jesus of Nazareth in due course proclaims the age of the Fishes. Now the formerly protected flocks of Aries must become creatures of the wild who know no master, slippery beings that can be caught only with difficulty, and even then only with their own connivance.

True, the zodiacal Fishes are bound together. The law of karma must continue to enchain them. Perhaps, too, they must remain enslaved by duality, crippled both inwardly and outwardly by their own fundamental psychic split.

For they are ourselves.

But in all other respects, reconceived in the womb of the deep, they must learn to find their own respective levels, be freed to pursue their several destinies.

They must choose—to be born or not to be born.

But that birth—that re-emergence, now imminent, from the coming pitcher of the age of Aquarius—is of the essence of the theme of transcendence. The very symbolism of the Fishes should make us suspect as much. From our Piscean freedom to enquire and explore we have gained a vast amount of knowledge and experience. Now we need as never before to use it to free ourselves from our former dualistic misconceptions. What is more, we need to do so at a time when we have still not fully broken free of the political and social hierarchies of the authoritarian age of Aries.

The need for transcendence, in consequence, is doubly urgent.

*Element Books, 1977.

Indeed, it is in danger of expressing itself in a paroxysm of violence so cataclysmic as to endanger humanity's very survival.

Once again, then, we have come up with the same answer. Whether you look at it philosophically or astrologically, transcendence seems to be the essential theme of the moment. That theme, then, needs to be acknowledged and responded to if we value our posterity.

And, as it happens, the signs are distinctly promising.

We have already noted the craze for record-breaking, the love-affair with flight, the great journey into the unknown with which space-flight has now captured the human imagination. In the sphere of fiction, too, our great cult-epics—with their hobbits and rabbits, their seagulls and astronauts—speak to us constantly of the archetypal pilgrimage of transcendence. All four species, in fact, are typical transcendent beings. The first two are subterranean dwellers that emerge into the light. The third is an earth- and sea-dweller that soars into the sky. And the last is a mortal being who leaves earth behind to journey among the stars.

At the more humble, everyday level, too, we increasingly feel the theme of transcendence to be of the essence. Revealingly, perhaps, we describe our very way of life as 'the rat-race'. By speaking in this way, we acknowledge that we are inwardly driven by a constant urge for self-betterment, for an ever-increasing standard of living. 'Growth' is the current watchword, notwithstanding the fact that unlimited expansion must eventually be self-defeating on a finite planet. And in response to that same drive, the masses of the so-called Third World and of the underprivileged have long since set out determinedly on their long march towards what they imagine to be a brighter future.

Once again we have become restless nomads. We must be ever on the move.

Reflecting the same theme, the young must now become mobile, and preferably motorised, at the first opportunity. Youthful western idealists, adopting the traditional role of penniless pilgrims, must set out on their hazardous journeys to the mystic shrines and cult-centres of the east. Others must undertake ritual summer-migrations to mass pop-festivals in the open air. And even for their more affluent parents, the focus of the whole year's efforts and labours, the symbolic beacon which gives meaning and purpose to their humdrum existence, increasingly becomes the annual package-tour to far-away lands.

Yet this, too, is a mere symbolic ritual. For it combines the twin motifs of flight and of perilous journey to some Shangri-la into a single, almost literal celebration of the traditional myth of transcendence.

Thus, while in the long-term view we are due for a rebirth of consciousness, it is transcendence that is currently of the essence for our cultural life. We feel a pressing urge finally to free ourselves from the shackles which the dead weight of tradition has imposed on us.

But then between transcendence and rebirth there is little, if any, difference. To break out of the womb is to transcend the pre-natal world. To break out of the tomb is to transcend death itself.

*　　*　　*　　*　　*

Meanwhile the broad epochs of historical time, whether astrological or otherwise, are themselves punctuated by briefer periods of cultural fashion. And here, too, a constant process of death, rebirth and transcendence continually operates.

At the beginning of our present, Piscean era, for example, the Roman Empire—with all its far-reaching consequences for the social, cultural and intellectual development of the west—was already about to enter its period of final decline. That is to say, it had passed through its resplendent period of expansion and transcendence, and had duly overreached itself. The time had come for the triumph of will and reason to be undermined by the long-neglected irrational side of human nature. The swashbuckling heroes were recalled to maternal Rome. The yelling hordes swept in from Asia.

But from the loins of that empire came the seed that was to give birth to a new dispensation. As the scattered lights of Christianity started to pierce the gloom of the Dark Ages, a new civilisation arose among the barbarians of Europe. With the Gothic era it reached its zenith. The pinnacles and spires of its mighty cathedrals bore mute yet eloquent witness to the ability of the very stones to transcend the constraints of terrestrial gravity. Many of them still do so today.

But that civilisation, too, you will recall, was to crumble in its turn. This time it was the Church and its irrational dogmas that over-reached themselves. The pendulum of awareness had swung to the other extreme. Witch-hunt, war and inquisition put the flames, not just to the heretic and infidel, but to the whole tottering edifice of belief and superstition that the Church had erected on the basis of the simple teachings of the Nazarene gospel of love.

The time was ripe for a new rebirth.

And so it duly occurred, exactly on cue. Indeed, we still know it today as the 'rebirth', or Renaissance. But this time it was once again the turn of human will and reason to triumph. The eventual fall of Constantinople to the Turks in 1453 produced an astonishing chain of revolutionary events. The peoples of Europe suddenly rediscovered from the Byzantine scholars the ancient cultural heritage of Rome and Greece. And, almost at the same time, such figures as Columbus, Cabot, da Gama, Magellan and Drake set out to discover a whole new world.

The return to Classical documentary sources was in due course to be reflected in a new, 'documentary' approach to Christianity—a movement that we now know as the Reformation. Out of this, in turn, there arose a strong trend towards puritanism. Meanwhile the renewed influence of Classical science—together with a new sense of physical mastery over the environment—was directing people's attention ever more and more to the mechanics of the physical world. Humanity came to see itself as the measure of the universe. And from it all came a tremendous explosion of psychic energy—energy which the Church had for so long kept seething and boiling under a heavy lid of dogma and repression. There was a new and almost universal confidence that humankind could somehow transform the world. The very cosmos must be tamed, cut down to size, made to conform to those dictates of human reason and order that we still know, even today, as the 'laws of nature'.

The conviction, certainly, died hard. The new-born infant proved sturdy and resilient. Yet by the early eighteenth century it, too, had overstayed its welcome. The age of reason had succumbed to a kind of hardening of the arteries. It was suffering from a rigid and sterile social order, a dry and dogmatic scientific rationalism that refused point-blank to venture out beyond the playpen of its senses. In the spiritual sphere, it had fallen victim to an almost rabid fundamentalism that was prone to confuse God with Holy Writ—refusing, as it were, to take its nose out of its book for fear of what it might see in the world outside. What had started out as an age of materialism had increasingly become an age of verbalism. The word and the concept, now finally defined and categorised for all time, were everything.

So that it is no surprise to find that this was the age which produced the first comprehensive, modern dictionaries.

In a sense, then, the age of rationalism had started to succumb to *rigor mortis* long before it finally died. To a large extent, *rigor mortis* was actually the cause of death. Yet, like every phase of evolution, the age of rationalism contained within it the seed of its successor. The rash of world-exploration that had started with the Renaissance brought a curious fact into western consciousness. There were many world societies which, for all their lack of sophistication and rationalism, somehow managed to produce happier people, and even a more equitable and just social order, than had been achieved at home.

And so, as the age of reason played out its death-throes on the stage of history, the myth of the 'noble savage' was already waiting in the wings.

Its moment duly came. The age of Romanticism was born. Once more it was the turn of the irrational and the intuitive to rule the European roost. The genius of the age turned out to be a familiar demon—none other than the human unconscious, resurrected and turned into a god. The arts started to flourish anew in a violent surge of creativity. In a dozen countries the existing social order was to be overthrown. Revolution became the order of the day, violence the new watchword. And in the great Napoleon Bonaparte the new age possibly found its supreme social expression.

Yet, moribund as it was, the former age of rationalistic materialism stubbornly refused to admit defeat. So carefully, so surely had its creators constructed their house of illusion, so closely did all its parts interlink and support each other, that it somehow managed to survive the awful shock. Perhaps it was because the Romantics, despite all their violence, had always hesitated to deliver the final death-blow. Even their greatest champions had always seen as their ideal, not a total victory for unreason and chaos, but a blissful wedding between reason and intuition, between head and heart. That, indeed, had been the guiding spirit behind the French Revolution. And the great Napoleon, too, constantly placed the vaulting steed of his intuition at the service of a more enlightened social order, apparently sensing that some such reconciliation is essential if the race is ever to re-attain its original wholeness.

At all events, it was while he was in the midst of his own supreme and highly symbolic pilgrimage of transcendence across the wastes of Russia that the forces of reaction saw their chance. Once again an age had over-reached itself. Once again it was to be brought crashing to the ground. The events of 1812 were symbolic of the coming end of an era. The safe world of rationalism was soon to re-establish its supremacy.

And now it was to be immeasurably reinforced.

For no sooner had the Romantic era started to decline than a vast new tide of materialism began to sweep the world. The rediscovery of steam power (first invented by the ancient Greeks), the growth of industrialisation, the spread of railways, the ever more rapid advance of science, the internal combustion engine, the telegraph, wireless, modern armaments, powered flight, modern medicine, nuclear power, astronautics—in all these the new god of matter rapidly turned itself into an ever more compulsive master.

Or rather into a mistress. For materialism is, literally, the religion of *mater*—the Great Mother.

And she, inevitably, was all that mattered.

In the socio-political sphere, too, materialism was the theme of the hour. With the rise of socialism and communism, whole civilisations must prostrate themselves in its worship. A whole new series of revolutions must therefore serve the concept.

Yet even in its earliest infancy the new materialistic age was starting to sow the seeds of its own destruction—a characteristic, this, of every age, as must by now be rather obvious, and as Karl Marx himself was to realise. It was the very investigation of the nature of matter that was to help lead, via Planck and Einstein, to the discrediting of materialism's mechanistic foundations. It was the medical investigation of the human organism that was to lead, via the physicians Freud and Jung, to the realisation that the essence of our being is psychic and irrational, not physical and rational. It was the physical and intellectual exploration of the world and its cultures that was to lead, via the encounter with oriental religious philosophies, to the undermining of the west's faith, not only in its basic religious and scientific assumptions, but also in the very processes of reason.

The age of rationalistic materialism, in short, is even now in the process of transcending itself. The physicist increasingly realises that it is necessary to go beyond physics. The astronomer looks more and more for a cosmic matrix behind the reality of the stars. The psychologist detects signs of further, intangible, collective processes underlying the very psyche. And even fundamentalist Christians—themselves as materialist in their way as the 'ungodly' whom they are so keen to convert—come to see that they must start looking for a deeper and more comprehensive reality that hides behind and beyond all religious texts and teachings.

*   *   *   *   *

And so in the cultural sphere, too—as in the larger, aeonic context of our social evolution—the theme of transcendence is today of the essence. Its supremacy as a motif for our age is therefore plain. Its psychological urgency is beyond question.

Yet it is not *mere* transcendence that is at issue. For to transcend is also to die to that which is transcended, and to die to one dispensation is to be reborn to another. And here there seems to be an important difference between our own era and those which have preceded it.

Every previous cultural phase seems to have cast itself in a heroic mould which, under the inexorable terms of the hero-archetype, has led it to over-reach itself. Consequently it has in due course been destroyed by its long-suppressed 'opposite'. But in our own society, by contrast, the heroic role is increasingly being discarded *quite voluntarily* under the imminent threat of humanity's self-extinction. We no longer think we know all the answers. Parents are no longer sure enough of their own standards to feel justified in imposing them on the children. And the young won't fight any more.

For the first time in millennia, a 'transcendent' world-society seems about to consent to its own 'death', its own initiation, for the sake of humanity's greater posterity.

And therein lies enormous hope for a new and major step in humanity's psychic evolution.

And so, in the cultural and social contexts particularly, our civilisation already shows signs of realising that a precondition for the glories of transcendence is its own ordeal and death—just as, in the wider sphere of human consciousness itself, that death is already with us, only waiting to be recognised for what it is.

Already the west is busy dismantling its societies. Old values and standards must, it seems, be undermined and abandoned, the law emasculated, distinctions blurred, traditional morality ridiculed and allowed to decay. Meanwhile we must do everything possible to scare ourselves to death. We must undergo ordeal by commercial sanction, ordeal by population-explosion, ordeal by pollution, ordeal by war and rumour of war, ordeal by nuclear threat. And as if that were not enough, we voluntarily submit ourselves to further ordeals in the guise of entertainment—ordeal by television documentary, by current-affairs programme, by horror-film, by football-crowd, by drugs. Ceaselessly we ask ourselves what is wrong with ourselves and our society, not what is right.

And since a thing's rightness or wrongness depends on the way in which you look at it, everything, not surprisingly, turns out to be wrong.

And so, like every dying civilisation before it, our society turns increasingly to its ancient beginnings in the hope of finding salvation. In the current craze for archaeology (itself a science that, in its present form, has arisen only in the last century or so), in our increasing anxiety to disinter the roots of our religion, of our culture, of our moral and intellectual assumptions, of our very consciousness and identity—why else are you reading this book?—we can detect the symbols of a prevalent and growing desire to 'return to the womb'. Even the current mania for water-sports—whether sailing, surfing, swimming or scuba-diving—may merely be symptomatic of a deeper, symbolic yearning for those ancient uterine waters of consciousness. The world of Jacques Cousteau, you could say, is the world of the foetus. And as for the world of the caver and pot-holer . . .

In almost every aspect of western society, in fact, we can detect the typical signs of a clear and ineradicable death-wish.

But that, as we have seen, is entirely as it should be.

What is more worrying, as you will appreciate, is the tendency to apply the tendency too literally. Through identifying ourselves too closely with our society and culture, we are only too prone to assume that, because *they* are in their death-throes, we too have only death and destruction to look forward to.

The assumption is perhaps understandable.

The gloom-and-doom industry, consequently, is in its heyday. Current population, resources and pollution statistics merely provide welcome grist to its mill. The question 'Has man a future?'*, despite the pie-in-the-sky blandishments of out-of-touch scientific optimists, increasingly finds a negative answer. Only the idealistic young, credulous and naive as they may sometimes appear to their elders, seem willing and able to carry off the practical act of faith involved in giving birth to a new order of society entirely. Fully conscious of the storm-clouds on the world's horizons, more and more of them are currently sacrificing both present affluence and alleged future 'career-prospects' to congregate in a growing number of experimental New Age communities all over the globe.

But then perhaps we should bear in mind that it is the credulous, not the incredulous, who will eventually discover the truth.

For conventional society, however, the smell of death is unmistakably in the air, and to a generation which assumes—on the basis, curiously enough, of Christian dogma—that, for terrestrial purposes, history is a straight-line graph and death is final, the prospects for the future look bleak indeed.

Today, as in the past, we humans need a guiding myth to remind us once more of the reality of eternal renewal. A myth capable of renew-

*Compare Bertrand Russell's book of the same title (Penguin, 1961).

ing the inner conviction that we have a vital and integral part to play in the larger evolution of our planet and of the universe as a whole. That conviction, despite the heroic—if indigestible—writings of Teilhard de Chardin*, can no longer be gained from the Christian myth which supported us for so long. Indeed, it is possibly the final abandonment of that myth that has done more than anything else to produce the current sense of bitter deception, of the utter purposelessness of life, of our own alienation from the ongoing process of the universe around us.

We have lost a religion and not yet found a faith.

Yet the universe will go on. The rebirth will come. Perhaps not in all spheres simultaneously. The social and cultural rebirth already with us in germ among the New Agers may well flower within a century or less. In the much longer-term sphere of human consciousness as such, the final return to total consciousness for humankind as a whole may take a good deal longer**.

What is of the essence at present, however, is to ensure that humanity as a whole is still here to enjoy it when it comes.

And so we in the west need to become aware, perhaps as never before, of the initiatory process to which, willy nilly, we have long since committed ourselves. We need to learn that death, rebirth and transcendence form a continual chain of becoming in which we are caught up at every level of our being. Indeed, to divide it up in this way into three stages is a mere artificial device. In reality the process forms an unbroken continuum whose essence is the theme of eternal renewal, and whose trademark is circularity itself.

But then, to give full credit where credit is due, we already seem to have a subliminal awareness of that fact too.

---

*For a readable digest, see his *Let Me Explain* (Fontana, 1974).

**For possible datings, compare Lemesurier: *Gospel of the Stars* (Element Books, 1977).

14. THE MAGIC CIRCLE

Plus ça change, plus c'est la meme chose.
French proverb

Nature abhors straight lines scarcely less than it abhors a vacuum. Any philosophy or religion, any way of life or political programme which ignores the fact inhabits a world of pure make-believe. Progress can never be a straight-line graph. There is no royal road leading directly from earth to heaven, from here to eternity.

Nor is there any point in believing otherwise. For in the end the reality will inevitably smash the illusion.

But will it also smash the deluded? That, perhaps, is the most pressing question of our day.

If our favourite illusions tend to follow straight lines, reality, as we shall see, is essentially curved or circular. So is our inner process of perpetual initiation. And our survival depends very largely on our recognition of the fact. There is no future for us if reality and our illusion are set on a collision-course.

And so, once again, there is actually some cause for optimism. For, whether you have noticed it or not, circularity is nowadays one of the themes of the moment in almost all areas of human activity.

Increasingly we conceive of existence in terms of cycles—the life-cycle, the ecological cycle, the historical civilisation-cycle. In cosmology, the dualistic opposition between the 'big bang' and 'steady state' theories of the universe is starting to give ground to a new and more all-embracing, 'cyclic' concept—that of the 'oscillatory universe', so long foreshadowed by the Hindu doctrine of the 'days and nights of Brahma'. At the religious level, too, the former view of the

159

cosmos as starkly divided between the powers of good and evil is as good as dead. In its place the popular mind has thrown up once again an ancient astrological paradigm which would impose upon the heavens, and consequently upon the earth too, a wheeling system of 'cycles of power'—a system which is neither good nor evil, but simply an ever-changing and inexhaustible index of cosmic possibilities.

Meanwhile, in the sphere of human life and death, the dualistic conflict between tyrannical God and wayward Devil is increasingly replaced by the concept of a universally self-imposed karmic cycle. The 'you only live once' mentality, with its single, one-way ticket to heaven or hell, is being ever more widely eroded by a growing belief in reincarnation.

Which is as circular a notion as you are likely to get.

Again, the traditional basis of scientific enquiry—namely that I am 'me', an independent observer, looking at 'that', some objective aspect of the universe 'out there'—has long since had the ground cut from under its feet. Research into the nature of the atom has already made it abundantly clear that there are no discrete 'things', but only interrelated processes'—and 'I' who attempt to observe them am as much a part of the processes I observe as are the processes themselves.

All that I can really observe is myself observing whatever I am observing.

Indeed, since only interrelationship *is*, there is nothing in the universe that can be defined other than in terms of the rest of the universe. Everything, in the last resort, is a function of everything else. The whole universe as we know it is ultimately holding itself up by its own bootstraps. Which is, of course, the circular argument to end all circular arguments.

As we humans, who started it, ought to be the first to realise.

Similar considerations even apply to the very language we use to talk about such things—the language on which our whole world-view is actually based. There is not a word in the dictionary whose meaning can be defined other than by further words in the dictionary.

Amateur linguists, it is true, are prone to seek sources of meaning through the process of derivation. The word 'derive' itself, for example, was originally formed on the basis of the Latin prefix *de-*, meaning 'down', and the root *riv-*, which denoted a river. Thus, the word 'derive' originally carried the idea of 'flowing from a source'. But establishing a word's former sense is not the same as establishing its present meaning. *Silly* no longer means blessed, nor *dinner* breakfast, nor *bureau* a piece of green cloth, nor *companions* people who eat bread together. Except to a person who is constantly aware of such things, a word's meaning is neither what it *used* to mean, not what it *might* mean if you took it to bits—nor, for that matter, what it *could* mean if you chose to look up those bits in other languages entirely.

Nor can we arrive at a word's meaning merely by 'defining' it. For the process can never get down from the airy round-dance of linguistic equivalents to the solid earth of reality.

Ultimately the meaning of the word *apple*, for example, is precisely that—what it means, its 'is-ness'—and even if you explore the fruit itself in all its aspects, as every baby instinctively does and must—how it looks, feels, tastes, smells, sounds—you are still only skimming the real meaning of the word, which covers a multitude of further associations and memories, symbolisms and attitudes reflecting the whole history not only of your racial, but also of your personal experience.

Which is one good reason why every dictionary is already out of date before it is even printed.

A word's meaning, in short, is what you make of it. But perhaps it is for that very reason that there is a growing band of writers and thinkers in our own day who are determined to prove that a word can mean absolutely anything at all.

And particularly, of course, what they want it to mean.

* * * * *

I refer, as you may already have guessed, to that intrepid band of esoteric scholars who insist on discovering 'hidden' meanings behind words (particulary those of the Bible) by converting them into numbers, or words of other languages, or places, or states of consciousness, or Tarot cards, or zodiacal symbols, or kabbalistic concepts*. It is an intriguing exercise, certainly. It opens up all sorts of possibilities. And there is absolutely no reason why you should not go on and use it to forecast tomorrow's weather, or to win the football pools, or to discover the winner of the two-thirty. What is more, you might even be right. For what both you and they are doing is merely discovering in the scriptures symbols for your own unconscious processes. And those processes have a remarkable way of ascertaining the apparently unascertainable.

Enjoy, then, if you must, this extension of the symbol-game. But do

---

*Compare, for example, John Michell: *The View Over Atlantis* and *City of Revelation* (Abacus, 1973), and Whone: *Church Monastery Cathedral* (Element Books, 1977).

not be deluded. You may discover a great deal about yourself, but you will discover next to nothing about the words themselves.

Except, perhaps, one curious fact.

For, with over four thousand million human beings between them speaking some four thousand different languages, it is almost inevitable that *every* basic combination of sounds or letters, examined across the whole spectrum of world language, must in fact have meant *everything* at some time or other.

Which is not only a splendid example of linguistic circularity. It is also philosophically exactly as it should be.

So perhaps it is not, after all, so unforgivable to treat language in this way. If it provides you with a row of new hat-pegs on which to hang unfamiliar sets of ideas, if it allows you to 'blow your mind' while still clinging to what seem to be traditional patterns of thought, if it opens up to you alternative mental circuits that bypass the filters and fuses of conventional rationality—then perhaps it is all to the good.

Something very similar, in fact, constantly happens in your dreams.

The unconscious, after all, is no respecter of linguistic rules and regulations. It puns shamelessly, plays unmercifully on words—or rather on the symbols that it prefers to substitute for words. That, indeed, is what dream symbolism is all about—the unlimited substitution of one image for another. That is how the unconscious constantly tries to make you aware of the vast universe of unrealised possibilities that lies beyond all language, out of reach of the searchlight of your present conscious mind.

Among modern esotericists, then, we merely see a process that has long been present in germ within the human unconscious. Language and logic, it seems, must no longer be treated as purely 'linear', but as 'circular'. And in this view of things we merely see a reflection of what is happening in almost every other sphere of basic human enquiry today. Interrelationship, on whatever level, is all. Circularity is of the essence. Everything must be seen as a function of everything else.

Perhaps it is significant, then, that the God of the migrating Israelites, the embodiment of the very ground of all being, should have revealed himself to Moses in the supremely circular phrase, 'I am that I am.'

Perhaps it is significant that, even in modern physics, the quantum-field of curved space-time is increasingly held to be, in Einstein's words, the only reality*.

* Quoted by Capra in *The Tao of Physics* (Fontana, 1976).

Perhaps it is significant that one of the prime symbols for that ultimate reality in world religions, as also for the wholeness of the Self in the dream-world of the psyche, has long been the circle.

*   *   *   *   *

And so it is distinctly encouraging to find that the theme of circularity is nowadays so much at the forefront of human thought. Indeed, it is reflected again and again in the typical cultural manifestations of our age.

Not only have our architects, in reaction against the fashionable cult of four-squareness, started once again to design circular churches and cathedrals. Not only have many of our New Age pioneers returned to the primitive igloo as a model for their geodesic domes and autonomous houses. We now devote more and more of our cultural resources to devising stereophony, quadrophony and surround-sound, to achieving stereovision, to immersing ourselves once again in the experience of theatre-in-the-round.

In music, too, the same circular motif can be observed. True, the ancient Indian *raga*, rather like the music of the Scottish bagpipes, was always essentially circular in form. It comprised an almost infinite series of variations on an everlasting bass-drone, with which it both started and finished. And in the process it took on a decidedly 'mythical' quality, seeming to symbolise the differentiation of the one ultimate reality into a whole kaleidoscopic universe, and then its final reversion to source.

But now the same basic ground-plan has been taken up by the new 'musicians of the spirit'. Their latest productions consist of circular and 'concentric' pieces designed to be played virtually *ad infinitum**—or at least until various natural necessities intervene. On the pop-scene, too, it is now normal for its essentially circular musical numbers to fade away at the end rather than finishing, simply because with verse designed to lead into chorus, and chorus into verse (I use the terms loosely), there is no obvious place to stop. And the recent offerings of the classical avantgardists likewise tend to come to a halt rather than end.

Wherever you look, in fact, the emphatic sense of four-squareness and finality typical of the age of Beethoven seems to be lost for ever.

Take the case of dancing, for example. Time was when dancing was a truly social activity. Any given musical number directly involved

*See Hamel: *Through Music to the Self* (Element Books, 1978).

everybody on the dance-floor. With the help of the music they became as one body.

Then disintegration set in.

By the time the age of rationalism arrived in the seventeenth and eighteenth centuries, the typical dance, appropriately enough, had become the square-dance. Long before our time, further disintegration had occurred. Dancing had become primarily an activity for private couples. The twosome had become the norm. Yet even that was not to last. Of recent years we have seen the arrival of an alienated form of individual dancing that represents the final disintegration of this formerly intensely social activity. Perhaps it is symbolic of what has happened to society itself.

For the literal meaning of disintegration is 'loss of wholeness'.

And it is that wholeness that the New Agers are now attempting to rediscover as they reinstate the round-dance and the spiral-dance at the heart of their group-rituals and celebrations.

Can it be by accident, then, that the image of the circle is nowadays appearing ever more frequently in modern art? Is it fortuitous that most of our competitive races, by whatever means of transport, are now circular in form—as they were not among the ancient Greeks, for example? Is it pure coincidence that the supreme aim of the yachtsman and yachtswoman is increasingly the circumnavigation of continent or globe—despite the apparent pointlessness of going through hell and high water in order merely to arrive back where you started?

You are at liberty to believe so. And yet the same theme constantly recurs, as we have seen, in the favourite myths of our age. We can detect it in the cosmologists' black holes and oscillating universes, in the Einsteinian curvature of space-time, in the astrologers' cyclic view of history, the esotericists' doctrine of reincarnation and the ecological cycle so beloved by the Friends of the Earth. We can sense it in the increasingly fashionable proposition that we humans need to learn to reintegrate the two disparate hemispheres of our neocortex— analytical left and holistic right—into a single, balanced brainsphere, capable of calling on both the intellectual and the intuitive aspects of our consciousness*. We may suspect its presence in the international reports which increasingly insist that the world's rich northern and poor southern hemispheres must be economically reintegrated into a single,

---

*See Sagan, C.: *The Dragons of Eden* (Coronet, 1977) and Ornstein, R.E.: *The Psychology of Consciousness* (Cape, 1975).

spherical planet if humanity itself is to survive*.

Even Jung's own theory of synchronicity—the idea that everything that happens in the universe is somehow a function of everything else—is a basically circular concept, no less than the 'bootstrap-universe' of the quantum-physicists. The motif of circularity is there all around us, in these waking dreams of ours, even if we choose to ignore the fact. And in this we may see a sign of great hope.

For, as Jung constantly pointed out, the image of the circle frequently appears in dreams as an effective symbol of imminent healing.

And its typical form is the *mandala*.

A *mandala* is a Buddhist contemplative design, generally circular in form. Possibly it is distantly related to the ancient Yin-Yang diagram of the Taoists, which represents the *Tao* (or the universal essence) in a state of dynamic equilibrium:

But the typical Buddhist *mandala* has a distinct and ornate form of its own. It is used as an aid to achieving inner stillness and as a preliminary to penetrating to deep levels of awareness.

*Compare, for example, the Independent Commission on International Development's *North-South: A Programme for Survival* (Pan, 1980), better known as the 'Brandt Report'; also John V. Taylor's *Enough is Enough* (SCM, 1975).

Just as the Navaho Indians use sand-paintings of similar design to stimulate the process of physical healing (see the diagram opposite), so the Buddhists use the *mandala* as an object of meditation designed to lead to *inner* wholeness. It is the awareness of the circle that, in both cases, somehow acts as the vital catalyst.

Perhaps, then, it is a similar awareness of the circularity of existence

166

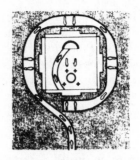

that may yet heal the human race as a whole. Perhaps what we need above all is a renewed sense of revolution—that perpetual revolution about the centre that is the very essence of the circle.

In fact we should have saved ourselves much anguish if we had acquired that sense already.

Take a particular case in point.

*   *   *   *   *

The received teaching of Christianity is that each of us has only one life. This assumption, of course, reflects a linear, not a circular view of existence. Everything simply has a beginning and an end, and that is that. The bird that is the soul flies out of the winter's night into the lighted banqueting-hall of life, and then flies out once more into the dark.

And during that single life, some are blessed with health, riches or intelligence, while others know only disease, starvation or brute ignorance.

It is all so monstrously unfair.

And so philanthropists and charitable organisations have felt moved to make almost superhuman efforts on behalf of the deprived. In order to better the lot of those whose supposed 'one chance' at life has been blighted at the outset, we now have welfare states, national health services, programmes of social reform and international aid.

No doubt that is all to the good. Even though healing the sick so often seems merely to add to the numbers of the starving, feeding the hungry to add to the masses of the helpless, educating the ignorant to add to the hosts of those who feel oppressed.

But then this very sense of oppression is also largely due to the same 'one-way' view of life. To it we owe the exaggerated feelings of social and human injustice which fuel the flames of most inter-class hatred. In it we can find the causes of most international socialist/capitalist confrontation and, consequently, of the resulting wars and brutal guerilla-campaigns too. Because of it we have in our schools today a strong egalitarian trend which insists that, since nobody can be allowed to fail, nobody can be allowed to succeed either.

If you *will* preserve a dualistic, class-based distinction between 'success' and 'failure', what else do you expect?

Yet consider what would have happened had western society been a Hindu or a Buddhist one.

For a start there would have been an almost universal belief in the 'circular' process of reincarnation. With the prospect of other lifetimes to 'balance the accounts', the inequalities of a single lifetime would no longer have loomed so important. The unrealistic and misleading assertion of the American Declaration of Rights that 'all men are created equal' would never have seen the light of day. The consequent struggle to impose such illusions on reality would have produced less envy and hatred, fewer confrontations and wars. The class-conflict might have been much less venomous, the civil rights campaigns less bitter. And our modern world might not have found itself divided down the middle by an Iron Curtain of political dogma.

Which is not to say that it would not have been divided by something else.

But then it is no use indulging in wishful thinking. The world is as it is. Humanity is gravely ill. And so it is doubly urgent now that the race as a whole should become aware again of its inner *mandala*—that circular symbol of healing which human culture now seems to be exuding at every pore.

*　*　*　*　*

The typical *mandala*, as we have already noted, is circular in shape. But imposed on this basic design there is generally a square, or some other manifestation of fourness. The illustration on page 166 demonstrates this quite clearly, as does the Navaho sand-painting on page 167. Moreover, the same thing often happens in dreams.

According to Jung, the circle generally stands for psychic wholeness, the square for physical existence. Thus the *mandala*, in whatever form, comes to you as a sign of hope. It points to the imminent reconciling of your inner and outer realities, of you and the universe.

That is why the eventual biblical 'heavenly city', or 'New Jerusalem', likewise takes the form of the 'squared circle', as John Michell has demonstrated in a dazzling display of esoteric mathematics*. It is the Bible's way of symbolising the final re-attainment of our former state of integrated bliss, our long-lost Garden of Eden.

The idea is even more superbly demonstrated in three dimensions by the Great Pyramid of Giza, the relationship of whose height to its square base-perimeter is exactly that of a circle's radius to its circumference**. For the Great Pyramid, too, it seems, is a mighty symbol for the destiny of humankind.

So that it is not very surprising to learn that the same, sacred motif of squared circle was taken up again and again by the medieval alchemists. Their constant efforts to transmute base metal into gold were, after all, merely an allegory of the ceaseless quest to rediscover the noble metal of the Self.

And even in our own day the theme of inserting symbolic circle in equally symbolic rectangle continues to surface out of the depths of the collective unconscious. Indeed, it lies at the basis of the sacred ritual that is unquestionably dearest to today's anonymous masses across much of the world. The mysteries of that rite arouse the passions of millions well beyond the boundaries of its sacred precinct. It is a truly religious celebration that can devastate our means of transport, inundate our media and tear out the very heart of our cities.

And it is called professional soccer.

Absurd, you may say, to suggest that a mere ball-game could have such religious or psychic significance. Absurd, but true. For just such a sacred ball-game was central to the religion of the ancient Maya. And who is to say that soccer does not share that significance? Who will deny that it has all the necessary ritual characteristics?

The magic precinct. The solemn hymn-singing. The entry of the symbolic celebrants out of the bowels of the earth. The battle between the representatives of light and darkness. The ritual chanting. The waving of banners and consecrated scarves. The total self-forgetfulness, the emotional identification of the masses of the faithful with the archetypal drama as it remorselessly unfolds before their eyes.

And, at the heart of the whole process, a ball. A single sphere which must eventually achieve—quite literally—its goal: one of two rectangular openings each attached to a net. Can you think of a better symbol for the psyche's long quest to 'place itself' in the physical

---

*Michell, *City of Revelation* (Abacus, 1973).

**Lemesurier, *The Great Pyramid Decoded* (Element Books, 1978).

world, currently ruled as it is by the powers of duality, and ensnared in the mesh of linguistic illusion?

The suggestion may seem fantastic and unreal. Equally fantastic, perhaps, is Jung's own theory about flying saucers. The current craze for Unidentified Flying Objects, he once hypothesised, represents the surfacing of natural circular symbols out of the depths of the submerged psyche. Not that this necessarily means that UFOs are totally imaginary. Merely that they have not hitherto been so readily seen because their conceptual paradigm was lacking in the human psyche. The primitive Tierra del Fuegans, you will recall, were unable at first to 'see' Darwin's ship, the *Beagle*, because nothing in their conceptual inheritance had predisposed them to do so.

But the image of the circle certainly *is* now manifesting itself in the contemporary psyche. The motif of circularity and of eternal renewal runs ever more strongly through the pattern of our culture. The time is ripe for us to wake up to the fact. And, in particular, the moment is at hand for us to realise that the death and rebirth of planetary initiation is not something to be feared and resisted, but merely a further stage in our collective evolutionary development—indeed, in the saga of the cosmos as a whole.

The caterpillar that refuses to become a chrysalis simply doesn't turn into a butterfly.

But mere knowledge and awareness of the cosmic process of initiation is not enough by itself. Involvement is of the essence. With the death, or at least the senile decay, of the Christian Sky-Father—a gradual disappearance long ago noticed by Jung in his patients' dreams—we now stand in need of a new myth. A living, breathing myth that we can celebrate and believe in.

As a man's faith is, claims the Hindus' *Bhagavad Gita*, so he is. And it follows, if true, that non-existent faith is liable to lead to non-existent humanity.

*　　*　　*　　*　　*

Writing at the end of his long life, Jung was above all concerned with the current need for a *metanoia*, a change-over of the gods, to give renewed strength and meaning to human existence. The time, indeed, was already over-ripe. Perhaps, he suggested, a new myth would shortly emerge from the human unconscious to satisfy that need. A myth capable of restoring our race's long-lost psychic wholeness.

He need not have worried. The human psyche can always be trusted to come up with the goods, given even half a chance. All the while we

170

remain in touch with our own deeper nature, in contact with our own psychic roots, we are unlikely to go far wrong.

It was in 1961 that Jung eventually died at the ripe old age of 85. And it was in that same year that humanity, in the very act—strangely enough—of using *conscious* science and technology to run away from itself and its whole planetary culture, finally came back down to earth.

And found that new myth staring it full in the face.

Part III
The New Initiation

Admittance: Pass, Friend!

Once you at last admit the Self into the camp, you are struck by a sudden realisation.

There are no longer any foes.

Perhaps they were entirely imaginary all along. Perhaps they were never there at all.

It is as if the perimeter of the camp has expanded to take in the whole of your space and time. Beyond its borders there now lies nothing. Not even a beyond.

No longer, then, is there any point in the camp's existence.

The watchmen can go home, the defenders lay down their arms. The swords can be beaten into ploughshares, the spears into pruning-hooks. War and division are no more. The wolf can lie down with the lamb, the leopard with the kid, the calf with the young lion. Everyman can sit unmolested under his vine.

'They shall not hurt or destroy in all my holy mountain,' says the Lord of the Christian Bible, from which these images are culled.

The same Lord who also says, 'I am Alpha and Omega, the first and the last.'

But who is this Lord, in reality?

He is Jehovah. EHYEH.

The I that truly AM.

And that, surely, is the beginning and the end of it.

15. RETURN TO SOURCE

That's one small step for a man; one giant leap for mankind.
Neil Armstrong, July 20th 1969

Not that it was the first time that the son of a carpenter had changed the world. Yet even Yuri Gagarin, as he made his way to the waiting space-rocket that fateful morning, can hardly have realised the full significance of what he was about to undertake.

True, it was a momentous hour for the Soviet Union. True, it was to be a day of historic, even epic importance for hitherto earthbound humanity. But it was not just a matter of conquering outer space. Far more important were to be the consequences of his act for the human psyche, its effects on his race's quest for its own deeper self.

The conquest of inner space.

At 9.07 a.m. on April 12th, 1961, the great rocket finally lifted off. The shining metal colossus lumbered into the sky. Faster and faster the flat landscape of the Soviet Union dropped away below, dwindled into the encircling embrace of an ever-receding horizon, finally faded into a fleeting, almost indistinguishable patch on an ever more rapidly spinning globe.

By lunch-time it was all over.

Parachuted back to earth and quickly located by the recovery-crews, the returned space-hero was soon being examined and debriefed. Triumphantly the news of his achievement was flashed around the globe. What most serious scientists had thought impossible only ten years previously had turned out to be not only possible, but established fact. Humanity had succeeded in putting itself into orbit.

In Moscow the flags were out. The hero was duly fêted.

175

But that was not the end of the story. Indeed, it was only the beginning. During his brief, 18,000 mph orbit in Vostok I at a maximum altitude of only 187 miles, it is doubtful whether the first cosmonaut had had much time to look around him, much opportunity fully to take in what he could see out of the spacecraft's porthole. The early cosmonauts and astronauts were still too intimately bound to earth fully to realise what they had achieved, to see what it truly was that they had left behind them.

It was not until Apollo 8's first venture into deep space in December 1968—that first, tentative, three-man voyage around the back of the moon and out of sight of Earth—that earthbound humanity's umbilical cord was finally cut, and we could look back as it were 'from outside' to take in at a single glance our ancestral planetary home.

'The good earth', the returning astronauts were to call it. And that, perhaps, was the real moment of truth.

For as they rounded the barren lunar globe for the tenth and last time, and the resplendent half-earth once again rose from behind that now familiar curved and rocky horizon, what they saw slowly coming up to meet them was somehow strangely familiar.

An image straight out of the racial memory. A god out of the world of the archetypes.

It was none other than the rounded form of the Great Mother, Earth herself, clad in the same flowing robes of shimmering blue and white that had been those of mother-goddesses of earth and sea and sky throughout human history—and not least that most recent of mother-goddesses, the Virgin Mary herself.

Freed from the maternal embrace, infant humankind had dared for the first time to hide behind the back of the celestial armchair—only to discover, as every child does, that mother is none the less there for being unseen, and ready to welcome it back with open arms.

It is scarcely surprising, then, that the theme of the hour was to be essentially that of the return to the womb. Almost as though in anticipation of the fact, the three-day return-journey to Earth started on Christmas Eve. The homeward flight coincided with the immemorial northern festival of the rebirth of light from the womb of winter darkness. In astronauts Borman, Lovell and Anders, the Three Wise Men, in pursuit of their star, were once again to discover an earthly nativity.

For that eventual entry into deep space coincided with the dawning of a new realisation on earth—the realisation that, like the Christ-child in the Christmas cave, our race must now be reborn from the womb of

176

the Earth-Mother if it was to fulfil its destiny.

Even the astronauts themselves seem to have been overawed with the astonishing aptness of the occasion. From the depths of far space there came for the first time human voices. And what they read out to the watching and listening peoples of Planet Earth were the ancient words of the Genesis creation-account: 'In the beginning God created the heaven and the earth . . .'

Certainly new beginnings were in the air.

And, as ever, external events had arranged themselves in such a way as to reveal to humanity the emergent contents of its own collective unconscious.

For perhaps it was at that moment that we humans first fully realised the extent to which *genus homo* was truly a child of its planet, undivided by national boundaries or ideologies or Iron Curtains. A single, blue planet whose very spheroidal shape proclaimed with archetypal force a message of planetary healing and wholeness. A single, piebald planet whose steady and constant revolution from day to night and back again spoke clearly of the essential, underlying unity of humanity's own 'light' and 'dark' sides, and of the continual process of initiation, of death and rebirth, that alone could reconcile the two.

*   *   *   *   *

Among primitive tribes, you will recall, initiation has a social purpose. It frees the adolescent from the control of father and mother and replaces their psychic image with another. For, much as they may desire total freedom, human beings can never be entirely free of the instinctive need for a parent-figure. Modern adolescents seek their parent-substitutes in gang or friendship-group. Their elders seek theirs among workmates, in trade-union, club or political party. Eventually the family-group itself becomes a kind of parent-figure, a being that we feel to be bigger than any individual, a protective god to be appeased, a sacred entity whose requirements are paramount. For the primitive, it is of course the tribe itself that becomes the new 'parent'.

In all these cases, the postulant must first 'die' to his or her former parents and be 'reborn' to the new. Some form of initiation-ceremony is generally performed to reflect the fact. And in the ancient traditions the basic theme of this initiation was that of the Mother-Goddess, to whose womb the candidate must symbolically return and from which, after due confinement, the new-born initiate must be released again.

But humanity, too, has now reached the end of its long adolescence. It has reached the point where it needs to be freed at last from the control of its immemorial psychic 'parents'. Those parents are, of course, already well known to you. They are none other than our race's own, wilful, rational, 'masculine' conscious mind on the one hand, and the intuitive, irrational, 'feminine' unconscious on the other, whose warring natures threaten even now to tear our world apart and destroy us

Humanity, then, must now die to the old and be reborn to the new—must seek once again the comforting embrace and reassuring womb of the Great Mother. That womb is of course identical with the celestial pitcher of Aquarius. Just as, with the dawning of the Aquarian age, the pitcher must be emptied, so from the womb of the Great Mother must pour forth the waters of life.

The time has come, in short, when the earth itself must take over the role of racial parent. The time has come when, if humanity is to survive at all, it must learn to see itself as nothing less than a child of its planet. For once it has truly become a child of the earth, then there is nothing on earth to which it can legitimately oppose itself.

Which is not, of course, to say that our race will not in due course find extra-terrestrial powers to fight against. The need for further initiations will probably never cease. Later on, humanity will need to become successively a child of the solar system, a child of the galaxy, a child of the universe itself . . .

Yet a journey of a thousand miles, in the words of the *Tao Te Ching*, starts under your own feet. And so it is entirely appropriate that humankind's present initiation of consciousness finally got under way at about the time when those three astronauts of Apollo 8 finally came back down to earth.

*　*　*　*　*

For that was the very period that also marked the beginning, quite literally, of the Great Return to the Earth. It was the era when, under rapidly growing pressures in the spheres of population, resources and pollution, the infant science of ecology finally took off. Conservation and preservation rapidly became the watchwords of the hour.

The young started to become appalled at the materialistic self-indulgence of their elders, their squandering of the earth's limited fossil fuels and mineral resources to satisfy artificially-stimulated demands that were rooted in sheer capitalistic greed. In reaction, they began to turn away in disgust from the accepted values of western civilisation in order to found their own alternative societies. In increasing numbers they gravitated towards experimental communes based on organic farming and direct attunement to the rhythms of the earth and the cycle of the seasons.

Even among some of their elders, there was a growing movement to reject mass-produced, chemically-adulterated 'junk-foods'. Instead, so-called 'wholefoods' started to come into favour—crops drawing their natural nourishment from the soil instead of merely using it to hold themselves up while being deluged with artificial fertilisers and pesticides. E.F. Schumacher was already formulating his philosophy of 'Small is Beautiful'*, of non-violent, 'intermediate' technology with a human face, of 'economics as though people mattered'.

Science and industry, our very institutions and culture, it was beginning to be realised, must become earth-orientated and human in scale if there was to be any worthwhile future.

Like their elders, it is true, the young had long since started to look earthwards in the matter of philosophy. Materialism, you could say, was in vogue. Yet there was a difference. Western civilisation had already ditched Christianity's spiritual transcendentalism—the myth of the Father-God 'out there'—in favour of a crass materialism, an applied existentialism. 'Things are as they are because they are—so we might as well enjoy them, or at least put up with them in comfort.' Such, you could say, was the 'normal' view of things.

But, for the young, this was not enough. Increasingly they looked beyond such dead-end philosophies towards a deeper reality underlying physical existence itself. And so they sought their new myth in the relatively practical and down-to-earth teachings of oriental religions such as Buddhism and Hinduism. At the same time they pursued the quest for new levels of consciousness with the aid both of traditional meditation-techniques and of the various plant-drugs.

Not that this attitude was any the less materialistic in essence. But then we have no right to expect it to be. In an age long since wholly committed to the physical, the new myth and its ritual adjuncts must take equally physical form. Mere airy-fairy ideas and projected spiritual entities are not enough. The physical earth and physical experience are alone capable of supplying modern humanity with the sense of reality and conviction demanded of an effective myth.

For it is of the essence of any healing myth that it must be believed in. Faith is a *sine qua non*. As a man's faith is, so he is.

And so, if we have long since lost the ability (as we think) to believe in anything beyond our own senses, it is in the world of the senses that

*Schumacher, E.F.: *Small is Beautiful* (Abacus, 1975).

our new myth must inevitably be grounded. For that is the way things are. Nobody is entitled to attempt to *impose* a healing myth on humanity—even though that can be done temporarily and to a limited extent. If Christianity and Marxism both succeeded in their day, it was because they deliberately adapted themselves to the myths that were already in vogue. And their eventual decline, like that of Nazism, will come about through their failure to adapt to the myths that eventually succeed them.

There is no future in resisting the flow, in wishing that a *fait accompli* were not so, in seeking to restore a bygone order of things.

And so the indubitable fact that materialism is already, in one form or another, the current reigning religion of almost the entire civilised world should make it quite plain where our new loyalty must lie, where our new myth will have to be found.

For materialism is none other than the worship of *materia*. It is the cult of that which pertains to *mater*.

The Great Mother.

* * * * *

The earth-cult, in short, must supply the new myth for our era. Not that the word 'new' is particularly appropriate. For the cult of the Earth-Mother reflects one of the oldest of human myths.

No doubt for that reason there are many who will see the new myth as a retrogressive development, a return to some dark, primitive, telluric religion. But then any given development can be 'retrogressive' only if you are hooked on 'progress'. 'Going back' is a bad thing only if you are obsessed with 'moving on'. And if you take a typically Christian and western view of history as a straight-line graph, then any development that does not fall squarely on that line is bound to seem an aberration, a catastrophe.

Yet human history, as we have already seen, is not linear, but cyclic. Humanity constantly takes one step back in order to take two steps forward. Such is the very essence of the initiatory process which is central to our race's whole evolution.

And so it is no more 'retrogressive' that we should return to our terrestrial roots in search of refreshment and renewal than that we should have to sleep at night. The conscious mind returns constantly to its unconscious wellsprings in search of initiation. Even the 'soul'—in the reincarnationist view, at least—has to 'return to source' between incarnations to recharge its batteries and seek fresh instructions.

Initiation, in fact, is of the essence for our ongoing development at

180

every level. It is simply the human equivalent of the political process known in Maoist circles as 'perpetual revolution', a truth similarly reflected in the ancient funereal formula, 'Ashes to ashes, dust to dust . . .'

'Earth', it could have added, 'to earth'.

Certainly the myth of the Earth-Mother is acceptable to most of modern humanity in a way that the religions of the recent past are not. The object of the exercise, after all, is the achievement of psychic wholeness for the human race as a whole. Consequently, no religion which stresses its own rightness and everybody else's wrongness is even remotely suitable for the task. For this reason, both Christianity and Islam as traditionally formulated must be ruled out of account.

True, the 'Christian' theme of love will be of vital importance in the coming years as a force for healing and reconciliation. Through it we can start learning to accept the 'dark' side of the world 'out there', and thus the 'dark' side of ourselves too. But then Christianity by no means has a monopoly of love. Indeed, it has never succeeded in approaching even the level of practical love recommended and demonstrated by its own founder.

Love, in fact, is a basic theme of every religion. And not least of that of the Earth-Mother.

But then, love has not been the only theme of the world's major religions. They have also preached spirituality. At every conceivable opportunity the message has been rammed home that all aspects of life must be subordinated to the demands of the spirit, or alternatively to the wishes of some insubstantial god or gods 'up there'. The concept was basic to the early animistic religions. It is still basic to Hinduism, to Judaism, to Christianity and Islam. Only in Buddhism has there been any serious attempt to wean people from their dependence on transcendental beliefs and to teach them to live life for what it is, here and now.

The true Buddhist, it has been remarked, is a mystic only because he or she is too much of a sceptic to be a materialist.

Yet even the Buddha's teaching has, in Mahayana Buddhism at least, long since been overlaid with rabid other-worldliness of every description—not excluding the most primitive forms of magic and superstition.

The cult of Mother Earth, on the other hand, is strictly practical. It accepts reality for what it is. It asks a humanity that has explored both the depths of matter and the vastnesses of space to accept nothing that does not square with its new-found material knowledge and experience.

It proposes no fiction, demands no blind faith, imposes on the conscious mind no need for superstitious beliefs.

For the earth *is* our mother. Where previously the idea was a mere religious dogma, a convenient ritual fiction, now we know it to be literal fact. Our science points inevitably to that conclusion.

We are literally the fruit of the womb of Planet Earth.

And so, increasingly, we have come to realise that we must worship her and cherish her if we wish her to continue nurturing and protecting us. We are flesh of her flesh, blood of her blood. And until we are ready to leave the terrestrial womb for good, our lives and hers must inevitably be intertwined.

Sewn together, it may be, with the thread of myth.

And not least with the Christ-myth. For the Christ-myth is a measure of humanity itself. Last Adam and First Adam are one and the same.

* * * * *

We have already traced the links between the Christ-story as it has come down to us and the procession of the archetypes within the mind of each of us. We have seen, too, how that inner pageant is constantly acted out upon the stage of world history by humanity at large.

To start with, the hero must set out to perform his prodigies, the Messiah to perform his miracles, the human conscious mind to transform the earth. It is a healthy development, and one which is essential to our further evolution. Yet the hero-myth is also a myth of separation, and it carries within itself a warning of what will happen if it is taken too seriously. There are dangers in pursuing too far the UDI of consciousness.

As humanity at large is just beginning to realise.

And so the stage is eventually reached where a change of archetypes is called for. Hero, Messiah and conscious mind are alike threatened by their very achievements. Initiation becomes due. And with it a new order arises, a new law takes over.

And we have the choice of resisting or coming quietly.

The hero must admit defeat, the Messiah must undergo death and entombment, the conscious mind must return to its unconscious source. Only thus can the resurrection follow. Only thus can our kind have life more abundantly.

The king is dead. Long live the king!

And it is this second part of the Christ-myth that is above all appropriate to our present needs. It is the initiatory theme of death and

182

resurrection that must supply our new, healing elixir of life.

And that theme, essentially, is that of the return to the maternal womb.

'Unless a man has been born again,' says Jesus at John 3:3, 'he cannot see the kingdom of God.'

* * * * *

But we seem unconsciously to know that already. Already, wittingly or otherwise, we have committed ourselves to that rebirth. Already we defer in almost countless respects to the religion of the Earth-Mother.

Ceaselessly we sacrifice ourselves at the altar of matter, seek in the depths of Earth's womb the oil, coal and minerals that are the basis of our civilisation. True, we have shifted the frantic rites of human ordeal and sacrifice to the blast-furnace and factory-floor. We have transferred the dark mysteries of the sacred cave to the deep recesses of the mines, transplanted the sexual rites of the gods and high-priestesses to the novel and the cinema, turned the holy pilgrimage to the spring of earthly self-renewal into a mere annual seaside holiday. Even the myth of eternal death and rebirth has been transformed into a doctrine of perpetual social and political revolution. Yet in all these respects we still show ourselves to be physically and practically the devoted servants of the cult of the Earth-Mother.

Only the sense of the religious and the mystical is lacking.

In all this we may detect a deep, unrecognised longing for initiation. It seems to symbolise a return to the unconscious wellsprings of life, to those dark, irrational powers which must ultimately fuel the psychic spaceflight of human consciousness even to the furthest borders of rationality itself.

And certainly such a return is needed. Indeed, it is already under way.

In science, the rationalistic world-view to which Newton, despite his own misgivings, was to bequeath his name, has given way to the almost bottomless uncertainties of Einsteinian physics. The mechanistic veil is even now being removed from the deep face of cosmic relativity. And the deeper we probe into the cosmos, the more we realise that we are really looking into the depths of our own mind.

In modern art, formal photographic techniques have largely given way to the expression of humanity's own chaotic, unconscious depths. The techniques used range from random arrangements of concrete objects and images on the one hand to purely 'abstract' assemblages on the other. And the results often bear strange similarities to the crystalline substructures and sinusoidal wave-forms of atomic physics, almost as though it were the *same* reality that underlies both the human psyche and the physical world itself.

In psychology, the old rational certainties of human behaviour have long since given way to a more humane view based on recognition of the vital role of the unconscious. Even the relatively mechanistic approaches of Freudianism on the one hand and Behaviourism on the other have started to give ground to the more numinous insights of Jung.

In religion, the ancient theological edifices founded on dry human reason are fast collapsing under the onslaught of less rational but none the less real experiences. Meditation and personal self-discovery are the themes of the moment. And even within the fold of Christianity the charismatics are on the move—or, as the title of one book puts it, The Pentecostals are Coming*.

At the same time, the citadels of reason are being shaken by a violent explosion of 'irrational' esotericism and 'dark' occultism. Witch-doctors and faith-healers are back in vogue. UFOs and extraterrestrials are taken seriously, not merely by national defence ministries and American Presidents, but by the United Nations itself**. Indeed, this tendency towards extreme credulity can even be observed within established science. The theories of space and time, of quantum mechanics and cosmic origins nowadays advanced in scholarly journals by serious scientists often far outdo for sheer speculative wildness the most way-out propositions of the science-fictionists, let alone the relatively harmless romancings of Erich von Däniken. By comparison, even the vast metaphysical speculations of the medieval kabbalists and alchemists often seem small beer indeed.

Even in the very structure of our society, the long supremacy of 'rational' man over 'irrational' woman is at last being questioned and occasionally reversed. Already we have women prime ministers, women terrorists, women airline pilots and cosmonauts. Women have scaled Everest, circumnavigated the globe single-handed. And often their activities are associated, not surprisingly perhaps, with extraordinary violence. The Amazons are abroad once more. In Indira Gandhi, Margaret Thatcher, Golda Meir and Ulrike Meinhof we can see the resurgence of a vigorous female archetype that is truly 'red in

*Wagner: *Look Out! The Pentecostals are Coming* (Coverdale, 1973).
**Daily Telegraph, 30/11/77.

tooth and claw'.

The spiritual Father-God (*spiritus*) is all but dead. The day of the maternal Mother-Goddess (*mater*) is at hand.

* * * * *

In almost every respect, in short, the human unconscious, like the legendary Kraken, is arising out of its age-long sleep to claim its pound of flesh. The era of rational control by the 'higher self' threatens to give way to an age of irrational chaos dominated exclusively by the 'lower self'.

But then what else do you expect a resurgent irrationality to be but irrational? How should it be other than chaotic? How can it help but be violent and murderously dangerous?

Already our planet has had an ominous foretaste of what we may be in for. The dark forces unleashed by Hitlerism on an unsuspecting world were a direct expression of the uncontrolled resurgence of the 'occult' side of human nature*. The atomic mushroom-cloud over Hiroshima was nothing less than the mighty exclamation-mark finally punctuating the story of our race's deliberate confrontation with the very ground of nature. That confrontation, whether in the socio-political sphere, in psychology, in art, in literature or in science, can be both positive and perilously negative in its effects. It brings with it the possibility of chaos, of psychosis, of disintegration, even of utter annihilation.

Nobody, say the scriptures, can see God and live**.

And yet the case is perhaps over-stated. We *can* see God and live. The ground of nature *can* be explored. The deeper aspect of the psyche *can* be revealed for what it is. Mother Earth *can* be allowed her say—indeed, she cannot be denied it much longer.

But only in the presence of Father Sun.

* * * * *

The sun is the primordial consort of Mother Earth. Her very existence revolves about the solar fire. Ultimately that fire is the source of all terrestrial life, the Adam without whom terrestrial Eve (life) would never have arisen in the first place. But for Father Sun, standing 'outside' and watching from afar the convolutions of Mother Earth, there would

---

*Compare Ravenscroft: *The Spear of Destiny* (Corgi, 1974).
**Ex. 33:20.

be no days and nights, no earthly seasons. But for him, Gaia would be a dead planet spinning aimlessly through the depths of outer chaos.

So it is, too, with the psyche. In our integrative re-encounter with the long-suppressed, 'feminine' unconscious it is absolutely essential that we retain a firm hold on our 'masculine', conscious side as well. It is integration that we are after, not an alternative form of disintegration.

Wholeness demands a resolving of duality, not a mere pendulum-swing to the other extreme. It is no use encountering the ground of your being if you propose to let go of your very reason.

Perhaps that is why those who, in the past, have claimed to come face to face with God have so often lapsed into insanity.

Consequently the typical, healing *mandala*, as we have seen, comprises not merely a circle, but a square or rectangle as well—or, alternatively, some other symbol of 'fourness'. The psyche, in other words, must be 'squared' with physical reality. Dissociation must be replaced by association—a harmonious attunement of inner self with outer universe. That, no doubt, is why the paradoxical notion of the 'four corners of the globe' so often appears in dreams, myths and rituals as a symbol for the integrated Self.

And so, if we are to return to the ancient myth of the Earth-Mother, then it is plain that her 'dark' and 'irrational' cult must be balanced and illuminated by that of Father Sun. Without him, after all, there would be no myth to celebrate. The initiation-myth which is central to the telluric cult is essentially that of night and day, of the terrestrial seasons, of the annual death and rebirth of nature.

And all of them are a direct function of the sun itself.

It was no doubt this idea that was already reflected over three thousand years ago in Akhenaten's heretical solar religion of love. And if St. Francis of Assisi stopped short of calling the sun his father, no doubt it was largely because that role had already been pre-empted by the Christian Father-God.

Perhaps, indeed, the saint should have gone on to make the obvious association.

For that, increasingly, is what seems to be happening today. Just as most of us nowadays spend all our working days worshipping the Earth-Mother (*mater*), so also we tend to spend more and more of our leisure-time worshipping the sun. Our holidays are spent searching for it. Our bodies crave it. And even our technology is starting to reflect the psychological fact that to place all our eggs in the single basket of Mother Earth is to court disaster, and that the aid of Father Sun must

186

also be called in if we are to avoid scrambling an almighty terrestrial omelette.

Virgin-birth is for gods, not mortals.

I refer, of course, to the current, much-publicised energy-crisis. Having disembowelled our planet in search of its precious fossil-fuels, we are rapidly coming to realise that we are, quite literally, digging the ground from under our own feet. Earth alone is incapable of satisfying our enormous and ever-growing demands for energy—demands which follow almost inevitably from our current social and technological megalomania. And so, if we persist in following that road, we must turn to alternative energy-sources—sources which would long ago have been our primary ones had we not been so obsessed with questions of low-cost economics as opposed to *real* economics.

For in what I term 'real economics' the quality of human life is assigned an over-riding and pre-eminent value and not, as is currently the case, a virtual zero-rating.

Conventionally, the main sources of 'alternative energy' are reckoned to be wind-power, tidal power, wave-power and direct solar power. But then *all* these energy-sources are to a large degree solar in origin.

It is solar heating that is responsible for the rise and fall of atmospheric pressure that produces the world's wind and weather patterns. It is the sun's gravitational pull that is at least partly responsible for the rise and fall of the earth's tides, even though the major credit for the tidal ebb and flow has, of course, to go to the sun's lunar *alter ego*. It is the sun's heat that is responsible for the fact that the seas are liquid enough to produce large tides in the first place. Meanwhile wave-power, which is generated by the force of wind on water, is just as solar in origin as is the direct solar heating which completes the quartet—whether collected on the planetary surface or beamed in out of space from orbiting satellites.

Apart from these, geothermal heating, based on the collection of the earth's own interior heat, is as yet of unproven effectiveness for general purposes; and nuclear power—derived, like the fossil fuels, from the earth's own mineral resources—involves almost ludicrous risks of contamination and long-term pollution.

So that we are left only with the doubtful benefits of controlled nuclear fission, in the form of the giant particle-accelerator. I say 'doubtful', partly because the system has not as yet proved its effectiveness, but more especially because it merely duplicates the process which is already going on in the sun itself, and which we therefore have only to 'tune in to' to collect all the energy we could possibly want for millennia ahead.

It is all very well wanting to steal fire from heaven, but in this case what is the point? It is rather like trying to produce water in a solar still while living under a waterfall.

However, at least the particle-accelerator has one useful function to perform. Representing, as it does, our own feeble attempt to duplicate the solar processes, it helps to remind us once again that our future cannot lie solely in becoming children of the earth. Whether directly or merely in symbol, we also need to become sons and daughters of the sun.

Nature, you could say, is once more arranging its external phenomena to act as images for the emergent archetypes of our own psyche. And it is telling us unmistakably, in a myriad different ways, that the next step in our march towards total consciousness involves not merely a return to the depths of the 'maternal' unconscious, but also the bringing of its contents under the full searchlight-glare of the 'paternal' conscious mind.

Only then will the archaic, artificial division between conscious and unconscious at last be resolved. Only then will the great psychic Iron Curtain at last be torn down. Only then will the final veil be removed from reality, and the full light of total consciousness dawn to reveal a new world of psychic harmony and wholeness.

If Beauty can learn to love the Beast, it will turn into a handsome prince. Even our deepest and most ferocious hidden instincts must be accepted, faced and brought into the realm of consciousness if our story is truly to have—as every story eventually must—a happy ending.

16. THE CULT OF EARTH AND FIRE

It is only through earth-awareness that we
can reach higher levels of consciousness . . .
You have to be grounded before you can fly.
Lyall Watson: *Gifts of Unknown Things*

And so it is in the simple cult of earth and sun that we need to seek the new myth for our age. Already, as we have seen, we defer to them physically in large degree. If we stop short of mythologising them and regarding them as living entities able to enter into the life of our very soul, then perhaps it is merely because we no longer fully believe in that soul.

We can accept the fact of their physical influence on us. We jib only at committing ourselves to willing and active participation in the reality of their myth.

Yet a myth is what we now need above all. A healing myth that we can believe in, involve ourselves emotionally with, act out, celebrate in ritual and art and poetry and music, in play and festival and imagination. And such a myth, for us, needs to centre around physical realities and scientific facts.

Nor is there any reason why it should not do so.

In the case of the myth of Mother Earth and Father Sun—unlike so many other myths—we do not need to be put off by the conviction that they are mere, dead entities, or that 'things are not really so'. Ultimately, as we now know, the sun is truly our father, and the earth just as truly our mother, even in the most concrete and scientific terms. We are truly children of the earth, sons and daughters of the sun.

Nor are they dead.

Sun and earth together still contain life, exude life, brim with life just as much as ever they did. We need not doubt, therefore, their capacity to exert an influence—even a spiritual influence—upon us. For 'spirit', too, as we have seen, is nothing more or less than life itself.

If, then, sun and earth truly confer life upon us, and if their adoration and celebration truly enables us to have that life more abundantly, who can complain that our actions are childish, superstitious or irrational? Since when was the accepted criterion of truth other than practical usefulness?

Nor will the adoption of the cult of earth and sun be as irrational as it may seem. For it should by now be clear enough what is involved. To immerse ourselves in its ritual will simply mean identifying ourselves with Earth herself, her daily cycle, her seasonal rhythms, her annual self-renewal. In celebrating the daily death, rebirth and noonday glory of the sun, in participating in the yearly death, rebirth and flowering of nature herself, we shall merely be expressing in the most natural way the archetype of initiation.

And the activation of that archetype is now of supreme importance for us if terrestrial evolution is not to come to a dead end in our own lifetime. Letting go of our pride in our conscious achievement, we need above all now to acknowledge our humble, physical origins, to come— quite literally—back down to earth.

Again, we are in urgent need of some clear symbol of inner wholeness—a symbol which, as we have seen, pre-eminently appears in the form of a circle.

Yet both sun and earth are archetypally circular. We always knew the sun to be. But now, in our transcendent technical ecstasy, we have plumbed the depths of space and walked among the stars. And, looking back, we have seen the good Earth in all her rounded beauty, hung amidst the night. The globe that is the archetypal blue-robed Mother, the Gaia, the Isis, the Mary of our most ancient dreams.

Our primal symbol of wholeness.

In the cult of earth and sun, then, we can return without the slightest intellectual qualms to our most ancient myths and symbols in order to irradiate ourselves once more with their life-giving power—but fully aware, perhaps for the first time, of what we are about. Conscious, in fact, that we are using them as mere local symbols for the universe itself, of which both they and we are inextricably part.

That same universe which, in us, seeks consciousness.

The new cult, then, will be nothing less than a kind of 'psychodrama' designed to resolve our inner conflicts. It will be a symbolic play, a piece of projection, designed to objectivise our inner life and put it into its true, over-all, psychocosmic perspective.

To this extent it will truly partake of the nature of a religious myth—a myth in which we immerse ourselves totally during its performance, emotionally identifying ourselves with it as actors identify with their roles. But actors do not forget their own identities—not, at least, once the performance is over. And we, too, shall remain conscious of immersing ourselves quite deliberately in the great ritual drama for psychotherapeutic reasons. We shall retain in our minds the intellectual realisation that it merely symbolises a psychic reality that is beyond the power of our conscious minds and their linguistic symbols to grasp at all.

Thus the new cult will involve investing an ancient myth with knowledge, illuminating a dark 'irrationality' with the light of reason. It will represent a knowing ignorance, a sophisticated primitiveness, a deliberate losing of the self in order to find it again.

A true initiation.

*　*　*　*　*

And so, at first in the great new age centres, and later in the world community at large, we can expect to see a return to the simple, primordial realities of earth and sun—indeed, to nature in all its manifestations—not merely in the physical sense, but in the emotional and spiritual sense as well. People will start, not merely to work with Mother Earth, but actually to commune with her; not merely to use Father Sun, but actually to attune themselves to him and his rhythms.

People may even find themselves talking to the earth-spirit, praying to the solar Logos—conscious that, if the process will not necessarily adjust cosmic reality to them, at least it may help them to adjust to cosmic reality.

At which point you may well think that the whole thing has gone too far.

Yet a moment's thought will reveal that talking to sun or earth is really no more ridiculous than praying to an imagined God 'out there'—a God who is in reality no more than a projected part of your own psyche. Indeed, since that psyche is undeniably real—the only reality, in fact, that we can be sure of—it is not unduly surprising to find that prayer, ridiculous as it may perhaps seem, not infrequently appears to work.

Perhaps, in other words, sheer practicality demands that you *should* speak to your own psyche, even if you have projected it onto Mother

191

Earth or Father Sun . . .

Certainly, however, we may expect a tremendous upsurge of co-operation and communion with the various orders of nature. Talking to plants and animals is already in vogue. Talking to pots and pans and inanimate machines is by no means unheard of. Full attunement to the devic beings underlying plant and animal, river and hill, building and artefact, group and community, planet and sun—even the very solar system and cosmos themselves—will come to be seen as of the essence for the full advancement of the great, evolutionary, cosmic plan.

Even if those mighty devic beings are really only yourself in disguise.

Already, in new age communities all over our planet, the great ritual has commenced. In prayer and chant, in song and dance, in art and play, in procession and meditation, the ever-changing geo-solar paradigm is already celebrated and reflected. A meditation for sunrise, a prayer for noon, a silence for sunset. The autumn equinox becomes a rite of death and self-recollection; the winter solstice a Christmastide of re-affirmed identity; the spring equinox an Easter celebration of rebirth and renewed vigour; the midsummer solstice a heady season of joy and abundance.

So it is that, in the processional cycle of the great geo-solar festivals, the soul-gardeners of Findhorn in Scotland—perhaps the archetypal seed-centre of the coming New Age—celebrate the seasons of human consciousness*.

And in the process the world is transformed. The community that started out by growing cabbages now devotes itself to growing people**.

But neither crop can of course be grown by the mere use of artificial nutrients and chemical additives. What are needed are light and air, water and wholesome food. And love.

Love, perhaps, above all.

For ultimately it is love alone that can bring about eventual unity and harmony between us and the universe, between me and you, between you and yourself. Love, after all, is the essence of attunement. Through love we can learn to accept the 'dark' side of the outer world, and thus the 'dark' side of ourselves. Conversely, by learning to love even the 'dark' side of ourselves, we can learn to accept the 'dark' side of the world 'out there'.

*Compare Spangler, D.: *Festivals in the New Age* (Findhorn Foundation, 1975).
**See Hawken: *The Magic of Findhorn* (Fontana, 1976).

And so the process of full self-opening to others lies at the basis of the educational programme of many a new age community. And the total and open-armed acceptance of genuine and selfless love in all its forms, uncramped and unwarped by conventional notions of morality, likewise underlies their developing web of everyday, intracommunal relationships.

'Love', in the words of Rumi, 'is the astrolabe of heavenly mysteries.' 'Make love, not war', is merely 'Love your enemy' in a new disguise.

* * * * *

Not that such an approach is without its risks. The uninformed and uneducated—and especially those who do not *want* to understand—will, as usual, confuse the mere physical symbols with psychocosmic reality itself. Even the diners, in Watts's words, may tend to eat the menu instead of the dinner. Even the travellers may sometimes tend to climb up the signpost instead of following it.

There will be a danger of a return to primitive pantheism.

The point will need to be continually stressed that the dual cult of earth and sun is merely a Janus-mask superimposed upon an underlying cosmic unity. Father Sun and Mother Earth are only symbols of the Cosmic Being itself—that all-encompassing entity which is unseen, unnamable and unknowable except through its inner and outer manifestations.

Yet, in the light of modern physics and astronomy, it should not be too difficult for people at large to realise the fact. Now in its transcendent phase, our science has long since demolished the idea that mere matter and energy are somehow the basis of existence itself. At every level we are today aware as never before that the physical world is merely one manifestation of a deeper reality—whether Einstein's quantum-field, the religionist's spirit or the new ager's Cosmic Being.

What we are here concerned with is not a return to mere, crass materialism, but the inception of a new age of *spiritual* materialism*.

And so the cult of earth and sun does not necessarily deserve to be tarred by materialists with the brush of religious superstition. Nor do religionists need to regard it as a retrogressive step—a betrayal of the

---

*Not to be confused with the subject of Chögyam Trungpa's *Cutting Through Spiritual Materialism* (Watkins, 1973), which is really about materialistic, or ego-based, spirituality.

claims of spiritual truth. The universe can speak to us as legitimately through the world of matter as it can through that of spirit. Both, after all, are equally *it*. In a similar way, the psyche itself continually speaks to us through the world 'out there'.

Indeed, this very parallel should give us cause to wonder whether Jung's 'collective unconscious' might not in some way be identical with that ultimate reality itself.

And certainly the geo-solar cult does not have to be seen as a 'new religion'. The day of religions is past. No return to them is needed. The story of spirit, it becomes increasingly clear, is identical with that of the cosmos and of the human psyche itself. No longer, then, do we need to latch on to a reality beyond the stars, to seek a truth that once was or that one day shall be.

This is it, and we are it. Here and now.

All that is needed is that we should at last realise and act upon the fact.

Initiation, as we have seen, must forever succeed initiation. The cosmos, through us, must lose itself in order to find itself again, looking through our eyes at the nature of reality and so, eventually, achieving self-awareness. Consequently we must descend into the swirling, initiatory mists of our private, symbolic underworld. From these mists we shall emerge only when we have allowed ourselves to 'die' to our beloved world of illusion.

And to be reborn to the world of reality.

And so human consciousness must be prepared to accept the 'death' of all its achievements—to acknowledge the futility and relativity of its rigid systems of cognition, the non-viability of its cultural assumptions—if it is truly to become one again with the collective unconscious of all humanity and of all ages throughout the history of our planet. The individual human psyche—virtually identical, it seems, with the religionist's 'soul'—must accept the demise of its much-vaunted independence in favour of a willing coalescence with the underlying spirit, the basic life of humanity, which is also that of earth itself and of the cosmos as a whole.

*   *   *   *   *

Death, then, is very much the theme of the moment. And death, for human beings, has always been associated with a return to the earth.

Ashes to ashes, dust to dust . . . The link is truly an apt one. For only from the womb of the Earth can the new life of spring arise.

194

Yet westerners in particular find death hard to accept. For us it is a taboo subject. Long divorced from the circularity—or rather, the spirality—of reincarnationist teaching, we imagine death to be the end, not the beginning. We lack the wisdom of the Persian sage who long ago perceived that 'death is a festival'. Identifying ourselves exclusively with the achievements of our conscious mind, we fail to realise that our deeper nature will survive their 'death', and that the mighty unconscious will ever remain.

We can rely upon it. In more ways than one.

For should we fail to accept the great initiation which now stares us in the face, the collective unconscious will inevitably take matters into its own hands. Should our recalcitrant conscious mind resist the impending death and the consequent rebirth, then the 'maternal' unconscious will impose that death upon us in the most literal form, only to drag us screaming from the womb again into the light of day. Our psyche, our culture and the very foundations of our society will be torn apart, uprooted, scattered to the four winds. The human race itself may come near to extinction.

It will be the story of Noah's flood all over again.

But it may be that we shall see the light in time. By submitting willingly to the initiatory archetype, we may forestall the otherwise inevitable catastrophe. Through close, even ritual attunement to the daily 'initiation' of the sun, the annual death and rebirth of earthly nature—even the monthly cycle of the moon—we may succeed in realising the literally vital need to 'ride with the flow', to let go, to be where the action is instead of where we would like it to be. A positive commitment, even now, to founding a new age and culture based on co-operation with Mother Earth in all her many guises may be enough to exorcise the need for a total social and cultural collapse.

Such a return to earth will have many practical benefits too. Live close to the earth, and you don't have far to fall. Become partially self-sufficient, less dependent on complex social structures, and you have less to fear from their collapse. Learn to live in true harmony with Planet Earth, and it follows that you will live in harmony with yourself too.

Even if we do nothing, the great initiation will duly take place. If we do *something*, we may help the process along and perhaps make it less painful.

But one way or the other it has to come.

As the ancient psalmist realised, the 'valley of the shadow of death' has to precede the celestial banquet and the final anointing—the coronation—of the son of man*.

All initiations, we have seen, involve a circular process. Candidates leave the light, enter the darkness and then re-emerge into the light—but this time transformed by their acquired knowledge. It is the same initiation that we now have to undergo in the service of our own psychic evolution.

We have long since left behind the unconscious world of instinctive behaviour-patterns and entered the realms of rational dissociation—the ordeal of our present 'hell'. In the process we have gained knowledge. Knowledge of the outer universe. More recently, too, knowledge of our inner selves.

Now we must first realise the extent of our present 'death', then return. Return to those basic instinctive behaviour-patterns which are still—and will always remain—an essential part of our nature as human animals. Return, in short, to the ancient archetypes, the stuff of our primeval myths. But this time consciously, and informed by our newly-acquired knowledge. Intent on bringing about the final psychic reintegration which alone can open to us the doors of the next stage of our journey towards our cosmic destiny.

In this way the enormous quantities of energy that we have so far wasted on inner conflict can at last be released. Freed, they can then be re-directed to the achievement of higher realms of being entirely. Instead of forever fighting the unconscious self, humanity can consciously descend into it and there make contact with a further order of psychic reality whose very existence has hitherto been all but unsuspected.

And so the consciousness of the entire race can be groomed for a further evolutionary leap into a future of resplendent and as yet undreamed-of possibilities.

*Psalm 23.

17. THE GREAT AWAKENING

The purpose of life is information-processing.
Arthur C. Clarke: *The View from Serendip*
Knowledge is our destiny.
Jacob Bronowski: *The Ascent of Man*

And so we have reached the crossroads of human destiny. Not that reaching that crossroads is anything unique. Every generation stands at its own crossroads. Every generation has to decide, in the light of its own vision, what heritage—both physical and purely visionary—it will leave to its successors.

For leave it it must.

But perhaps we have an opportunity that was denied to so many of our ancestors. We have knowledge. A knowledge, admittedly, that is still limited—but one which, nevertheless, can stop us falling prey to certain illusions.

The illusion that reality corresponds to our language. That the world is as we think it is.

The illusion, too, that we are who we think we are—or rather who we should like to be.

In the current breakdown of ancient systems and dogmas, in the demolition of accepted values that is above all characteristic of our own age, there is an unparalled opportunity, a new and shining hope. The chance to see reality, for the first time in millennia, as it really is. The chance to recognise ourselves as we truly are. And thus the opportunity to bring to bear on the evolution of human consciousness the almost unimagined powers that will flow from our attainment of a new, psychic wholeness, a new and transcendent aliveness.

And here our new-found knowledge comes to our aid.

For our advances in high-energy physics, in astronomy, in linguistics, in psychology, in our understanding of the evolutionary processes of Planet Earth and of human history—not to mention our investigation of the world's spiritual and esoteric traditions—all tend increasingly to come up with similar conclusions. And with one conclusion in particular.

The world 'out there' can in no way be separated from the world 'in here'. In the celebrated formula so beloved of Hinduism, 'Thou art that'. No longer is it possible to separate what is 'real' from what is 'just psychological'. Indeed, since, for all practical purposes, reality does not exist outside the psyche's perception of it, *everything* is psychological.

Which explains a great deal.

It explains, for a start, what must by now have become blindingly obvious—namely that the story of the psyche is in almost every respect identical to the story of the soul itself, as outlined in the opening chapters of this book.

Like the soul, the psyche appears to be a mere individualisation of a larger entity which we have called the 'collective unconscious'. Like the soul, too, the psyche seems to feel a compulsive need to hide behind a veil of self-imposed illusion, a mask of rationality fashioned by the conscious mind. Indeed, it tends to identify itself totally with that mask, while denying its own reality. And so it cuts itself off from all other beings—all other aspects of itself—in the name of a purely imaginary individuality.

As a result it has to undergo a continual process of initiation—of death, gestation and rebirth—until such time as it has re-attained its original state of wholeness; just as the soul itself must similarly undergo, it is said, the continuing, karmic process of reincarnation. True, there is a difference of timescale. But that difference may merely reflect the fact that psychologists and reincarnationists tend to concentrate on different areas of the spectrum of time.

But then perhaps it is not so very surprising that the stories of psyche and soul should be so similar. *Psyche*, after all, is merely the Greek for 'soul'.

Yet the similarities do not stop there. If it is the destiny of the individual psyche to undergo a perpetual process of initiation, the same applies, at a deeper level, to the collective unconscious itself. The same process of initiation applies, in other words, to the deeper, general consciousness of mankind as a whole.

198

And here we can trace a direct parallel to the earlier story of 'spirit'.

For the collective unconscious, it is increasingly clear, can no longer be confined—as Jung, out of deference to scientific respectability, sometimes tended to confine it—to a mere, inherited bundle of psychic instincts and behaviour-patterns. It seems to be a living, breathing entity in its own right, a kind of 'megapsyche' or Great Mind which, exactly like the supposed cosmic 'spirit' itself, experiences a need to dismember itself into 'separate' entities in order to acquire experience and ultimately gain full self-awareness.

Individual human beings, in other words, are merely the physical tools which the collective unconscious, relaying its commands through the various archetypes, uses as its eyes and ears, its arms and legs, its hands and feet. It is through them that, reincarnated through generation after generation, the mighty Being moves on its inexorable way towards achieving the light of full consciousness. It is through the myriad individualities that are the antithesis of its wholeness that it is destined eventually to produce a new synthesis.

And that synthesis will mark its entry into even higher dimensions of wholeness, the beginning of yet another cycle of initiation.

But then this is no more than the same archetypal process in which the universe itself, too, is continually involved.

The great galactic star-systems appear to be nothing more or less than the means whereby the ultimate unity that is the underlying quantum-field of space-time periodically dismembers itself into apparently separate entities. 'No-thing' must become polarised into positive and negative, space-time differentiated into matter and energy. In the furnaces of the stars, simple hydrogen must be transmuted to form successively the whole gamut of the natural elements. Life must arise, the organic compounds be formed, and at length, through the agency of their product—*homo sapiens*—even further, artificial elements must be produced.

Nor does the process of differentiation have to stop there. For *homo sapiens* is quite capable of taking it even further.

The human race may yet succeed in blasting apart even the planet on which it lives . . .

And yet the process of cosmic differentiation and disintegration is merely the reverse side of the coin of ever-growing complexity and interrelatedness. From it arises an evolutionary synthesis which eventually ensures that, out of the 'separate' psyches of individual men and women, a new, planetary humanity will one day emerge. Already we are searching for those stones that are the archetypal symbols of our deeper selves. Soon we shall put them all together again to build a mighty, psychic edifice, a spiritual Great Pyramid founded on the common earth, a monument to our re-achievement of the ancient oneness of the great, primeval Self.

And in the process we shall eventually bring about the realisation of an ancient dream—the achievement of full, galactic self-awareness, of total cosmic consciousness.

Meanwhile the same cosmic process of initiation is reflected in human experience itself at every level.

With the aid of language, as we saw earlier, we divide reality into discrete concepts, separate 'this' from 'that', 'then' from 'now', 'self' from 'other', 'good' from 'bad'. From this innocent symbol-game arises at length the whole edifice of our rational science and technology and the continual, initiatory rise and fall of our successive cultures and civilisations.

Yet the forbidden fruit of the tree of the knowledge of good and evil is the same knowledge that now promises to help us transcend the limitations which we thereby impose on ourselves. Increasingly we learn to perceive the unreality of the 'real', to sense the unity which underlies diversity. The veil of our self-built temple of illusion is rent asunder, and there in the Holy of Holies of human consciousness we come face to face with the very heart of reality.

Only to find that it is literally nothing. No-thing. Total undifferentiation.

All is one, all is whole again. And in that realisation we can finally let go of our age-old illusion, let go of ourselves. For at last we realise that we too partake of that ultimate wholeness.

* * * * *

And so the advance of knowledge in every sphere has now brought humanity to a crucial point in its evolution. The point where the underlying oneness of all phenomena—whether physical, psychological or spiritual—finally demands to be recognised. The development of the universe out of undifferentiated oneness, the evolutionary process of earth itself, the slow unfolding of human history—all are mere expressions of the same inner process that is central to your experience and mine.

That is why the great cultural symbols—the Great Pyramid, the Zodiac, the ancient legends and mythologies, the world's great scriptures—can all be interpreted in any or all of those senses*.

What is unfolding out there amid the depths of the universe, no less than across the surface of our planet itself, is in its essentials the story of our own collective psyche. That psyche without which, as far as we are concerned, there would in any case be no story, no universe, no earth, indeed no humanity in the first place.

And so the time has come for a truly shattering realisation to dawn.

Far from the psyche being merely our tool for learning about life, the whole of life as we experience it is merely the psyche's tool for learning about itself.

Mind, in other words, is not possessed by us. It is we who are possessed by Mind.

And so you could quite happily describe the whole of reality as we know it as a mere dream in the mind of *homo sapiens*—or of God. For if the view that I have just put forward is valid, then it follows that the fundamental realities touched upon by physics, psychology and religion are all identical—as, indeed, they must be if they are truly reality.

And, in particular, quantum-field, collective unconscious, cosmic spirit and inconceivable God are all one and the same—mere symbols, or manifestations, of a single, *psychocosmic* continuum which lies at the basis of all our experience, and out of which the whole world as we know it is therefore ultimately created.

* * * * *

In whatever form, in fact, it is Mind that—like the Hindus' dreaming Vishnu—dismembers itself into the individual 'souls' which are its scattered arms and legs, hides itself behind the mask of personality, subjects itself to the karmic law of cause-and-effect, and is reborn continually, as it believes, in the succeeding generations of humankind.

It is Mind that divides up reality—i.e. itself—into illusory parts via the technique of linguistic discrimination, and that then attempts to rediscover its primal unity via techniques such as meditation.

It is Mind that envisages everything that seems to come into being through its dreams and visions—and not least through its archetypes.

And it is Mind that then manifests those equally psychic events which are their eventual historical fulfilments.

* * * * *

*Compare Lemesurier: *The Great Pyramid Decoded* (Element Books, 1978) and *Gospel of the Stars* (Element Books, 1978).

And now, as the moment for Mind's re-awakening to full self-consciousness draws near, the psychic dream intensifies, raising the fever of illusion to the point at which it must finally break. There are explosions in the spheres of communications, of travel, of technology, of population, of stress, of political and social change, of occultism, of scientific knowledge. And at last, working through the evolution of the universe, the unrolling of history, the development of human physics and psychology, of religion and astronomy, of space-technology and philosophy, Mind contrives to transcend its own self-imposed limitations, and rediscovers—or rather re-members—itself at the heart of all experiential reality.

And so, for us, the conclusion is obvious. There is only one God. There is but a single, cosmic reality. *There is only Mind.*

But from this realisation a further conclusion follows.

Mind—and not least the human mind—*can directly manipulate matter itself.* This fact, which lies at the basis of what we have termed the Law of Creation, could yet have unimagined consequences for the future both of our race and of our universe.

* * * * *

If, meanwhile, there is an initiation to undergo, whether for cosmos, humanity or Planet Earth, then it is ultimately Mind that has to undergo it. Using concrete reality as its postulant at the altar of evolution, it dies and is reborn, loses itself in order to find itself again.

And we are inevitably part of that process. Indeed, we have a crucial role to play in it.

For it is through human consciousness alone—so far as we know—that Mind can become aware of itself again. It is human self-awareness that alone can supply the key which will open the door of its self-imposed prison. It is the two-edged blade of human perception that alone is sharp enough to rend the veil of its hidden sanctuary and show the Cosmic Psyche once again that it stands at the very heart of reality itself.

And so, for humanity, awareness is of the essence. Consciousness is all. Necessarily so—for it is only of consciousness itself that we can ever be conscious. Aware, in particular, that that consciousness, that Cosmic Psyche, asleep through all the aeons of the universe, is now, in us, gradually stirring into full wakefulness.

Already, it seems, Vishnu is rising with the dawn. Already the scattered members of the long-dead Osiris are being re-assembled into a living body by the maternal, blue-robed Isis who is Earth herself. Already the dismembered arms and legs of God are being resurrected to form the body of Christ on earth.

The time has come for the son of man to appear, restored to life and health and clothed in the robe of true glory. His coming, say the scriptures, will be like lightning from the east, flashing as far as the west*.

A flash of truly oriental insight, no less.

The dawning of the realisation that we are our own 'lower' nature no less than our 'higher' nature. The realisation that we are children of the earth, offspring of the sun. The realisation that we are ultimately the universe itself, as the universe is us. And consequently the practical living out, here and now, of the fundamental truth, not merely that I am you and you are me, but that, in everything that is, simply and eternally, I AM.

That, indeed, is the only real answer to the question, 'Who are you?' It is the truth which, once known, can set us free.

It is by making I AM the way, the truth and the life that our race will finally fulfil its destiny.

*Matt. 24:27.

18. OVER TO YOU

It is not I at the door, but You;
grant access, open the door to Yourself.
Jalal'ud-Din Rumi: *Shamsi Tabriz*

So it is that from the cradle, through the initiatory labyrinths of language, history and technology, and eventually out into primordial starlight, humankind continues to pursue its ancient dream. At the same time it pursues it deep into the secret fastnesses of the inner atom and the darkest wells of its own psyche.

And always what it discovers there is simply its own awareness, its own consciousness.

In short, itself.

And so where does it all leave *you*, this outward odyssey, this inward exploration? Where does it leave Joe Soap, the student, the office-worker, number three in the hierarchy, the person who lives at number twenty-seven, the owner of the blue Suzuki, Jane's cousin?

Surprisingly, perhaps, it leaves them—and you—exactly where you started.

Here and now.

For there is no other reality. Nor was there ever. Nor will there ever be.

'Here' is merely the point at which consciousness impinges on the space that it carves for itself out of infinity. 'Now' is the point at which that same consciousness impinges on the time that it snatches for itself out of eternity. And since consciousness can never, by definition, be conscious of anything other than what it is conscious of, reality can never be other than here and now.

Yet, by the same token, here and now is what you yourself make of it.

By expanding and developing your consciousness, you can expand 'here' until it takes in not only 'there', but everywhere else as well. Everywhere, after all, of which consciousness is directly and intimately conscious is, by definition, 'here'.

Similarly, it needs only a simple shift in your awareness to realise that 'now' can take in not merely 'then'—any given point in the past or future—but the whole of eternity itself. For any moment of which consciousness is directly and intimately aware is, by definition, 'now'. It follows, therefore, that this 'nowness' must travel with consciousness itself for as long as consciousness exists.

And consciousness, by its own terms, can of course have no known beginning or end.

It is quite possible, for example, to take the view that there has really only ever been one day since the world began—one single hemisphere of solar illumination that, relatively speaking, has revolved about our planet since the beginning of what we call time.

And this is it.

This, in other words, is the day on which the Great Pyramid's foundations were laid, the day when the Buddha achieved enlightenment, when Jesus of Nazareth was born, when Rome finally fell to the barbarians, when William the Conqueror landed at Pevensey Bay, when Joan of Arc was burnt at the stake, when Columbus set out for America, when Shakespeare completed *Hamlet*, when the Bastille fell to the Paris mob, when Hitler marched into Austria, when the atomic bomb exploded over Hiroshima, when men first set foot on the moon.

All these events took place during the same, endless today which you and I too are now sharing.

And so, in the event, it is how you look at it—your mode of awareness—that decides whether you see the whole of recorded history as one day or two million.. Look at it from 'outside', and the pattern changes considerably.

Perhaps, then, there is something to be said for applying the same technique to yourself—looking from the outside in, rather than from the inside out. Or, better still, from all angles at once.

That, after all, is what total consciousness is all about.

By expanding your consciousness until it is no longer merely *your* consciousness, but consciousness itself, you can annihilate space and time. For where there is no separate knower and known, but only simple knowing, there is no more discrimination or separation. There is only pure consciousness—the universe at peace, knowing itself. And so the primal bliss of cosmic wholeness is re-achieved.

Here becomes infinity. Now is forever. Thou art that.

* * * * *

But how can you achieve that vital transformation of consciousness? How can you realise in yourself the universe's vision of wholeness?

One thing is quite plain. The mere intellectual realisation that you and the universe are one is not enough. Mind has by now become totally entrapped in the alienated thought-forms of its own creation. As a result, what seems to be the concrete evidence of your senses is more than strong enough to swamp any purely mental realisation that things are not really as they seem. Thanks to the Law of Creation, your own symbolic projections have long since become full-bodied creatures of flesh and blood. Your ancestral language-patterns continually hold their carving-knife of discrimination at your throat. And, faced with this self-imposed threat, your unaided intellect—your conscious mind that is at last trying to burst out of its ancient chains—is too easily cowed into submission to make its final dash for freedom.

There is no question, either, of using that same mental realisation of oneness to operate on yourself 'from outside'. The you that would do the operating is, after all, the same you on whom you would operate. You cannot force *yourself* to do anything, since the you that is applying coercion is the same you that is doing the resisting. Any attempt at consciousness-expansion which operates in terms of a dual you, a 'split-personality', is merely reinforcing the inner psychosis which lies at the root of the problem in the first place.

There is no future, as we saw earlier, in saying 'Pull yourself together.'

Indeed, the real answer, paradoxically, lies not in 'getting a grip on yourself' at all, but in letting go. Letting go, that is, of your conditioning, of your illusion, of your mask of personality, of your imagined individuality, of your very soul. Letting go, in short, of everything that alienates you from the rest of humanity, the rest of the universe.

As Jesus of Nazareth is on record as suggesting, he who would save his soul is lost, while he who is prepared to let go of his soul discovers his true self*.

Meditation could serve as a useful first step. It may not abolish your

---

*Matt. 16:25. The Bible's term *psyche* means both 'life' and 'soul'.

symbolic world entirely, but at least it tends gradually to reinforce your sense of cosmic oneness, your awareness that your thoughts and ideas are not you. It even has a mildly initiatory effect, comprising as it does an initial self-forgetting, a period of voluntary confinement in the state of meditation, and an eventual release. And by avoiding the use of language it can help you, for limited periods of time at least, to steer clear of the original cause of the trouble.

But knowing is one thing, acting quite another. Your new, holistic awareness is a tender plant. And if your everyday actions continue to proclaim a world of opposites, whether inner or outer, that plant will at best become stunted and at worst wither away and die. Come to that, perhaps it is *preferable* that it should wither away and die—for if you are dedicated mentally to wholeness and harmony, and physically to duality and conflict, you are merely adding a new dimension to your psychosis, and not healing it at all. That is why drug-induced trips to Elysium generally cause even more problems than they solve.

How, then, can you act without forcing yourself to act? How can you apply the remedy while at the same time seeming not to?

The answer seems to lie in the ancient oriental concept of 'non-action'.

*   *   *   *   *

Curiously enough, this doesn't mean just doing nothing. Merely sitting cross-legged never boiled an egg, let alone solved the world's problems.

What it does mean is flowing with the universe, being where the action is—in short, letting events come to you, rather than trying to manipulate events 'from outside'. You, after all, are part of the universal process anyway; and exercising your individual will, screwing up your personal determination, will affect your involvement in it not one iota.

You, for example, have already felt moved to read this book. Already it will have suggested to you certain ideas that attract or interest you. Probably, too, there are others that repel you.

What else would you expect of a dual world?

Nevertheless, at the end of this chapter you will find a classified list of books giving more information on various of the topics that we have discussed. Most of those titles are in relatively cheap editions. Some of them may even seem to you worth getting hold of. At some future date you are bound to see one or more of those books, or other books on similar topics, on a bookstall, and in your pocket will be sufficient money to buy them. Or perhaps you will be given the opportunity to borrow one of them. Better still, you will possibly meet somebody with personal experience of one of the topics in question.

If you then feel drawn to do so, that will be the moment to act. Indeed, it is then of the greatest importance that you should. Fatalism and a belief in karma are all very well, but saying 'If it's meant to happen, it will' too easily ignores the point that your own action may be part of what is 'meant to happen'. When the time is right, in fact, positive thought and action are vital. That action in turn will lead, in due course, to other actions of various kinds, all in their due time. And so you will eventually be led, with little or no active effort on your own part, to whatever path is ultimately right for you.

And your world will never be the same again.

When the pupil is ready, says the ancient proverb, the guru will appear. And the true guru is any 'catalyst', be it animate or inanimate, that brings you one step further along your chosen evolutionary path. It is your own thoughts, your own needs, your own deep desires that will manifest appropriate gurus for you throughout your life.

Such is the Law of Creation.

Think positively, then, lest all that you manifest be opposition and negativity. Do not oppose.

Propose.

But be quite clear about one thing. There is no single, 'right' path. There is no evolutionary panacea, no royal road of spirituality, no unique highway of consciousness. Your road is *your* road, and where it will lead nobody except you can ever find out.

Do not ask others, then, for final answers. The only answer you will get is the one that you eventually discover for yourself.

And yet perhaps you will not have too far to look. For the universe itself is now poised for a new initiation. Through its agent, humankind, it is at this very moment in the process of returning to source, of rediscovering its primal identity. As one of the manifestations of that process, our race is already embarking on a great return to the earth, a new realisation of common wholeness. Meanwhile it is the world of symbols that has, eventually, to supply the first aid of the human soul, the catalyst of healing. And perhaps it is in some aspect of the overall process of global self-rediscovery that you will eventually discover your own healing talisman.

The outer world, in other words, may yet supply you with the means of rediscovering your inner self. All that is demanded of you is that you should allow yourself to experience it.

208

It is a simple case of striking while the iron is hot.

* * * * *

All around you, in fact, the symbols of wholeness are beginning their ritual dance of cosmic initiation. Wherever you turn, the instruments of salvation are staring you in the face.

If your thing is manual labour, an ever-growing number of new age communities are longing to show you how to use it as a means of rediscovering yourself[1]. If it is plants and the soil, a whole 'back to earth' movement is there to minister to your needs[2]. If science, then opportunities for research into ecology, high-energy physics and astronomy are opening up to help lead you towards the realms of bliss[3].

If your current problem is emotional stress and consequent physical diseases, healing groups using such approaches as bio-energetics, transactional analysis, psychodrama, yoga, gestalt and encounter-therapy are available to help you put yourself back on the road to health and inner wholeness[1]. If you feel drawn to activities of a more overtly spiritual nature, a whole range of mainly meditation-based and religious groups stands at your disposal . If your inclinations are mainly musical, a whole new musical technology is arising to help re-open the long-lost highways to the self[4]. And even the simplest of 'growth-games' can help you to stretch your consciousness to the extent of be-ing in your body instead of merely in your head[5].

Meanwhile there are always the books. Books on astrology, on religions of every type, on the occult, on the Great Pyramid, on medita-tion, on the New Age, on Jungian psychology, on reincarnation, on self-awareness techniques . . . the list is endless[6].

Not that reading books can ever be a substitute for reality. But then, neither can any of the other activities that I have listed. They are all mere symbolic techniques for facing yourself 'out there' with various

---

[1] Compare Annett: *The Many Ways of Being* (Abacus/Turnstone, 1976).
[2] Compare Saunders, N.: *Alternative England and Wales* (N. Saunders, 1975).
[3] See Capra, F.: *The Tao of Physics* (Fontana, 1976) and Gribbin: *White Holes* (Paladin, 1977).
[4] Compare Hamel: *Through Music to the Self* (Compton Press, 1978).
[5] Compare Lewis & Streitfeld: *Growth Games* (Abacus, 1973).
[6] See the classified list of suggested titles at the end of this book.

aspects, or manifestations, of the truth that ultimately lies 'in here'—of facing yourself, in short, with yourself. They can provide you with the means of breaking your alienating conditioning, your inherited addiction to duality and the world of opposites. Each offers you one key to freeing yourself from your self-imposed conviction, your life-sentence. By operating on your physical body, on your emotions, and even on your intellect, they can provide you with a range of outer symbols with which you can at least start to operate on your inner self.

And books, in particular, can help you to construct a vision of what, eventually, the Law of Creation will turn into undoubted fact.

And so the choice is yours. By exposing yourself to any one of a number of sets of external situations you may, if you feel drawn to do so, indirectly apply to yourself a whole range of symbolic tools—tools that will help you to achieve that Self-realisation which, it is now clear, is the very reason for your existence in the first place. And even if you feel moved to do absolutely nothing at all—merely to sit and wait and see what happens—you need not fear. The universe will inevitably catch up with you sooner or later.

There is a time and place for everything.

And eventually the realisation will come home. The realisation that the time is now, that the place is here.

And that everything is you.

It is less a universe, you could say, than a YOU-niverse.

And it is with the full dawning of that realisation at every level of your being—physical, emotional, intellectual and psychic—that you (the real you, that is) may at last blossom and live happily ever after.

* * * * *

Yet the expression is of course misleading.

Eternity is not merely an endless future. Much rather is it an endless present, an eternal now. Only in being fully conscious of yourself as you truly are, here and now, in this instant—and not as you think yourself to be on the basis of past experience or imagine yourself to be on the basis of future expectation—are you likely to achieve that ultimate bliss, that happy ending, without which no story is truly complete.

Your *real* nature, which is subject neither to space nor to time, neither to separateness nor to becoming, is not a function of memory or of anticipation. It is neither a has-been nor a will-be, but an IS.

An IS that is also the very IS of the cosmos itself, timeless and infinite.

210

And that IS is to be found not in the hereafter (as some religions claim) nor in the heretofore (as numerous legends might seem to suggest), but in the here-and-now—in the experiential reality that is the on-going process of your total awareness.

Truly the end of time.

The literally self-evident truth strides in big letters across the secret pages of the deepest human experience.

IN THE ETERNAL *NOW* ETERNITY EVER IS.

This, then, *is* heaven. This *is* the Garden of Eden. We never left it. It was our Divine awareness, our 'godness' that fell asleep. Some ancient shift of consciousness that closed our race's eyes to reality and plunged it into a deep slumber.

Perchance to dream.

And so we have only ourselves to blame if we dream that we are in hell, borne on our nightmares through the depths of Hades.

Yet even dreams must retreat before the coming of day. Soon the new dawn will start to break. Already the planetary consciousness stirs in anticipation of that event. Already the first cockerels are crowing. Soon there will be a stretching, a yawning, an opening of the eyes.

And awakening at last from its age-old slumbers, Earthchild will go forth to meet the sunrise.

CLASSIFIED SUGGESTIONS
FOR FURTHER READING
(all in paperback apart from the works asterisked)

Alternative Medicine
*Blythe, P., *Drugless Medicine* (Arthur Barker, 1974)
Eagle, R., *Alternative Medicine* (Futura, 1978)

Astrology and the Zodiac
Gauquelin, M., *Cosmic Influences on Human Behaviour* (Futura, 1976)
Lemesurier, P., *Gospel of the Stars* (Element, 1977)

Brain-Hemisphere Function
Ornstein, R.E., *The Psychology of Consciousness* (Harcourt Brace, 1977)
Sagan, C., *The Dragons of Eden* (Coronet, 1977)

Buddhism
Humphreys, C., *Buddhism* (Pelican, 1951)
Rampa, T.L., *The Third Eye* (Corgi, 1956)
Saddhatissa, H., *The Buddha's Way* (Allen & Unwin, 1971)
Trungpa, Chögyam, *Cutting Through Spiritual Materialism* (Watkins, 1973)
Watts, A.W., *The Way of Zen* (Penguin, 1970)

Christianity and Judaism
Däniken, E. von, *Miracles of the Gods,* Chapter 2 (Corgi, 1977)
*Lemesurier, P., *The Armageddon Script* (Element, 1981)
New English Bible, Matthew's and John's gospels (Penguin, 1974)
Powell Davies, A., *The Meaning of the Dead Sea Scrolls* (Mentor, 1956)
Schonfield, H.J., *The Passover Plot* (Futura, 1976)
Schonfield, H.J., *Those Incredible Christians* (Bantam, 1969)
Vermes, G., *The Dead Sea Scrolls in English* (Penguin, 1968)
Weatherhead, L.D., *The Christian Agnostic* (Hodder & Stoughton, 1963)

Gematria and Sacred Geometry
Charpentier, L., *The Mysteries of Chartres Cathedral* (RILKO)
Michell, J., *City of Revelation* (Abacus, 1973)
Michell, J., *The View over Atlantis* (Abacus, 1973)

The Great Pyramid
Lemesurier, P., *The Great Pyramid Decoded* (Element, 1978)
Tompkins, P., *Secrets of the Great Pyramid* (Penguin, 1979)
Valentine, T., *The Great Pyramid: Man's Monument to Man* (Panther, 1977)

Hinduism
Mascaró, J. (tr.), *The Bhagavad Gita* (Penguin, 1962)
Mascaró, J. (tr.), *The Upanishads* (Penguin, 1965)
Sen, K., *Hinduism* (Pelican, 1961)

Islam
Dawood, N.J. (tr.), *The Koran* (Penguin, 1956)
Pickthall, M.M. (tr.), *The Meaning of the Glorious Koran* (Mentor)

Language and Linguistics
Potter, S., *Language in the Modern World* (Pelican, 1960)
Sapir, E., *Language* (Harvest, 1921)
Saussure, F. de, *General Course in Linguistics* (Fontana, 1974)

Meditation
Krishnamurti, J., 'The Only Revolution' in *The Second Penguin Krishnamurti Reader* (Penguin, 1973)
Saddhatissa, H., *The Buddha's Way* (Allen & Unwin, 1971)
Trungpa, Chögyam, *Meditation in Action* (Watkins, 1969)

New Age Movements and Communities
Annett, S., *The Many Ways of Being* (Abacus/Turnstone, 1976)
Hawken, P., *The Magic of Findhorn* (Fontana, 1976)
Matson, K. (Ed.), *The Encyclopaedia of Reality* (Paladin, 1979)
Saunders, N., *Alternative England and Wales* (N. Saunders, 1975)
Saunders, N., *Alternative London* (Wildwood House & N. Saunders, 1974)
Spangler, D., *Revelation: the Birth of a New Age* (Findhorn Press)
Wright, B., & Worsley, C., *Alternative Scotland* (Wildwood House, 1975)

Oriental Religions in General
Capra, F., *The Tao of Physics* (Fontana, 1976)
Watts, A.W., *The Way of Zen* (Penguin, 1970)

Prediction

Carter, M.E., *Edgar Cayce on Prophecy* (Paperback Library, New York, 1968, available in U.K. from Adele Spero, 80, St. James Road, Surbiton, Surrey)
*Dixon, Jeane, *My Life and Prophecies* (Muller, 1971)
*Glass, J., *The Story of Fulfilled Prophecy* (Cassell, 1969)
*Lemesurier, P., *The Armageddon Script* (Element, 1981)
Lemesurier, P., *Gospel of the Stars* (Element, 1977)
Lemesurier, P., *The Great Pyramid Decoded* (Element, 1978)
Lindsey, H., *The Late Great Planet Earth* (Zondervan, 1970)
Sabato, M. de, *Révélations* (Pensée Moderne, 1975)
Sabato, M. de, *25 Ans à Vivre?* (Pensée Moderne, 1976)

Psychology

Harris, T.A., *I'm OK—You're OK* (Pan, 1973)
Jung, C.G., *Man and His Symbols* (Aldus/Jupiter, 1964)
Jung, C.G. *Memories, Dreams, Reflections* (Fontana, 1967)

Reincarnation

*Cerminara, G., *Many Mansions* (Morrow, 1950)
Grant, J. & Kelsey, D., *Many Lifetimes* (Corgi, 1976)
Langley, N., *Edgar Cayce on Reincarnation* (Paperback Library, New York, 1967, available in U.K. through Adele Spero, 80, St. James Road, Surbiton, Surrey)
Leek, S., *Reincarnation: the Second Chance* (Bantam, 1975)
Stevenson, I., *The Evidence for Survival from Claimed Memories of Former Incarnations* (M.C. Peto, 4 Oakdene, Burg Heath, Tadworth, Surrey, England, 1961)
Weatherhead, L., *The Christian Agnostic*, chapter 14 (Hodder & Stoughton, 1965)

Religion, Cosmology and Science

Capra, F., *The Tao of Physics* (Fontana, 1976)
Gribbin, J., *White Holes* (Paladin, 1977)
*Johnson, R.C., *The Imprisoned Splendour* (Hodder & Stoughton, 1953)
*Le Shan, L., *The Clairvoyant Reality* (Turnstone, 1980)
Watson, L., *Lifetide* (Coronet, 1980)
Watson, L., *The Romeo Error* (Coronet, 1976)
Watson, L., *Supernature* (Coronet, 1974)

The Search for the Self

Jung, C.G., *Memories, Dreams, Reflections* (Fontana, 1967)
Watts, A.W., *The Book on the Taboo against Knowing Who You Are* (Abacus, 1973)

Self-Awareness Techniques
Hamel, P.M., *Through Music to the Self* (Element, 1978)
Lewis, H.R. & Streitfeld, H.S., *Growth Games* (Abacus, 1973)

Taoism
Lao Tsu, *Tao Te Ching* (tr. Gia-Fu Feng & Jane English, Wildwood House, 1973)
Watts, A.W., *The Way of Zen* (Penguin, 1970)

Tibetan Religion
David-Neel, A., *Magic and Mystery in Tibet* (Corgi, 1971)
Evans-Wentz, W.Y. (Ed.), *The Tibetan Book of the Dead* (O.U.P., 1960)
Govinda, Lama A., *The Way of the White Clouds* (Rider, 1966)
Rampa. T.L., *The Third Eye* (Corgi, 1956)
Trungpa, Chögyam, *Born in Tibet* (Penguin, Inc., 1971)